AROUND THE WORLD
IN EIGHTY SWEATERS

SUE BRADLEY

AROUND THE WORLD IN EIGHTY SWEATERS

HENRY HOLT AND COMPANY
NEW YORK

Copyright © 1988 by Johnson Editions Ltd,
15 Grafton Square, London SW4 ODQ, England
Knitwear designs copyright © 1988 by Sue Bradley

Published in the United States by Henry Holt and Company, Inc.,
115 West 18th Street, New York, New York 10011.

Published in Canada by Fitzhenry & Whiteside Limited,
195 Allstate Parkway, Markham, Ontario L3R 4T8.

Published in Great Britain under the title *Travellers' Yarns*.

Library of Congress Cataloging-in-Publication Data
Bradley, Sue.
  Around the world in eighty sweaters.
  1. Sweaters. 2. Knitting—Patterns. I. Title.
TT825.B678 1988   746.9'2   88-9001
ISBN 0-8050-0456-4

First American Edition

Typesetting by Fowler Printing Services
Colour separation by Fotographics London–Hong Kong.
Printed and bound in Italy by Arnoldo Mondadori Editore
10 9 8 7 6 5 4 3 2 1

ISBN 0-8050-0456-4

CONTENTS

INTRODUCTION

In this, my third book, I have been inspired by the costume, art and textiles of many different cultures to create an imaginary knitted journey around the world.

We set off from northern Europe with traditional costumes from England and Scandinavia and wind our way through eastern Europe with a Russian cossack jacket and peasant shirt, on to western Asia and some richly patterned designs from Turkestan and Iran. We continue through India with hot, bright colours and a sequinned kaftan jacket to visit the Far East and take inspiration from Japanese fabrics and crafts. In Australia we find motifs and colours from Aboriginal bark paintings, and in North and South America take ideas from cowboys and Indians and Inca legends respectively. The journey ends in Africa with some bold and colourful beadwork designs.

The garments use a wide variety of styles and colour combinations. Some take inspiration directly from costumes, for example the 'Japanese' sweaters, which make use of typical kimono shaping; others are influenced not so much by shapes as by textile patterns, like the 'North American' designs with motifs taken from Navajo rugs and other Indian artefacts.

There are garments to suit every occasion, warm winter coats, stylish jackets and cardigans, sweaters for day and evening, waistcoats and cool summer tops. A vast range of different yarns has been used: cotton, wool, mohair, linen, aran and tweed, plus some interesting metallic lurex and fancy slub fibres. Different types of yarn are often used together to create unusual and intriguing textures. The collection in each chapter is complemented with accessories – not only hats and gloves but also knitted headbands, bangles and earrings – and alternative versions are given for some designs, showing a change in colour or style. There are more than 80 patterns in all.

So be inspired and let me transport you to far-away places. Follow the patterns in this book and you can knit you way around the world.

I hope you will enjoy your journey as much as I have enjoyed creating it – *bon voyage!* (And don't forget to pack the knitting needles!)

Sue Bradley

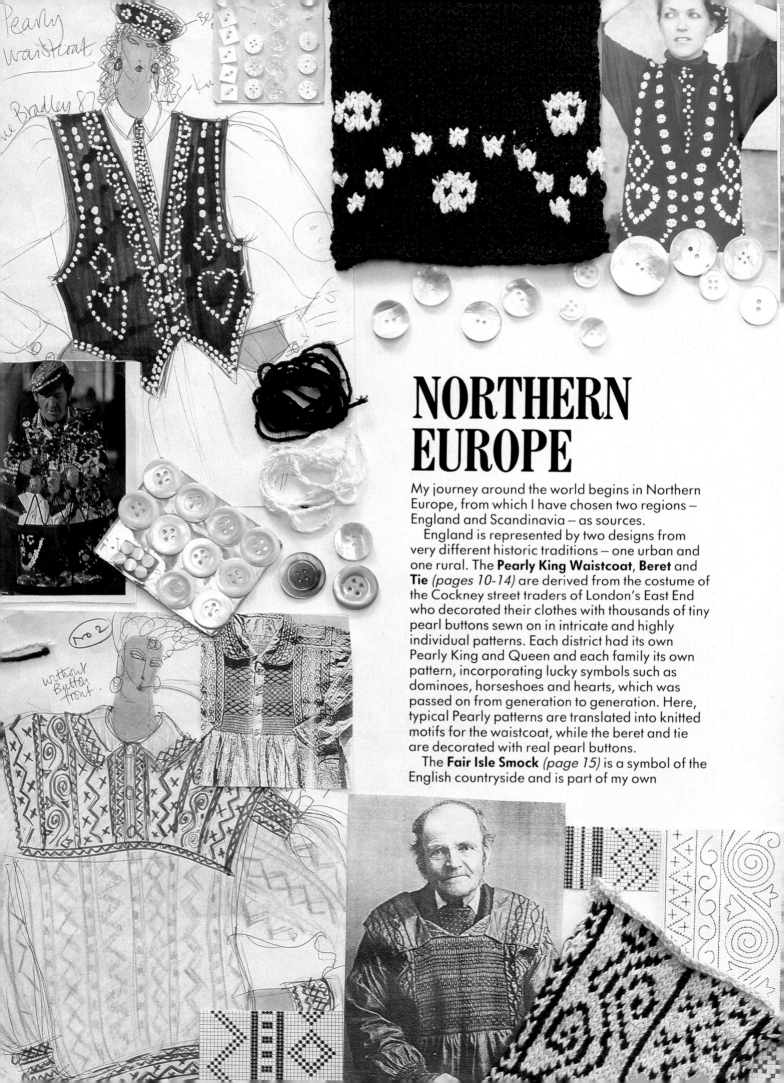

NORTHERN EUROPE

My journey around the world begins in Northern Europe, from which I have chosen two regions — England and Scandinavia — as sources.

England is represented by two designs from very different historic traditions — one urban and one rural. The **Pearly King Waistcoat**, **Beret** and **Tie** *(pages 10-14)* are derived from the costume of the Cockney street traders of London's East End who decorated their clothes with thousands of tiny pearl buttons sewn on in intricate and highly individual patterns. Each district had its own Pearly King and Queen and each family its own pattern, incorporating lucky symbols such as dominoes, horseshoes and hearts, which was passed on from generation to generation. Here, typical Pearly patterns are translated into knitted motifs for the waistcoat, while the beret and tie are decorated with real pearl buttons.

The **Fair Isle Smock** *(page 15)* is a symbol of the English countryside and is part of my own

heritage, as I was born and brought up in Somerset, the heart of the West Country. Smocks, however picturesque they look to us today, were the normal workwear of agricultural labourers in the eighteenth and nineteenth centuries. They were loose garments made from natural-coloured coarse cotton or linen, cut economically in rectangles and shaped by gathering and smocking. The plain cloth was decorated with embroidery, and typical motifs included sheaves of corn, ploughs, pitchforks, hearts and flowers. Valuable and much-treasured garments, they were handed down from father to son. My interpretation of the smock uses flat Fair Isle patterning in black to suggest the intricate stitchery of the original.

The **Scandinavian Sweater**, **Gloves** and **Bobble Hat** *(pages 18-22)* are based on the traditional colour knitting of peasant communities in Norway, Sweden and Denmark. Knitted in thick wool, their simply shaped garments had crew or roll necks for warmth and combined a pattern of 'seedings' or all-over dots with bold motifs of reindeer, trees and stars, directly inspired by their natural surroundings. This sweater uses authentic colours, with cream Aran-weight wool as the base and dark, rich shades for the pattern.

PEARLY KING WAISTCOAT

MEASUREMENTS
To fit bust: 81-91cm/32-36in and 91-102cm/36-40in

Please see page 145 for actual garment measurements.

VERSION 1 ★ ★

MATERIALS
Yarn
Any **Aran-weight** yarn can be used as long as it knits up to the given tension.
425(475)g/15(17)oz black cotton (A), 75(100)g/3(4)oz cream cotton (B)

Needles and other materials
1 pair each 4mm (US 5) and 5mm (US 7) needles
1 circular 4mm (US 5) needle
3 pearl buttons
Crochet hook (optional)

NOTE
When knitting this garment *do not* strand yarn across wrong side of work.

TENSION
18 sts and 25 rows to 10cm/4in on 5mm (US 7) needles over st st.

BACK
With 4mm (US 5) needles and A, cast on 90(96)sts and work from **back chart** (see pages 12-13 for all charts) as follows, working between appropriate lines for size required:
Rows 1-4: Work in K1, P1 rib in A.
Change to 5mm (US 7) needles and starting with a K row, cont in st st following chart until row 54(58) has been worked, thus ending with a WS row.

Shape armholes
Keeping chart correct, cast off 8 sts at beg of next 2 rows.
Now dec 1 st at each end of next row and foll 3 alt rows – 66(72)sts.
Now cont straight following chart until row 124(128) has been worked, thus ending with a WS row.

Shape shoulders
Cast off 6(7)sts at beg of next 6 rows.
Cast off rem 30 sts for back neck.

FRONTS
With 5mm (US 7) needles and A, cast on 2 sts and starting with a K row, cont in st st and work from **front charts**, working between appropriate lines for size required, and working all shapings as shown.

TO MAKE UP
Sew in ends and press pieces carefully following ball band instructions.
Join shoulder seams together.

Armhole edgings
Alike. With 4mm (US 5) needles and A and with RS facing, pick up and K 64 sts evenly around armhole edge on each side of shoulder seam – 128 sts.

Work in K1, P1 rib for 4 rows.
Cast off fairly loosely ribwise.

Front band
With the 4mm (US 5) circular needle and A and RS facing, pick up and K 120 sts from row 30 (bottom of straight front edge) of right front to shoulder seam, 28 sts across back neck and finally 120 sts down from shoulder seam to row 30 (bottom of straight front edge) on left front – 268 sts.
Work 3 rows in K1, P1 rib.
Buttonhole row: (RS facing) Rib 4, cast off 3, rib 12, cast off 3, rib 12, cast off 3, rib to end.
Next row: Rib, casting on 3 sts over cast-off sts on previous row (3 buttonholes worked in all).
Work 3 more rows in rib.
Cast off fairly loosely ribwise.

To complete
Join side seams and armhole edgings. Sew on buttons to correspond with buttonholes. The pointed waistcoat fronts may be left as they are or finished off with a crochet edging in A to prevent them from curling.

VERSION 2 ★
IN ONE COLOUR
(see page 23 for illustration of versions 2 and 3)

MATERIALS
Yarn
Any **Aran-weight** yarn can be used as long as it knits up to the given tension.
500(575)g/18(21)oz of chosen colour.
Needles and tension as for **Version 1**.

METHOD
Work exactly as for **Version 1**, omitting all reference to B and working in one colour only.

DECORATION
If required, small pearl buttons could be sewn on in position of chart motifs to give a real pearly effect, or create your own design.

VERSION 3 ★ ★
PEARLY KING JACKET

MATERIALS
Yarn
Any **Aran-weight** yarn can be used as long as it knits up to the given tension.
650(700)g/23(25)oz black cotton (A), 75(100)g/3(4)oz cream cotton (B)
Needles and tension as for **Version 1**.

BACK AND FRONTS
Work exactly as for **Version 1**.

Pearly King Waistcoat: This light-hearted waistcoat in cotton yarn is inspired by the intricately patterned traditional costumes of the Pearly Kings and Queens of London's East End. Its button motifs are knitted in, while the matching tie and jaunty beret are decorated authentically with tiny pearl buttons.

PEARLY KING WAISTCOAT BACK CHART

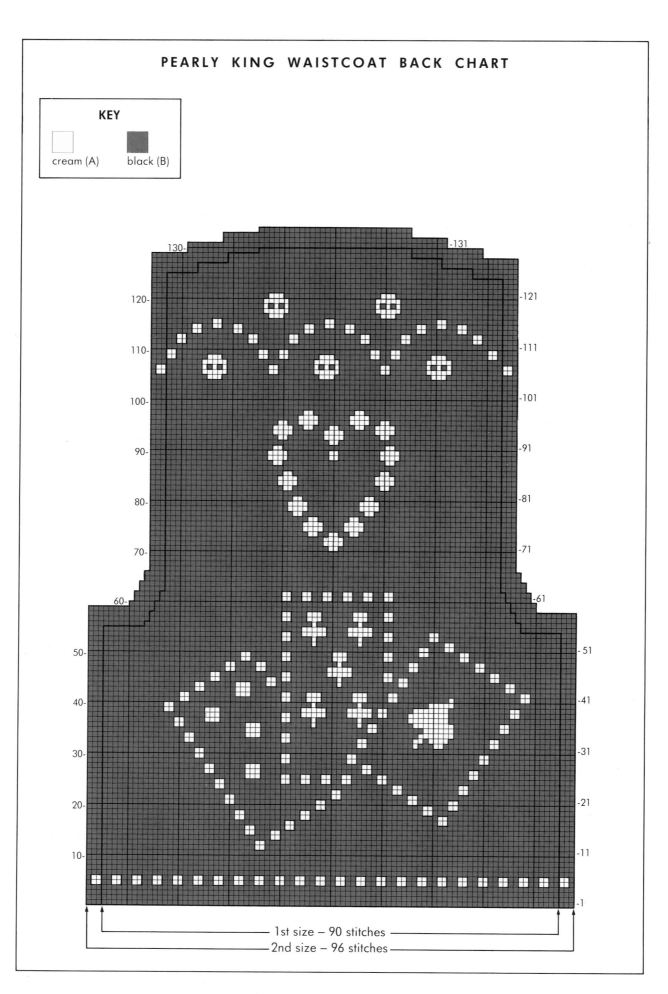

KEY

cream (A)   black (B)

1st size – 90 stitches
2nd size – 96 stitches

12

PEARLY KING WAISTCOAT FRONT CHARTS

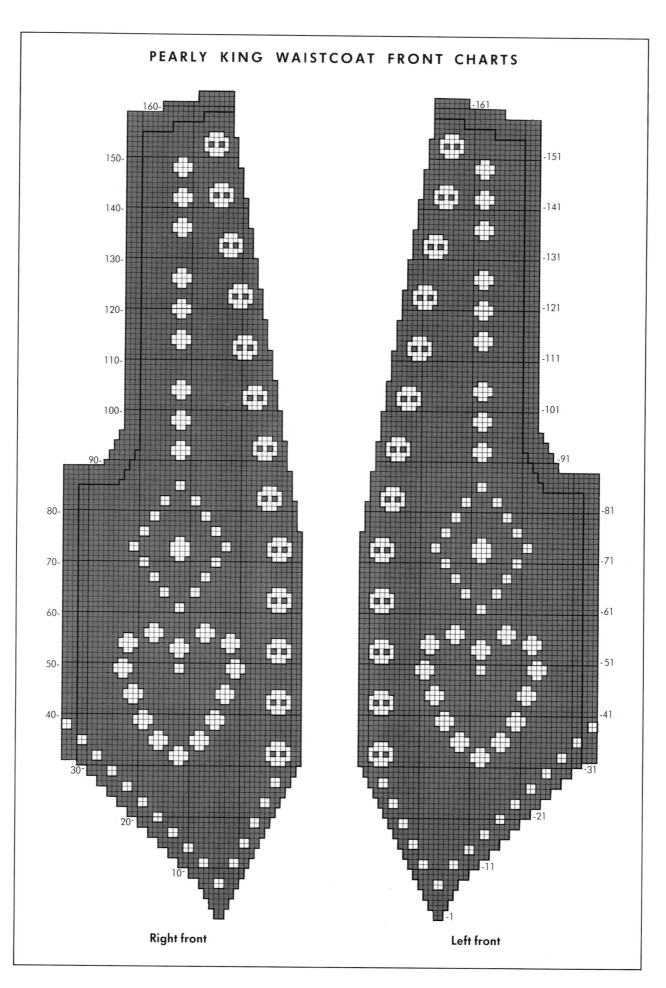

Right front

Left front

SLEEVES

Make 2. With 4mm (US 5) needles and A, cast on 48(52)sts and work in K1, P1 rib for 4 rows.
Change to 5mm (US 7) needles.
Row 1: (RS facing) K1A, *K2B, K2A, rep from * to last 3 sts, K2B, K1A.
Row 2: P1A, *P2B, P2A, rep from * to last 3 sts, P2B, P1A.
Now starting with a K row, cont in st st in A only, inc 1 st at each end of next row and then every foll 3rd row until there are 98 sts on the needle.
Now cont straight until sleeve measures 43(46)cm/17(18)in from cast-on edge, ending with a WS row.

Shape top

Cast off 8 sts at beg of next 2 rows – 82 sts.
Now dec 1 st at beg of foll 8 rows. Cast off rem 74 sts fairly loosely.

TO MAKE UP

Sew in ends and press pieces carefully following ball band instructions.
Join shoulder seams. With centre of cast-off edges of sleeves to shoulder seams, sew sleeves carefully into armholes.

Front band

Work as for **Version 1**.

To complete

Join side and sleeve seams. Then work as for **Version 1**.

PEARLY KING BERET ★★

MEASUREMENTS

To fit average adult head

Please see page 145 for actual garment measurements.

MATERIALS

Yarn
Any **Aran-weight** yarn can be used as long as it knits up to the given tension.
125g/5oz black cotton
Needles and other materials
1 pair each 4mm (US 5) and 5mm (US 7) needles
Approx 74 small pearl buttons
Approx 10 large pearl buttons

TENSION

18 sts and 25 rows to 10cm/4in on 5mm (US 7) needles over st st.

METHOD

With 4mm (US 5) needles, cast on 90 sts and work in K1, P1 rib for 8 rows.
Increase row: Rib and inc 1 st in every 4th st across row to last 2 sts, rib 2 – 112 sts.
Change to 5mm (US 7) needles and starting with a K row work in st st until work measures 5cm/2in from cast-on edge, ending with a WS row.
Increase row: Inc 1 st in every 8th st across row – 126sts.
Starting with a P row cont in st st until work measures 7·5cm/3in from cast-on edge, ending with a WS row.
Increase row: Inc 1 st in every 7th st across row – 144sts.
Starting with a P row cont in st st until work measures 11cm/4½in from cast-on edge, ending with a WS row.

Split for sections

1st row: (RS facing) **K24, turn, and work on this first set of sts only.
2nd row: P.
3rd row: K1, sl 1, K1, psso, K to last 3 sts, K2 tog, K1.
Rep last 2 rows until 4 sts remain.
P 1 row.
Next row: (K2 tog) twice.
Next row: P2.
Slip yarn through rem sts.**
With RS facing rejoin yarn to rem sts, rep from ** to ** 5 times more.

TO COMPLETE

Press carefully following ball band instructions. Join all seams.
Decorate with pearl buttons as required.

PEARLY KING TIE ★

MEASUREMENTS

Please see page 145 for actual garment measurements.

MATERIALS

Yarn
Any **Aran-weight** cotton yarn can be used as long as it knits up to the given tension.
75g/3oz black cotton
Needles and decoration
1 pair 4mm (US 5) needles
Approx 35 small pearl buttons

TENSION

20 sts and 28 rows to 10cm/4in on 4mm (US 5) needles over moss stitch.

METHOD

With 4mm (US 5) needles, cast on 8 sts and work in moss stitch as follows:
Row 1: *K1, P1, rep from * to end.
Row 2: *P1, K1, rep from * to end.
Rep these 2 rows until tie measures approx 140cm/55in, or required length.
Cast off in moss stitch.

DECORATION

Starting approx 43cm/17in up from one end, dot the buttons at regular intervals or in a diamond pattern, or other pattern of your choice – finishing at tie end (this part will show when the tie is knotted).

Fair Isle Smock Sweater: The traditional English farm worker's smock is brought fashionably up to date to create a modern heirloom. This long, loose, easy-to-wear sweater has full sleeves gathered into deep cuffs and a flattering wide collar. Natural-coloured linen/cotton mix yarn is knitted in a textured design of vertical panels, with contrasting black wool used for the flat Fair Isle pattern that recreates the effect of the elaborate embroidery stitches and smocking of the original garment.

FAIR ISLE SMOCK SWEATER

MEASUREMENTS
To fit bust: 81-87cm/32-34in and 97-102cm/38-40in

Please see page 146 for actual garment measurements.

VERSION 1 ★ ★ ★ ★

MATERIALS
Yarn
Any **double-knit** yarn can be used as long as it knits up to the given tension.
800(850)g/28(30)oz cream cotton/linen mixture (A),
150(175)g/6(7)oz black wool (B)
Needles
1 pair each 3¼mm (US 3) and 4mm (US 5) needles
Spare needle

TENSION
26 sts and 25 rows to 10cm/4in on 4mm (US 5) needles over Fair Isle pattern.
26 sts and 28 rows to 10cm/4in on 4mm (US 5) needles over textured pattern.

TEXTURED PATTERNS
Worked throughout in A.

PATTERN 1 (worked over 5 sts)
Row 1: (RS facing) K1, P3, K1.
Row 2: P1, K3, P1.
Row 3: K5.
Row 4: P5.
These 4 rows form **pattern 1**, repeated as required.

PATTERN 2 (worked over 17 sts)
Row 1: (RS facing) P2, K6, P1, K6, P2.
Row 2: K2, P5, K1, P1, K1, P5, K2.
Row 3: P2, K4, (P1, K1) twice, P1, K4, P2.
Row 4: K2, P3, (K1, P1) 3 times, K1, P3, K2.
Row 5: P2, K2, P1, K1, P1, K3, P1, K1, P1, K2, P2.
Row 6: K2, (P1, K1) twice, P5, (K1, P1) twice, K2.
Row 7: As 5th row.
Row 8: As 4th row.
Row 9: As 3rd row.
Row 10: As 2nd row.
These 10 rows form **pattern 2**, repeated as required.

PATTERN 3 (worked over 19 sts)
Row 1: (RS facing) P2, K9, (P1, K1) 3 times, P2.
Row 2: K2, P2, (K1, P1) 3 times, P7, K2.
Row 3: P2, K7, (P1, K1) 3 times, K2, P2.
Row 4: K2, P4, (K1, P1) 3 times, P5, K2.
Row 5: P2, K5, (P1, K1) 3 times, K4, P2.
Row 6: K2, P6, (K1, P1) 3 times, P3, K2.
Row 7: P2, K3, (P1, K1) 3 times, K6, P2.
Row 8: K2, P8, (K1, P1) 3 times, P1, K2.
Row 9: P2, (K1, P1) 3 times, K9, P2.
Row 10: As 8th row.
Row 11: As 7th row.
Row 12: As 6th row.
Row 13: As 5th row.
Row 14: As 4th row.
Row 15: As 3rd row.
Row 16: As 2nd row.
These 16 rows form **pattern 3**, repeated as required.

BACK
With 3¼mm (US 3) needles and A, cast on 96(120)sts and work in K1, P1 rib for 6 rows.
Increase row: K in A and inc 24 sts evenly across row – 120(144)sts.
P 1 row in A.
Change to 4mm (US 5) needles and starting with a K row work in st st from **chart 1**, repeating the 12-stitch patt across row.
Cont as set until the 26 rows of chart have been worked, thus ending with a WS row and on *1st size* inc 1 st and on *2nd size* dec 1 st on last row worked – 121(143)sts.
Now place textured patterns as follows:

1st size only
Row: 1 (RS facing) work across row 1 of the following patterns:
1, 3, 1, 2, 1, 3, 1, 2, 1, 3, 1.
Row 2: Work across row 2 of the following patterns:
1, 3, 1, 2, 1, 3, 1, 2, 1, 3, 1.

2nd size only
Row 1: (RS facing) Work across row 1 of the following patterns:
1, 2, 1, 3, 1, 2, 1, 3, 1, 2, 1, 3, 1.
Row 2: Work across row 2 of the following patterns:
1, 3, 1, 2, 1, 3, 1, 2, 1, 3, 1, 2, 1.

Both sizes
The textured patts are now placed.
Cont working from appropriate patts, repeating the

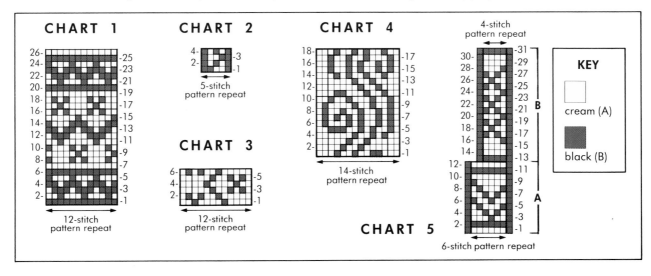

CHART 1 CHART 2 CHART 4 CHART 3 CHART 5

KEY
cream (A)
black (B)

12-stitch pattern repeat
5-stitch pattern repeat
12-stitch pattern repeat
14-stitch pattern repeat
4-stitch pattern repeat
6-stitch pattern repeat

16

relevant patt rows as required until back measures 44(46)cm/17½(18)in from cast-on edge.

Place coloured markers at each end of last row to indicate armholes.

Now cont straight in patts as set until back measures 49(51)cm/19¼(20)in from cast-on edge, ending with a WS row, and on *1st size* dec 1 st and on *2nd size* inc 1 st on last row worked – 120(144)sts.

Place Fair Isle yoke charts as follows:

Starting with a K row cont in st st and work rows 1-6 as **chart 1**. Now work across row 1 of the following yoke charts:

charts 2, 3, 2, 4, 2, 3, then from **chart 5** – work 1 st before the solid line, rep the 6-stitch patt 2(6) times, work 1 st beyond the solid line – now work across **charts 3, 2, 4, 2, 3, 2.**

The charts are now set.

Cont to follow appropriate charts, repeating the relevant chart rows, noting that **chart 5 section A** is a 6-stitch patt repeat and **section B** is a 4-stitch patt repeat.

Cont as set until back measures 74(78)cm/29¼(30¾)in from cast-on edge, ending with a WS row.

Shape shoulders

Keeping charts correct, cast off 10(12)sts at beg of next 8 rows.

Cast off rem 40(48)sts for back neck.

FRONT

Work as for back until 34 rows of **chart 5** have been worked in all, thus ending with a WS row.

Shape front neck

Next row: Patt 50(59)sts, cast off centre 20(26)sts, patt to end of row and cont on this last set of sts only, leaving rem sts on a spare needle.

****Keeping patt correct, dec 1 st at neck edge on every row until 40(48)sts remain.

Now cont straight until front measures the same as back to beg of shoulder shaping, ending at side edge.

Shape shoulder

Keeping patts correct, cast off 10(12)sts at beg of next row and foll 3 alt rows.

With WS facing rejoin yarn to rem sts and work as for first side from ** to end.

SLEEVES

Make 2. With 3¼mm (US 3) needles and A, cast on 36(48)sts and work in K1, P1 rib for 6 rows.

K 1 row in A, P 1 row in A.

Change to 4mm (US 5) needles and starting with a K row work in st st from **chart 1**, repeating the 12-stitch patt across row.

Cont as set until the 26 rows of chart have been worked, thus ending with a WS row and inc 39(49)sts evenly across last row – 75(97)sts.

Now place textured patterns as follows:

1st size only

Row 1: (RS facing) Work across row 1 of the following patterns: 1, 3, 1, 2, 1, 3, 1.

Row 2: Work across row 2 of the following patterns: 1, 3, 1, 2, 1, 3, 1.

2nd size only

Row 1: (RS facing) Work across row 1 of the following patterns: 1, 2, 1, 3, 1, 2, 1, 3, 1.

Row 2: Work across row 2 of the following patterns: 1, 3, 1, 2, 1, 3, 1, 2, 1.

Both sizes

The textured patts are now placed.

Cont working from appropriate patts, repeating the relevant patt rows as required, *at the same time* inc 1 st at each end of every foll alt row until there are 139(161)sts on the needle, working inc sts into st st on either side, and ending with a WS row.

Decrease row: K32, now K across the 75(97)sts of textured patts but dec 39(49)sts evenly across this section, K32 – 100(112)sts.

Place Fair Isle top

Next row: (WS facing) P32A, P36(48)B, P32A.

Next row: Inc in 1st st, K until there are 33 sts on RH needle, K1B, then work across 1st row of **chart 2**, then work from **chart 5** repeating the 6-stitch patt 4(6) times, then work across 1st row of **chart 2**, K1B, K to end of row in A, inc in last st.

The charts are now set.

Cont to follow appropriate charts, repeating the relevant chart rows, noting that **chart 5 section A** is a 6-stitch patt repeat and **section B** is a 4-stitch patt repeat, *at the same time* cont to inc 1 st at each end of every foll alt row until there are 134(146)sts on the needle and 33 rows of **chart 5** have been worked in all.

Cast off all sts fairly loosely in A.

TO MAKE UP

Press pieces carefully following ball band instructions and sew in ends. Carefully join both shoulder seams. With centre of cast-off edges of sleeves to shoulder seams, sew sleeves carefully in position between coloured markers, stretching slightly to fit. Join side and sleeve seams matching patts on welt and cuffs.

Collar

With 3¼mm (US 3) needles and A, cast on 120(132)sts and work in K1, P1 rib for 5cm/2in.

Change to 4mm (US 5) needles.

Next row: (RS facing) rib 6A, K108(120)A, rib 6A.

Next row: Rib 6A, P108(120)A, rib 6A.

Rep last 2 rows until collar measures 13cm/5in from cast-on edge ending with a WS row.

Next row: Rib 6A, now work across the 12-stitch patt on row 1 of **chart 1** 9(10) times, rib 6A.

Keeping rib borders correct, work from chart as set until 6 rows have been worked in all.

Next row: (RS facing) Rib 6A, K108(120)A, rib 6A.

Next row: Rib 6A, P108(120)B, rib 6A.

Next row: Rib 6A, K108(120)A, rib 6A.

Now work 4 rows in K1, P1 rib in A across all sts.

Cast off fairly loosely ribwise.

To complete

Carefully press collar. Starting at centre front, carefully sew cast-on edge of collar around neck edge, stretching to fit. Join the 5cm/2in of rib together at centre front and leave remaining edges of collar free to fold over onto right side of garment.

VERSION 2 ★ ★ ★ ★

BLACK WITH CREAM FAIR ISLE PATTERN

(see page 23 for illustration)

This is worked exactly as for **Version 1** except B is used in place of A, and A is used in place of B and yarn amounts are altered correspondingly.

SCANDINAVIAN SWEATER

MEASUREMENTS

To fit bust: 81-91cm/32-36in and 97-102cm/38-40in

Please see page 147 for actual garment measurements.

VERSION 1 ★ ★ ★

MATERIALS
Yarn

Any **Aran-weight** yarn can be used as long as it knits up to the given tension.
725(825)g/26(29)oz cream (A), 100(125)g/4(5)oz navy (B), 75(100)g/3(4)oz each of rust (C), brown (D) and green (E)
Needles

1 pair each 4½mm (US 6) and 5½mm (US 8) needles
Spare needle

TENSION

22 sts and 22 rows to 10cm/4in on 5½mm (US 8) needles over main pattern.

BACK

With 4½mm (US 6) needles and A, cast on 72(80)sts and work in K2, P2 rib for 10cm/4in.
Increase row: Rib and inc 44 sts evenly across row – 116(124) sts.
Change to 5½mm (US 8) needles and starting with row 1 (K row), work in st st from **chart** (see page 20), working between appropriate lines for size required. Work straight following chart until row 120(126) has been worked.

Shape shoulders

Keeping chart correct, cast off 12(14)sts at beg of next 2 rows.
Cast off 12(13)sts at beg of foll 4 rows.
Cast off rem 44 sts for back neck.

FRONT

Work as for back until row 110(116) on chart has been completed.

Shape front neck

Next row: (RS facing) Patt 47(51)sts, turn and work on this first set of sts only, leaving rem sts on a spare needle.
****Keeping patt correct, dec 1 st at neck edge on every row 11 times, *at the same time*, when front measures the same as back to beg of shoulder shaping ending at side edge, cont as follows:

Shape shoulder

Keeping patt and neck shaping correct, cast off 12(14)sts at beg of next row. Patt 1 row.
Cast off 12(13)sts at beg of next row and foll alt row.

Scandinavian Sweater: Reindeers and snowflakes are popular motifs of Scandinavian peasant knitwear. For this attractively chunky sweater they are incorporated into a colourful pattern in deep, rich shades on a cream ground. Knitted in Aran-weight wool, it has a deep ribbed roll collar for warmth and is partnered by a cosy bobble hat and gloves with extra-long cuffs.

With RS facing return to rem sts, cast off centre 22 sts, patt to end of row.
Now work as for first side from ** to end.

SLEEVES
Make 2. With 4½mm (US 6) needles and A, cast on 40(44)sts and work in K2, P2 rib for 10cm/4in.
Increase row: Rib, inc 1 st in every st of row – 80(88) sts.
Change to 5½mm (US 8) needles and starting with row 1 (K row) work in st st from chart, working between appropriate lines for sleeve size required, *at the same time*, inc 1 st at each end of 2nd row and then every foll 3rd row. Cont as set until row 24 has been worked.
Now rep rows 25-40 to form the patt, inc as set until there are 136(144)sts on the needle, working inc sts into the patt on either side.
Work a few rows straight until sleeve measures approx 48(51)cm/19(20)in from cast-on edge ending with a WS row and a complete motif worked.
Cast off all sts fairly loosely in A.

TO MAKE UP

Press pieces carefully following ball band instructions. Sew in all ends. Join left shoulder seam.

Polo neck

With 4½mm (US 6) needles and A and RS facing, pick up and K 44 sts from back neck, 13 sts down left front neck, 22 sts at centre front and finally 13 sts up right side of front neck – 92 sts.
Change to 5½mm (US 8) needles and work in K2, P2 rib for 20cm/8in. Cast off fairly loosely ribwise.

To complete

Join right shoulder seam and polo neck, reversing seam for turn-back.
With centre of cast-off edges of sleeves to shoulder seams, sew sleeves carefully in position. Join side and sleeve seams matching patterns.
Roll over polo neck to right side of garment.

VERSION 2 ★ ★ ★

MAN'S CREW-NECK SWEATER WITH BLACK BACKGROUND

(see page 23 for illustration)

MEASUREMENTS
To fit chest: 97-102cm/38-40in

MATERIALS
Yarn

Any **Aran-weight** yarn can be used as long as it knits up to the given tension.
850g/30oz black (A), 125g/5oz cream (B), 100g/4oz each of rust (C), brown (D) and green (E)
Needles and tension as for **Version 1**.

BACK, FRONT AND SLEEVES

Follow instructions for **Version 1**, *2nd size only*.
When working sleeves, make total length 56cm/22in.

TO MAKE UP

As **Version 1**.

Crew neck

Work as for polo neck on **Version 1**, but work only 8cm/3in in K2, P2 rib. Cast off fairly loosely ribwise.

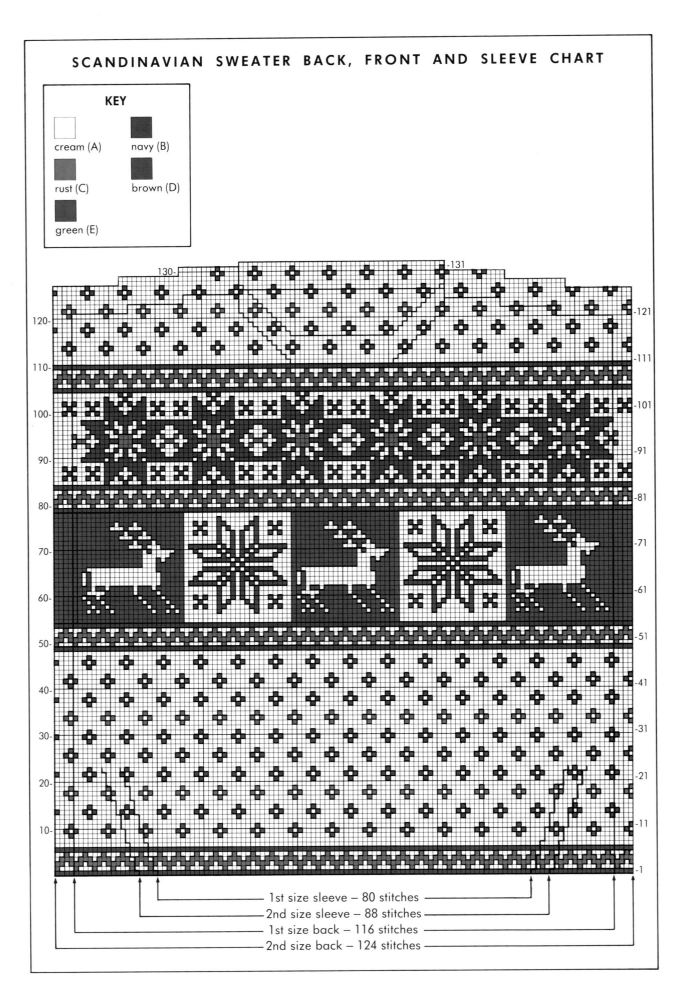

SCANDINAVIAN SWEATER BACK, FRONT AND SLEEVE CHART

KEY

cream (A) navy (B)

rust (C) brown (D)

green (E)

1st size sleeve – 80 stitches
2nd size sleeve – 88 stitches
1st size back – 116 stitches
2nd size back – 124 stitches

To complete
Join right shoulder seam and crew neck. Fold crew neck in half to inside and loosely slip stitch in position. Complete as for **Version 1**.

SCANDINAVIAN GLOVES ★ ★

MEASUREMENTS
To fit average adult hand

Please see page 147 for actual garment measurements.

MATERIALS
Yarn
Any **double-knit** weight yarn can be used as long as it knits up to the given tension.
75g/3oz cream (A), 25g/1oz each of green (B) and rust (C)
Needles
1 pair needles 3¾mm (US 4)
2 stitch-holders

TENSION
25 sts and 32 rows to 10cm/4in on 3¾mm (US 4) needles over st st.

RIGHT GLOVE
With 3¾mm (US 4) needles and A, cast on 48 sts and work in double rib as follows:
Row 1: (RS facing) *K2, P2, rep from * to end.
Rep this row 3 times more.
Change to B and work 2 rows in rib as set.
Change to A and work 4 rows in rib as set.
Change to C and work 2 rows in rib as set.
Rep these 12 rows once more and then the first 6 rows again (30 rib rows worked in all).
Rows 31-36: Starting with a K row work in st st in A.
Row 37: (RS facing) K2A, K19C (this places position of **chart** for motif on back of hand), K3A inc in next st, K1, inc in next st, K21.
Rows 38-40: Work in st st and follow chart over the 19 sts as set.
Row 41: K24, inc in next st, K3, inc in next st, K21.
Rows 42-53: Work from chart, on every 4th row inc 1 st at each side of gusset for thumb as set – 58 sts.
Rows 54-56: Work in st st.

Thumb
Row 57: (RS facing) K38, turn, and leave sts unworked on a stitch-holder, cast on 2 sts.
Row 58: P16, turn, and leave rem sts on a stitch-holder, cast on 2 sts – 18 sts.
Rows 59-80: Starting with a K row, work in st st.
Row 81: *K2 tog, K2, rep from * to last 2 sts, K2 – 14 sts.
Row 82: P.
Row 83: (K2 tog) across row.
Break yarn and thread through rem sts. Draw up and fasten off.
With RH needle, K up 4 sts at base of thumb, K across the sts on first stitch-holder.
Next row: P across sts, then P across sts on 2nd stitch-holder – 48 sts. Starting with a K row, work in st st for 8 rows (chart is now complete).

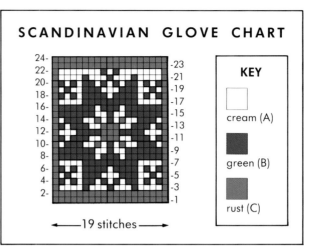

SCANDINAVIAN GLOVE CHART

24- -23
22- -21
20- -19
18- -17
16- -15
14- -13
12- -11
10- -9
8- -7
6- -5
4- -3
2- -1

←—19 stitches—→

KEY

cream (A)

green (B)

rust (C)

1st finger
Next row: (RS facing) K31, turn, and leave sts unworked on a stitch-holder, cast on 1 st.
Next row: P15, turn, and leave rem sts on a stitch-holder, cast on 1 st – 16 sts.
Starting with a K row work in st st for 20 rows.
****Next row:** (RS facing) *K2 tog, K2, rep from * to end – 12 sts.
Next row: P.
Next row: (K2 tog) across row.
Break yarn and finish as for thumb.**

2nd finger
With RH needle, K up 2 sts at base of 1st finger, K across 6 sts on first stitch-holder, turn and cast on 1 st.
Next row: P across these 9 sts and then 6 sts from the 2nd stitch-holder, turn, and cast on 1 st (16 sts), leaving sts unworked on stitch-holders.
Starting with a K row, work in st st for 24 rows.
Rep from ** to ** and finish as for 1st finger.

3rd finger
Work as for 2nd finger, but work 20 rows of st st.

4th finger
With RH needle, K up 2 sts at base of 3rd finger, K across rem 5 sts on first stitch-holder.
Next row: P across these 7 sts and then P rem 5 sts from second stitch-holder – 12 sts.
Starting with a K row, work in st st for 16 rows.
Next row: *K2, K2 tog, rep from * to end – 9 sts.
Next row: P.
Next row: (K2 tog) to last st, K1.
Break yarn and finish as for thumb.

LEFT GLOVE
Rows 1-36: Work as for right glove.
Row 37: (RS facing) In A, K21, inc in next st, K1, inc in next st, K3A, K19C, K2A (this places position of **chart**).
Rows 38-40: Work in st st and follow chart over the 19 sts as set.
Row 41: K21, inc in next st, K3, inc in next st, K24.
Rows 42-56: Work as for right glove.
Row 57: K34, turn, and leave sts unworked on a stitch-holder, cast on 2 sts.
Finish thumb and fingers as for right glove.

TO MAKE UP
Sew in all ends and press carefully following ball band instructions.
Carefully join all seams.

BOBBLE HAT

MEASUREMENTS
To fit average adult head

Please see page 147 for actual garment measurements.

VERSION 1 ★ ★

MATERIALS
Yarn
Any **Aran-weight** yarn can be used as long as it knits up to the given tension.
75g/3oz cream (A), 25g/1oz each of green (B) and rust (C)
Needles
1 pair each 4½mm (US 6) and 5½mm (US 8) needles

TENSION
22 sts and 22 rows to 10cm/4in on 5½mm (US 8) needles over pattern.

METHOD
With 4½mm (US 6) needles and A, cast on 116 sts and work in K2, P2 rib for 6 rows.
Change to 5½mm (US 8) needles and starting with a K row, work in st st following **Scandinavian Sweater Chart** (see page 20).
Start from row 79 and continue until row 110 has been worked, working between lines for *1st size*, and working green instead of navy (32 patt rows worked in all, thus ending with a WS row).
Now complete in A only:
Starting with a K row, work 2 rows in st st.

Shape top
Row 1: (RS facing) *K8, K2 tog, rep from * to last 6 sts, K6 – 105 sts.
Row 2 and every foll alt row:
Row 3: *K7, K2 tog, rep from * to last 6 sts, K6 – 94 sts.
Row 5: *K6, K2 tog, rep from * to last 6 sts, K6 – 83 sts.
Row 7: *K5, K2 tog, rep from * to last 6 sts, K6 – 72 sts.
Row 9: *K4, K2 tog, rep from * to end – 60 sts.
Row 11: *K3, K2 tog, rep from * to end – 48 sts.
Row 13: *K2, K2 tog, rep from * to end – 36 sts.
Row 15: *K1, K2 tog, rep from * to end – 24 sts.
Row 17: (K2 tog) to end – 12 sts.
Row 19: (K2 tog) to end – 6 sts.
Row 21: (K2 tog) to end – 3 sts.
Next row: K3 tog and fasten off.

TO COMPLETE
Sew in ends. Press carefully following ball band instructions. Sew up seam carefully matching patt.

TO MAKE POMPON
Cut 2 circles of card approx. 6cm/2½in in diameter. Cut a 2cm/¾in circle in centre of each circle of card.
Place the two circles of card together and wrap yarn around and around until the card is completely covered. Now cut in between the two circles and tie around the centre tightly with matching yarn leaving a long end with which to sew pompon onto hat. Trim into shape if necessary. Sew pompon to tip of hat.

VERSION 2 ★

IN ONE COLOUR WITH RIBBED TURN-UP

MATERIALS
Yarn
Any **Aran-weight** yarn can be used as long as it knits up to the given tension.
100g/4oz in chosen colour
Needles and tension as for **Version 1**.

METHOD
With 4½mm (US 6) needles, cast on 116 sts and work in K2, P2 rib for 10cm/4in.
Now starting with a K row, cont in st st until work measures 16cm/6½in from cast-on edge, ending with a WS row.
Now shape top as for **Version 1**.
Complete as for **Version 1** adding optional pompon.

EASTERN EUROPE

Inspiration for this chapter comes from several different countries – Russia, Hungary, Lithuania and Rumania – with designs mainly drawn from folkloric and peasant costume, although I have taken floral motifs from the rich brocades and patterned chintzes worn by the nobility at the Russian court. The overall look is pretty and feminine, with soft pastel shades harmonizing with lace and flowers.

Embroidery was a striking feature of traditional dress in Eastern Europe and each area had its own distinctive patterns and stitches. Particular colour schemes and motifs often indicate the place of origin: for instance, geometric motifs worked in red on a cream background were popular in Bulgaria and floral patterns were characteristic of the Ukraine, while animals and other figurative devices were common elsewhere in Russia.

The **Floral and Lace Cardigan** *(page 28)* is a
classic shape, fairly easy to knit. It is based on a
decorative apron, part of a woman's festive
costume from the Russian province of Vologda,
now in the Hermitage Museum, Leningrad. The
apron has layers of white lace alternating with
flowered silk ribbons. This translates well as a
knitted fabric, with openwork bands in white
cotton yarn contrasting with lines of simple
flower shapes.

The loose shape of the **Peasant Shirt** *(page 30)*
is typical of men's work shirts in Rumania and
Hungary; it is knitted in raw natural slub cotton,
with a Fair Isle border design in blue double-knit
cotton resembling traditional embroidery stitches.

The **Cossack Jacket** *(page 32)* combines the
style of Russian military tunics — notably the high
neck and dashing gold fasteners — with that of
women's loose, high-waisted quilted jackets
formerly worn in Russia and Lithuania. Touches of
gold lurex and silk add elegance, recalling the
richness of embroidered brocades, and the
Cossack Hat and **Gloves** complete the outfit.

FLORAL AND LACE CARDIGAN ★ ★

MEASUREMENTS
To fit bust: 81-91cm/32-36in and 97-102cm/38-40in

Please see page 148 for actual garment measurements.

MATERIALS
Yarn

Any **double-knit** weight yarn can be used as long as it knits up to the given tension.

375(400)g/14(15)oz cream cotton (A), 75(100)g/3(4)oz each of blue cotton (B), orange mohair (C), yellow cotton (D), 525(550)g/19(20)oz beige cotton (E), 50(75)g/2(3)oz green cotton (F)

Needles and other materials

1 pair each 3¼mm (US 3) and 4mm (US 5) needles
9 pearl buttons
2 safety-pins

TENSION
25 sts and 30 rows to 10cm/4in on 4mm (US 5) needles over pattern.

NOTE
When working flower motifs, use separate balls of yarn for each motif worked. Do *not* carry yarn across wrong side of work as this will make the garment very heavy. Stitch count varies on some rows, so take this into account when counting stitches.

BACK
With 4mm (US 5) needles and A, cast on 128(142)sts and work in lace pattern as follows:

Row 1: (RS facing) P2, *yrn, sl 1, K1, psso, K1, sl 1, K1, psso, yrn, P2, rep from * to end.

Row 2: *K2, P5, rep from * to last 2 sts, K2.

Row 3: P2, *K1, yf, sl 1, K2 tog, psso, yf, K1, P2, rep from * to end.

Row 4: As Row 2.

These 4 rows form one patt repeat. Rep them twice more.

Previous pages

Left *Floral Cossack Jacket: This stunning outfit is inspired by the dashing uniforms of the Cossack cavalry. It is knitted mainly in cotton, with gold lurex and silk yarn adding extra richness. Floral motifs twining across a soft blue background are derived from the sumptuous embroidered brocades worn at the Imperial Russian Court. Details include a peplum gathered on to a high waist, balanced by very full sleeves. The gold fasteners, matching hat and embroidered gloves complete the Cossack look.*

Centre *Peasant Shirt: A loose, flowing smock is knitted in textured cream cotton, suggesting the rough home-spun linen of traditional farmers' shirts in Eastern Europe. Dropped shoulders and full sleeves make it both graceful and comfortable to wear.*

Right *Floral and Lace Cardigan: Derived from the festive peasant costume of provincial Russia, this charming cardigan has lacy white cotton stripes alternating with subtly coloured bands of flowers, also knitted in cotton, with orange mohair used to add textural interest.*

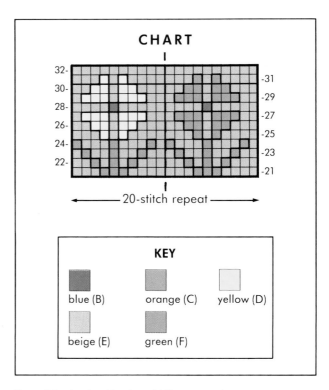

CHART

← 20-stitch repeat →

KEY

blue (B)   orange (C)   yellow (D)

beige (E)   green (F)

Row 13: In E, K, dec 8(2)sts evenly across row – 120(140)sts.

Row 14: In E, K.

Row 15: *K2A, K1B, K1A, K1B, rep from * to end.

Row 16: *P1A, P1B, P3A, rep from * to end.

Row 17: As Row 15.

Row 18: In E, P.

Row 19: In E, P.

Row 20: In E, P.

Now work in st st from **chart** as follows:

Row 21: (RS facing) *1st size only:* Rep the 20-stitch patt 6 times across row; *2nd size only:* Rep the 20-stitch patt 7 times across row.

Rows 22-32: Cont as now set until the 12 rows of chart are complete.

Row 33: In E, K.

Rows 34-39: As rows 14-19.

Row 40: P in A and inc 8(2)sts evenly across row – 128(142)sts.

These 40 rows form one pattern repeat.

Rep these 40 rows once more, but reverse colour of flowers, so they alternate with 1st row of flowers.

Cont to rep these 40 rows, alternating flowers as set until 5 complete patt repeats have been worked, thus ending with a 40th patt row, *but* work this last row across in E and *do not* inc sts – 120(140)sts (200 patt rows worked in all).

Shape shoulders
Cont in st st in E only, cast off 13(15)sts at beg of next 6 rows.

Cast off rem 42(50)sts fairly loosely.

RIGHT FRONT
With 4mm (US 5) needles and A, cast on 65(72)sts and work in lace patt to match back until row 12 has been completed.

Row 13: In E, K, dec 5(2)sts evenly across row – 60(70)sts.

Now cont as for back until row 20 has been completed.
Now work in st st from Fair Isle chart as follows:

Row 21: (RS facing) *1st size only:* Rep the 20-stitch patt 3 times across row; *2nd size only:* Work the 10 sts beyond the dotted line, then rep the 20-stitch patt 3 times.
(Flowers at front edge are in C(D), and therefore will match with back at side seams.)
Rows 22-32: Cont as now set until the 12 rows of chart are complete.
Rows 33-39: Work as for back.
Row 40: P in A and inc 5(2)sts evenly across row — 65(72)sts.
These 40 rows form one pattern repeat.
Cont to rep the patt, as for back, until 180 patt rows have been worked in all, thus ending with a 20th row of patt — 60(70)sts.

**Shape front neck
Next row: Cast off 12 sts, patt to end of row — 48(58)sts.
Keeping patt correct, dec 1 st at neck edge on next row and every foll row 9(13) times in all — 39(45)sts.
Now cont straight in patt until 5 complete patt repeats have been worked, thus ending with a 40th patt row *but* work this last row across in E and *do not* inc sts — 39(45)sts (200 patt rows worked in all).**
Now cont in st st in E only and K 1 row, thus ending at side edge.

Shape shoulder
Cast off 13(15)sts at beg of next row and foll 2 alt rows.

LEFT FRONT
Work as for right front working all lace patt rows as given.
Place Fair Isle chart as follows:
Row 21: (RS facing) *1st size only:* Rep the 20-stitch patt 3 times across row; *2nd size only:* Rep the 20-stitch patt 3 times, then work 10 sts before the dotted line.
(Flowers at front edge are in D(C), and therefore will match with back at side seams.)
Cont as for right front until 179 patt rows have been worked in all, thus ending with a 19th row of patt.
Now work as for right front from ** to **, then shape shoulder as right front.

SLEEVES
Make 2. With 3¼mm (US 3) needles and E, cast on 48 sts and work in K1, P1 rib for 6cm/2½in.
Increase row: K and inc 1 st in every st across row — 96 sts.
Next row: K in E.
Increase row: (RS facing) In E, K2, inc 1 st in every 2nd st to last 2 sts, K2 — 142 sts.
Next row: P in E.
Change to 4mm (US 5) needles and work in pattern as for back.
Cont straight working inc and dec rows and Fair Isle chart as for *2nd size on back* until 100(120) patt rows have been worked in all, thus ending with a 20th(40th) patt row; on *2nd size only,* work last row across in E and *do not* inc sts.
Cast off fairly loosely in E.

TO MAKE UP
Join both shoulder seams. Measure 23cm/9in down both back and front from shoulder seams and place coloured markers at side edges. Gather cast-off edges of sleeves until top sleeve measures 46cm/18in. Pin sleeves to side edges, between coloured markers, placing gathers to fall over shoulder seam area. Stitch

in position. Join side and sleeve seams matching pattern carefully. Do not press.

Left front band
With 3¼mm (US 3) needles and E, cast on 9 sts and work in single rib as follows:
Row 1: (RS facing) K1, *P1, K1, rep from * to end.
Row 2: P1, *K1, P1, rep from * to end.
Rep last 2 rows, until band, when slightly stretched, fits up left front to beg of neck shaping, sewing in position as you go along. Leave sts on a safety-pin.
On this band mark positions for 8 buttons (9th will be in collar). First to come 3cm/1¼in up from bottom edge, 8th to come 1cm/½in below neck edge and remainder spaced evenly between.

Right front band
Work as for left front band with the addition of 8 buttonholes worked when button positions are reached.
Buttonhole row: (RS facing) Rib 3, cast off 3 sts, rib to end.
Next row: Rib, casting on 3 sts over cast-off sts on previous row.
Complete as for left front band.

Collar
With 3¼mm (US 3) needles and E and RS facing, rib across the 9 sts of buttonhole band, then pick up and K 28 sts up right front neck, 43(49)sts across back neck, 28 sts down left front neck and finally rib across the 9 sts of button band — 117(123)sts.
Keeping rib correct as for front bands, cont in single rib for 6cm/2½in ending with a RS row, making a buttonhole on right front, as before, when collar measures 3cm/1¼in.
Next row: (WS facing) K to mark fold-line.
Now cont in single rib as before, making a buttonhole when collar measures 3cm/1¼in from fold-line.
When collar measures 6cm/2½in from fold-line, cast off fairly loosely ribwise.

To complete
Fold collar in half to inside along fold-line and carefully slip stitch in position, catching edges of top buttonhole together. Sew on buttons to correspond with buttonholes.

PEASANT SHIRT

MEASUREMENTS
To fit bust: 76-81cm/30-32in, 81-91cm/32-36in and 91-102cm/36-40in

Please see page 148 for actual garment measurements.

VERSION 1 ★ ★

MATERIALS
Yarn
Any **double-knit** weight yarn can be used as long as it knits up to the given tension.
550(575:600)g/20(21:21)oz textured cream cotton (A), 25(25:25)g/1(1:1)oz each of blue cotton (B) and brown cotton (C), 75(75:100)g/3(3:4)oz cream cotton (D)
Needles and other materials
1 pair each 3¼mm (US 3), 4mm (US 5) and 3¾mm (US 4) needles
4 pearl buttons
Safety-pin
Spare needle

TENSION
20 sts and 31 rows to 10cm/4in on 4mm (US 5) needles over st st using yarn A.

BACK
With 3¼mm (US 3) needles and A, cast on 104(110:116)sts and work in K1, P1 rib for 2.5cm/1in. Change to 4mm (US 5) needles and starting with a K row, work straight in st st until back measures 61(63:65)cm/24(24¾:25½)in from cast-on edge, ending with a WS row.

Shape shoulders
Cast off 11(12:13)sts at beg of next 6 rows.
Cast off rem 38 sts fairly loosely.

FRONT
Work as for back until front measures 31(33:35)cm/12¼(13:13¾)in from cast-on edge, ending with a WS row.

Place centre front panel
Next row: K38(41:44)A, K28C, K38(41:44)A.
Next row: P38(41:44)A, P28C, P38(41:44)A.
Now work from charts as follows:
Row 1: (RS facing) K38(41:44)A, now K across the 11 sts of row 1 of **chart 1**, K6D, now K across the 11 sts of row 1 of **chart 2**, K38(41:44)A.
Row 2: P38(41:44)A, P across the 11 sts of row 2 of **chart 2**, P6D, now P across the 11 sts of row 2 of **chart 1**, P38(41:44)A.

Divide for split
Row 3: K38(41:44)A, patt 11 sts from **chart 1**, slip middle 6 sts onto a safety-pin for front band, patt across the 11 sts from **chart 2**, K38(41:44)A.
Now cont on this last set of 49(52:55)sts only, leaving rem sts on a spare needle.
Cont to rep the 6 rows of **chart 2 keeping outer edge in A only as set, until front measures 53(55:57)cm/21(21¾:22½)in from cast-on edge, ending at centre front edge.

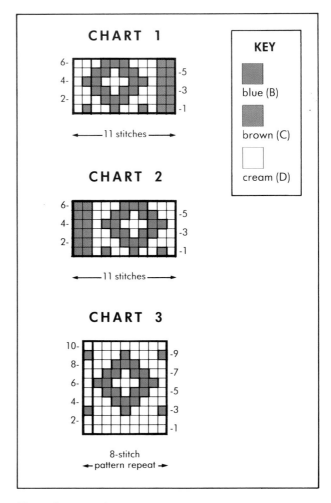

CHART 1 — 11 stitches

CHART 2 — 11 stitches

CHART 3 — 8-stitch ← pattern repeat →

KEY
blue (B)
brown (C)
cream (D)

Shape front neck
Next row: Cast off 7 sts, patt to end.
Keeping patt correct, dec 1 st at neck edge on every row until 33(36:39)sts remain.
Now cont straight until front measures the same as back to beg of shoulder shaping, ending at side edge.

Shape shoulder
Cast off 11(12:13)sts at beg of next row and foll 2 alt rows.
With WS facing rejoin yarn to rem 49(52:55)sts and work as for first side from ** to end, but keeping patt correct as for **chart 1**.

SLEEVES
Make 2. With 3¼mm (US 3) needles and C, cast on 48 sts and starting with a K row work in st st in C for 4 rows. Change to 4mm (US 5) needles and work in patt as follows:
Row 1: (RS facing) Work across the 8 sts of row 1 of **chart 3** 6 times.
Cont as set until the 10 rows are complete. Then rep these 10 rows once more (20 patt rows worked in all, thus ending with a WS row).
Change to C and K 1 row, P 1 row.
Change to A and K 1 row, P 1 row.
Increase row: (RS facing) In A K, and inc 1 st in every st of row – 96 sts.
Cont in st st in A only and inc 1 st at each end of 2nd row and then every foll 3rd row until there are 140 sts on the needle.

Now cont straight until sleeve measures 41(43:45)cm/16¼(17:17¾)in from cast-on edge, ending with a WS row.
Cast off all sts fairly loosely.

TO MAKE UP
Sew in ends and carefully press pieces following ball band instructions.

Left front band
With 3¼mm (US 3) needles and D cast on 6 sts and work in single rib as follows:
Row 1: (RS facing) *P1, K1, rep from * to end.
Row 2: K1, *K1, P1, rep from * to last st, K1.
Rep last 2 rows until band, when slightly stretched, fits up left front, from base of centre front opening to start of neck shaping, sewing in position as you go along.
Cast off ribwise.
On this band mark positions for 4 buttons. First to come 2cm/¾in up from base, last to come 2cm/¾in down from neck shaping and rem 2 spaced evenly between.

Right front band
With 3¼mm (US 3) needles and D and RS facing rejoin yarn to the 6 centre sts on safety-pin.
Row 1: (RS facing) *K1, P1, rep from * to end.
Row 2: *K1, P1, rep from * to last 2 sts, K2.
Rep last 2 rows and work as for left front band with the addition of buttonholes when button positions are reached.
Buttonhole row: (RS facing) Rib 2, cast off 2 sts, rib to end.
Next row: Rib, casting on 2 sts over cast-off sts of previous row.
Cont as set until 4 buttonholes have been worked.
Complete as for left front band.

Collar
Join both shoulder seams.
With 3¼mm (US 3) needles and C and RS facing and starting in middle of buttonhole band, pick up and K 26 sts along right front neck, 37 sts across back neck and 26 sts along left front neck to middle of button band – 89 sts.
P 1 row in C.
Change to 4mm (US 5) needles and work in patt as follows:
Row 1: (RS facing) Work across the 8 sts of row 1 of **chart 3** 11 times, then work 1 st beyond the solid line.
Row 2: Work 1 st before the solid line, then rep the 8 sts 11 times across row.
Cont as now set until the 10 rows of chart are complete thus ending with a WS row.
K 1 row in C.
Fold-line: K in C.
Change to 3¾mm (US 4) needles and D and starting with a K row work 10 rows in st st.
Cast off fairly loosely in D.

To complete
Fold collar in half to inside along fold-line, and slip stitch in place neatly enclosing ends. Press collar.
Measure 25cm/10in down both back and front from shoulder seams and place coloured markers at side edges. Gather cast-off edges of sleeves until top sleeve measures 50cm/20in. Pin sleeves to side edges, between coloured markers, placing gathers to fall over shoulder seam area. Stitch in position. Join side and sleeve seams, carefully matching patt on cuffs. Catch-stitch base of button band neatly in position behind buttonhole band. Sew on buttons to correspond with buttonholes.

VERSION 2 ★ ★ ★
BLUE WITH DEEP RIBBED WELT
(see page 37 for illustration)

MATERIALS
Yarn
Any **double-knit** weight yarn can be used as long as it knits up to the given tension.
575(600:625)g/21(21:22)oz textured blue cotton (A), 25(25:25)g/1(1:1)oz brown cotton (C), 75(75:100)g/3(3:4)oz cream cotton (D)
Needles, other materials and tension as for **Version 1**.

BACK
With 3¼mm (US 3) needles and A, cast on 84(90:96)sts and work in K1, P1 rib for 10cm/4in.
Increase row: Rib and inc 20 sts evenly across row – 104(110:116)sts.
Change to 4mm (US 5) needles and starting with a K row work straight in st st and follow pattern as for **Version 1**.

FRONT
Work rib and increase row as for back. Now work as for front of **Version 1**, but use C instead of B.

SLEEVES
Make 2. With 3¼mm (US 3) needles and C, cast on 48 sts and starting with a K row work in st st in C for 4 rows.
Change to 4mm (US 5) needles and work as for sleeves on **Version 1**, but work C instead of B.
Now complete as for **Version 1**.

FLORAL COSSACK JACKET

MEASUREMENTS

To fit bust: 81-91cm/32-36in and 97-102cm/38-40in

Please see page 149 for actual garment measurements.

VERSION 1 ★ ★ ★

MATERIALS

Yarn

Any **double-knit** weight yarn can be used as long as it knits up to the given tension.
625(650)g/22(23)oz deep blue cotton (A), 50(50)g/2(2)oz pale blue cotton (B), 25(50)g/1(2)oz yellow wool (C), 100(100)g/4(4)oz orange cotton (D), 25(50)g/1(2)oz brown cotton (E), 25(50)g/1(2)oz gold lurex used double (F), 75(75)g/3(3)oz aqua silk (G), 25(50)g/1(2)oz cream wool (H), 25(25)g/1(1)oz beige wool (I)

Needles and other materials

1 pair each 3¼mm (US 3) and 4mm (US 5) needles
1 circular 4mm (US 5) needle
7 gold metal clasp fasteners or braid frog fasteners

TENSION

25 sts and 28 rows to 10cm/4in on 4mm (US 5) needles over st st using yarn A.

NOTE

Gold lurex (F) is worked *double* throughout.
Background colour may be woven across back of work, but each leaf/stem/flower should be worked separately. Small areas of colour may be Swiss darned when garment is complete instead of being knitted, if preferred.

BACK

With 4mm (US 5) needles and A, cast on 112(118)sts.
Starting with a K row, work in st st from **back chart**, working between appropriate lines for size required. Cont as set until row 22(26) has been worked, thus ending with a WS row.

Shape armholes

Keeping chart correct, cast off 10 sts at beg of next 2 rows.
Now dec 1 st at each end of next row and foll 3 alt rows – 84(90)sts.
Now cont straight until row 100(104) has been worked, thus ending with a WS row.

Shape shoulders

Keeping chart correct, cast off 7(8)sts at beg of next 6 rows.
Cast off rem 42 sts for back neck.

RIGHT FRONT

With 4mm (US 5) needles and A, cast on 52(55)sts.
Starting with a K row, work in st st from **right front chart**, working between appropriate lines for size required. Cont as set until row 23(27) has been worked, thus ending at side edge.

Shape armhole

Keeping chart correct, cast off 10 sts at beg of next row.
Now dec 1 st at armhole edge on next row and foll 3 alt rows – 38(41)sts.
Now cont straight until row 86(90) has been worked, thus ending at front edge.

Shape front neck

Cast off 10 sts at beg of next row.
Keeping chart correct, dec 1 st at neck edge on next row and every foll row until 21(24)sts remain.
Now cont straight until row 101(105) has been worked, thus ending at armhole edge.

Shape shoulder

Keeping chart correct, cast off 7(8)sts at beg of next row and foll 2 alt rows.

LEFT FRONT

Work as for right front, but following chart for **left front**, and starting armhole shaping on row 23(27), neck shaping on row 86(90) and shoulder shaping on row 101(105).

PELUM

With 4mm (US 5) needles and A, cast on 60 sts. Starting with a K row, cont in st st and work from **peplum chart**,

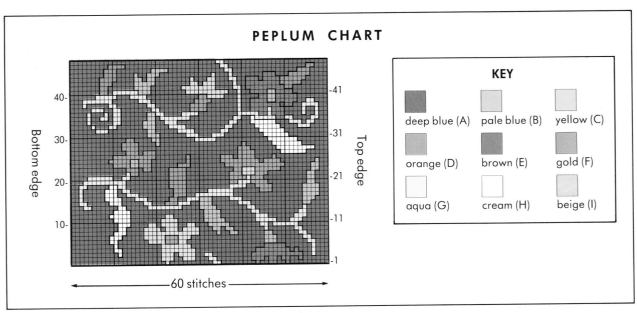

PEPLUM CHART

Bottom edge — 40- 30- 20- 10-

Top edge — -41 -31 -21 -11 -1

◄—— 60 stitches ——►

KEY

deep blue (A)	pale blue (B)	yellow (C)
orange (D)	brown (E)	gold (F)
aqua (G)	cream (H)	beige (I)

FLORAL COSSACK JACKET BACK/FRONTS CHART

KEY

- deep blue (A)
- pale blue (B)
- yellow (C)
- orange (D)
- brown (E)
- gold (F)
- aqua (G)
- cream (H)
- beige (I)

1st size – 52 stitches

2nd size – 55 stitches

Right front

1st size – 52 stitches

2nd size – 55 stitches

Left front

1st size back – 112 stitches

2nd size back – 118 stitches

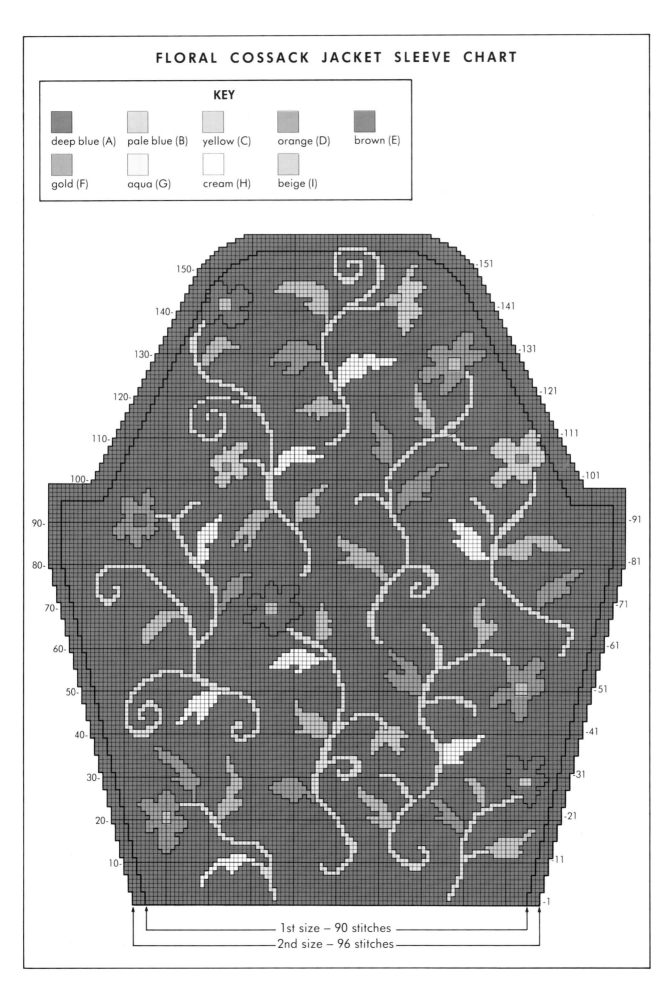

34

repeating the 48 rows of chart as required, until piece measures approx 152cm/60in from cast-on edge, ending with a WS row.
Cast off fairly loosely in A.

SLEEVES

Make 2. With 3¼mm (US 3) needles and H, cast on 44(48)sts and work in K2, P2 rib in the following colour sequence:
Work 2 rows A, and 4 rows D.
Rep these 6 rows twice more. Work 2 rows in A.
Next row: P in A.
Increase row: (RS facing) In A, (K1, P1) into every st of row – 88(96)sts.
Change to 4mm (US 5) needles and P 1 row in A, *on 1st size only*, inc 1 st at each end of row – 90(96)sts.
Now starting with a K row, work in st st following **sleeve chart**, *at the same time* inc 1 st at each end of 4th row and then every foll 4th row until there are 130(136)sts on the needle working inc sts into patt as shown.
Now cont straight until row 94(98) has been worked.

Shape top

Keeping chart correct, cast off 10 sts at beg of next 2 rows.
Now dec 1 st at each end of next row and every foll alt row until 58(64)sts remain.
Now dec 1 st at each end of next 4 rows, and then 2 sts at each end of foll 3 rows.
Cast off rem 38(44)sts in A.

TO MAKE UP

Sew in ends and press pieces carefully following ball band instructions. Join both shoulder seams. Gather up top shaped edges of sleeves with a gathering thread until sleeves fit armholes. Pin sleeves into armholes placing gathers over shoulder seam area. Sew sleeves into position. Remove gathering threads. Join side and sleeve seams. Press seams. Gather the *top edge* of the peplum with a gathering thread until it fits around lower edges of fronts and back. Pin, then carefully sew into place. Remove gathering thread.

Front edgings

Alike. With 3¼mm (US 3) needles and A and RS facing, pick up and K 60 sts along edge of peplum and 80 sts along edge of centre front – 140 sts.
Work in K2, P2 rib in the following stripe sequence:
Work 2 rows in A, 4 rows in D, 2 rows in A.
Cast off fairly loosely ribwise in A.

Neckband

With 3¼mm (US 3) needles and A and RS facing, pick up and K 8 sts along top of right front edging, 26 sts up right side of front neck, 40 sts across back neck, 26 sts down left side of front neck and finally 8 sts from left front edging – 108 sts.
Work in K2, P2 rib in the following stripe sequence:
Work 2 rows in A, 4 rows in D.
Rep these 6 rows once more, then work 2 rows in A.
Cast off fairly loosely ribwise in A.

To complete

With the 4mm (US 5) circular needle and A and RS facing, pick up and K 72 sts evenly around *bottom edge* of peplum from centre front to side seam, 144 sts across back to other side seams, and 72 sts to centre front – 288 sts.
Work in K2, P2 rib in A for 2 rows.

Cast off fairly loosely ribwise in A.
Press bottom edge out carefully, and sew fasteners to front edges as shown in photograph.

VERSION 2 ★ ★ ★

CREAM BACKGROUND WITH BUTTONS

(see page 37 for illustration)

Yarn, needles and tension as for **Version 1**, but work cream as main colour (A) and deep blue for (H).
7 buttons

METHOD

Work exactly as for **Version 1**. Instead of the clasp fasteners, buttonholes are made in the right front band as follows:
Pick up and K 142 sts along right front (instead of 140 on **Version 1**).
Work in K2, P2 rib in A for 2 rows, and then D for 1 row.
Next row: (RS facing) In D, rib 3, *cast off 4 sts, rib 18, rep from * five times more, then cast off 4 sts, rib 3.
Next row: In D, rib, casting on 4 sts over cast-off sts on previous row (7 buttonholes worked in all).
Rib 1 more row in D, then rib 2 rows in A.
Cast off fairly loosely ribwise in A.
Complete as for **Version 1**, but sew on buttons to correspond with buttonholes.

FLORAL COSSACK HAT

MEASUREMENTS

To fit average size adult head.

Please see page 149 for actual garment measurements.

VERSION 1 ★ ★

MATERIALS

Yarn

Any **double-knit** weight yarn can be used as long as it knits up to the given tension.
75g/3oz deep blue cotton (A), small amounts of pale blue cotton (B), yellow wool (C), orange cotton (D), gold lurex used double (F), aqua silk (G), cream wool (H), beige wool (I)
Needles and other materials
1 pair each 3¼mm (US 3) and 4mm (US 5) needles
Approx 56×15cm/22×6in iron-on interfacing
Lining fabric to match

TENSION

25 sts and 28 rows to 10cm/4in on 4mm (US 5) needles over st st using yarn A.

Please see **note** for **Floral Cossack Jacket** (page 32).

METHOD

With 4mm (US 5) needles and A, cast on 36 sts and starting with a K row, work in st st from **peplum chart** (page 32) for **Floral Cossack Jacket**, working the *last 36 sts only* of row.
Repeat the 48 rows of chart until piece is required

length to fit around head easily. Cast off fairly loosely in A.

TO MAKE UP
Sew in ends and press piece carefully following ball band instructions.
Cut the interfacing to fit and then carefully iron onto the wrong side of the knitting to stiffen it.

Bottom rib
With 3¼mm (US 3) needles and A and RS facing, pick up and K 128 sts along bottom edge and work in K2, P2 rib in the following stripe sequence.
Work 2 rows in A, 4 rows in D, 2 rows in A.
Cast off fairly loosely ribwise in A.
Join the short edges together.

Top of hat
With 4mm (US 5) needles and A, cast on 12 sts and starting with a K row work in st st shaping as follows:
Cast on 2 sts at beg of next 2 rows – 16 sts.
Now cast on 4 sts at beg of foll 2 rows – 24 sts.
Cast on 2 sts at beg of every row until there are 36 sts on the needle.
Inc 1 st at beg of every row until there are 48 sts on the needle.
Work 12 rows straight.
Now reverse shapings, by dec 1 st at beg of every row until 36 sts remain. Now cast off 2 sts at beg of every row until 24 sts remain.
Cast off 4 sts at beg of next 2 rows – 16 sts.
Cast off 2 sts at beg of foll 2 rows.
Cast off rem 12 sts.

To complete
Cut 2 pieces of lining fabric to fit top and lower sections of hat.
Carefully press knitted top section, then carefully stitch it onto lower section.
Now stab stitch all round top of hat at a distance of 2.5cm/1in from outer edge to form a raised rim.
Make up lining to match hat and carefully stitch lining inside.

VERSION 2
CREAM BACKGROUND

Yarn, needles and tension as for **Version 1**, but work cream as main colour (A) and deep blue for (H).

METHOD
Work exactly as for **Version 1**.

FLORAL GLOVES ★ ★

MEASUREMENTS
To fit average adult hand.

Please see page 149 for actual garment measurements.

MATERIALS
Yarn
Any **double-knit** weight yarn can be used as long as it knits up to the given tension.
100g/4oz blue cotton (A)
Needles and other materials
1 pair each 3¾mm (US 4) and 4mm (US 5) needles
2 stitch-holders
Small amounts of green, rust and yellow yarn for embroidery

TENSION
25 sts and 32 rows to 10cm/4in on 3¾mm (US 4) needles over st st.

RIGHT GLOVE
With 4mm (US 5) needles cast on 44 sts and work in lace pattern as follows:
Row 1: (WS facing) P.
Row 2: *Sl 1, K1, psso, K3 tbl, yf, K1, yf, K3 tbl, K2 tog, rep from * to end.
Row 3: P.
Row 4: *Sl 1, K1, psso, K2 tbl, yf, K1, yf, sl 1, K1, psso, yf, K2 tbl, K2 tog, rep from * to end.
Row 5: P.
Row 6: *Sl 1, K1, psso, K1 tbl, yf, K1, (yf, sl 1, K1, psso) twice, yf, K1 tbl, K2 tog, rep from * to end.
Row 7: P.
Row 8: *Sl 1, K1, psso, yf, K1, (yf, sl 1, K1, psso) 3 times, yf, K2 tog, rep from * to end.
Change to 3¾mm (US 4) needles and work in K1, P1 rib for 12 rows.
Increase row: (WS facing) Rib and inc 4 sts evenly across row – 48 sts.**
Now complete as for right **Scandinavian Glove** (see page 21) working from row 31 to end, and omitting all reference to chart.

LEFT GLOVE
Work as for right glove to **.
Now complete as for left **Scandinavian Glove** working from row 31 to end, and omitting all reference to chart.

TO MAKE UP
Sew in all ends, press carefully following ball band instructions.
Carefully join all seams. Embroider back of gloves with floral motifs, using chain stitch and lazy daisy stitch as shown on page 25.

Cossack Hat
Version
2.

Floral
Cossack
Jacket
Version 2.

Detail of
Front
Band

Peasant Shirt
Version 2.

WESTERN ASIA

Rich colours and intricate patterns characterize this chapter, whose varied sources include textiles from Turkestan, Persian miniatures and Islamic manuscripts. Two of the garments, the Persian Striped Coat and the Turkestan Coat, are derived from men's clothing, since in the Islamic world this was often much more elaborate and colourful than women's. Whereas, in nomadic societies in particular, men's status was displayed in their costume and in the rich decoration of their saddles and bridles, women had plainer clothes but wore their wealth in the form of jewellery, which represented an easily transportable and readily negotiable form of capital.

The **Persian Striped Coat** *(page 42)* is a simple classic style taken from the elegant and surprisingly modern-looking men's outer coats depicted in Persian miniatures. It follows the design of the original which was cut in rectangles, given shape by the gathered peplum skirt effect at the back. Double-breasted with square sleeves and a shawl collar, it is easy to knit, with stocking stitch used throughout.

The **Floral and Striped Sweater** *(page 43)* has wide dolman sleeves and a soft ribbed roll neck.

Front and back are each knitted in one piece, from cuff to cuff. The body has a central floral panel whose design was taken from decorative border patterns on Persian illuminated manuscripts. The sleeves have bands of scrolls and flowers alternating with stripes, creating a richly patterned effect.

The spectacular **Turkestan Coat** *(page 46)* has a large, bold all-over pattern inspired by the ikat-weave velvet of a male dignitary's coat from Khiva in Turkestan. The luxurious softness of the velvet is suggested by using mohair for the body of the coat, while the intricately embroidered cuffs and borders of the original garment are reproduced by a Fair Isle pattern knitted in double-knit wool for a finer, more detailed effect.

The coat, though very light, is warm to wear but could easily be lined for extra luxury – perhaps, like the original, in a flowered fabric or in plain satin in a toning colour. The matching **Shoulder Bag** repeats the pattern at the top of the coat sleeve and has multi-coloured fringes, recalling the fringed and frayed borders of antique oriental rugs. The little mohair **Hat** that completes this exotic ensemble was inspired by a dervish's cap.

PERSIAN STRIPED COAT

MEASUREMENTS
To fit bust: 81-91cm/32-36in and 97-102cm/38-40in

Please see page 150 for actual measurements.

VERSION 1 ★ ★

MATERIALS
Yarn
Any **double-knit** weight yarn can be used as long as it knits up to the given tension.
825(850)g/29(30)oz deep green (A), 200(225)g/8(9)oz red (B), 225(250)g/8(9)oz cream cotton (C)
Needles and other materials
For 1st size only
1 pair each 3¼mm (US 3) and 4mm (US 5) needles
1 circular 4mm (US 5) needle
For 2nd size only
1 pair each 3¾mm (US 4) and 4½mm (US 6) needles
1 circular 4½mm (US 6) needle
For both sizes
2 large pearl buttons
Snap fasteners

NOTE
The 2nd size is knitted exactly as the first size, the only difference being the size of needle required, and certain length measurements.

TENSION
22 sts and 30 rows to 10cm/4in on 4mm (US 5) needles over st st.
20½ sts and 28 rows to 10cm/4in on 4½mm (US 6) needles over st st.

BACK BODICE
With 3¼mm (US 3) [3¾mm (US 4)] needles and A, cast on 108 sts and work in K1, P1 rib for 8cm/3in.
Increase row: In A, rib and inc 1 st in every 3rd st of row – 144 sts.
Change to 4mm (US 5) [4½mm (US 6)] needles and starting with a K row work in st st in the following stripe sequence: 2 rows B, 2 rows C, 2 rows B, 12 rows A, 1 row B, 2 rows C, 1 row B, 12 rows A.

Previous pages
Left *Persian Striped Coat: This striking design is derived from the shape of Persian men's traditional outer coats. Knitted in double wool and cotton, using stocking stitch, it has wide sleeves, square armholes and a cross-over front. The back is gathered in at the waist to give a flattering skirted effect.*
Centre *Floral and Striped Sweater: Floral scrolls and stripes alternate on this beautiful, easy-to-wear sweater in wool and cotton. Worked horizontally from sleeve to sleeve, it has deep ribbed cuffs and waistband and a loose rolled cowl neck.*
Right *Turkestan Coat: This sumptuous coat has all the richness and romance of oriental rugs and textiles. The large-scale all-over pattern, inspired by Ikat-weave velvet, is knitted in luxurious soft mohair; double-knit wool is used for cuffs and borders whose smaller, more detailed Fair Isle pattern suggests intricate embroidery. A matching cap and shoulder bag complete the outfit.*

These 34 rows form the stripe patt and are repeated as required.
Cont straight in stripe patt as set until back measures 28(29)cm/11(11½)in from cast-on edge, ending with a WS row.

Shape armholes
Next row: Keeping patt correct, cast off 19 sts at beg of row, insert a coloured marker to indicate side seam, cast off a further 19 sts (38 cast off in all), patt to end of row.
Rep last row once more – 68 sts.
Now cont straight in st st and stripe patt until back measures 48(50)cm/19(19¾)in from cast-on edge, ending with a WS row.

Shape shoulders
Keeping patt correct, cast off 8 sts at beg of next 4 rows.
Cast off rem 36 sts.

RIGHT FRONT
(Worked sideways)
With the 4mm (US 5) [4½mm (US 6)] circular needle and A, cast on 220 sts and starting with a K row work in st st.
Work 8 rows in A.
Now work in the 34-row stripe patt as for back bodice, and *at the same time*, when 23 rows have been worked in all, cont as follows:

Shape front neck
Next row: (WS facing) Keeping patt correct cast off 4 sts at beg of row.
Patt 1 row.
Cont to rep these 2 rows until 116 sts remain – 74 rows worked in all.
Cast off these rem sts fairly loosely.

LEFT FRONT
Work exactly as for right front but reverse position of shaping by working 22 patt rows and then casting off the 4 sts at *beg* of every RS row.

SLEEVES
(Worked sideways)
Make 2. With 4mm (US 5) [4½mm (US 6)] needles and A, cast on 126 sts and starting with a K row work in st st in the 34-row stripe sequence as for back bodice.
Cont straight until sleeve measures 40(42)cm/16(16½)in from cast-on edge, ending with a WS row.
Cast off sts fairly loosely.
Place coloured markers on cast-on and cast-off edges 8.5(9.25)cm/3¼(3¾)in in from one side edge.

PEPLUM FRILL
With 4mm (US 5) [4½mm (US 6)] needles and A, cast on 116 sts and work in the 34-row striped st st pattern as for back bodice until frill measures approx 153cm/60in from cast-on edge ending on same stripe row as frill was started on so that stripes are symmetrical.
Cast off fairly loosely in A.

TO MAKE UP
Sew in ends and press carefully following ball band instructions. Join both shoulder seams. Using a gathering thread gather up one long side edge of the peplum frill until it fits onto the back bodice rib. Pin carefully and stitch into position. Remove gathering thread. Join side seams of back bodice and peplum frill to front edge leaving armhole edge free. Press seams

carefully as you go along. Join sleeve seams to coloured markers. Now placing coloured markers to markers on cast-off edges of armholes, sew sleeves carefully into square armholes, matching centre of sleeves to shoulder seams.

Hems

Turn a small hem around complete bottom edge of garment to the inside and slip stitch neatly in position. On the sleeves turn a hem to the inside, making sleeves required length and slip stitch neatly in position.

Right front band

With 3¼mm (US 3) [3¾mm (US 4)] needles and A, cast on 48 sts and work in K1, P1 rib in the following stripe sequence:
Work 14 rows A, 2 rows B, 2 rows C, 2 rows B, 14 rows A, 1 row B, 2 rows C, 1 row B.
Rep these 38 rows until band measures 53(56)cm/21(22)in from cast-on edge, ending with a WS row.
Buttonhole row: Rib 8, cast off 4 sts, rib 24, cast off 4 sts, rib to end.
Next row: Rib, casting on 4 sts over cast-off sts on previous row.
Now cont in rib as before until band, when slightly stretched, fits up right front to centre back neck, sewing in position as you go along.
Cast off fairly loosely ribwise.

Left front band

Work as for right front band, omitting buttonholes. Carefully join centre back seam. Sew on buttons to correspond with buttonholes. Sew snap fasteners onto front bands as required to hold front in position.

VERSION 2 ★ ★

IN ONE COLOUR

(see page 51 for illustration)

MATERIALS

Yarn
Any **double-knit** weight yarn can be used as long as it knits up to the given tension.
1225(1300)g/43(46)oz in one colour.
Needles, other materials and tension as for **Version 1**.

METHOD

Work exactly as for **Version 1**, but in one colour only, omitting all reference to stripes.

FLORAL AND STRIPED SWEATER ★ ★ ★

MEASUREMENTS

To fit bust: 81-91cm/32-36in and 97-102cm/38-40in

Please see page 151 for actual measurements.

MATERIALS

Yarn
Any **double-knit** weight yarn can be used as long as it knits up to the given tension.
125(150)g/5(6)oz each dark green (A) and light green (B), 50(75)g/2(3)oz red (C), 200(225)g/8(8)oz orange cotton (D), 175(200)g/7(8)oz cream (E), 50(50)g/2(2)oz each yellow (F) and mustard cotton (G)

Needles
1 pair each 3¼mm (US 3) and 4mm (US 5) needles

TENSION

23 sts and 27 rows to 10cm/4in on 4mm (US 5) needles over main pattern.

BACK

(Worked in one piece starting at right cuff)
With 3¼mm (US 3) needles and A, cast on 24(26)sts and work in K1 tbl, P1 twisted rib in the following stripe sequence: 2 rows A, 2 rows B.
Rep these 4 rows until cuff measures approx 10cm/4in, ending with 2 rows in A.
Increase row: (RS facing) In B, K and inc 1 st in every st across row – 48(52)sts.
Next row: P in B.
Change to 4mm (US 5) needles and starting with a K row, work in st st from **chart 1** (see page 44) as follows:
Starting from point as indicated, rep the 21-stitch patt twice, then work 6(10) sts beyond the dotted line.
The chart is now placed. Cont to rep the 44 rows of chart and *at the same time,* inc 1 st at *left-hand side edge* on every foll 3rd row (keeping right-hand side edge straight) until there are 84(87)sts on the needle, working inc sts into the patt at side edge.
Work 3(2) rows straight, thus ending with a RS row – 111(107) patt rows worked in all.
Now cast on 32(33)sts at beg of next row – 116(120)sts. Working these sts into the patt, and keeping both side edges straight, cont until 154 rows of patt have been worked in all (ending with 2 rows of B).**
Now starting with a K row, cont in st st and work straight from **chart 2**, working between lines for size required, until the 44 rows have been worked.
Now starting with 2 rows of B, work patt from **chart 1** in reverse to match first side. Cont straight until 41(45) patt rows of this chart have been worked, ending with a RS row.
Cast off 32(33)sts at beg of next row – 84(87)sts.
Work 2(1) row(s) straight. Now keeping patt correct, dec 1 st at *left-hand side edge* on next row and then on every foll 3rd row (keeping right-hand side edge straight) until 48(52)sts remain.
Cont straight until left sleeve ends on same patt row to correspond with beg of right sleeve (1 row F).
Decrease row: (RS facing) In B, K2 tog across row – 24(26)sts.
Next row: P in B.
Change to 3¼mm (US 3) needles and work in stripe

FLORAL AND STRIPED SWEATER
CHART 1

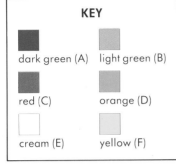

KEY

- dark green (A)
- light green (B)
- red (C)
- orange (D)
- cream (E)
- yellow (F)

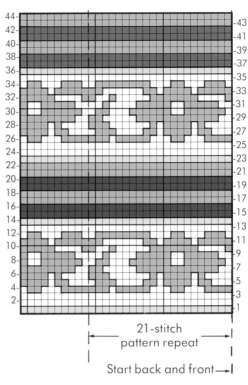

21-stitch
pattern repeat

Start back and front →

twisted rib patt to correspond with right cuff for approx 10cm/4in, ending with 2 rows A.
Cast off fairly loosely ribwise in A.

FRONT
(Worked in one piece starting at left cuff.)
Work as for back to **.
Now starting with a K row, cont in st st and work from **chart 2**.
Work 2 rows straight.

Shape front neck
Cast off 17 sts at beg of next row.
Keeping patt correct, dec 1 st at neck edge on every row 7 times – 92(96)sts.
Cont straight until row 35 has been worked.
Now inc 1 st at neck edge on every row 7 times.
Cast on 17 sts at beg of next row – 116(120)sts.
Cont straight until the 44 rows of **chart 2** are complete.
Complete as for back.

TO MAKE UP
Sew in ends and press pieces carefully following ball band instructions.
Join right shoulder and sleeve seam, matching pattern carefully.

Collar
With 3¼mm (US 3) needles and RS facing and A, pick up and K 72 sts evenly around front neck edge and 42 sts evenly around back neck edge – 114 sts.
Next row: P in A.
Increase row: In B, K and inc 1 st in every 4th st of row – 142 sts.

Next row: In B, *K1 tbl, P1, rep from * to end.
Change to 4mm (US 5) needles and work in twisted striped rib as for cuffs until collar measures approx 26cm/10¼in, ending with 2 rows in A.
Cast off fairly loosely ribwise in A.
Join left shoulder and sleeve seam and outer edge of collar, reversing seam for turnback.

Bottom ribbings
Alike. With 3¼mm (US 3) needles and A and RS facing, pick up and K 100(104)sts evenly along bottom edge of either back or front and work in striped twisted rib as for cuffs for approx 10cm/4in, ending with 2 rows in A.
Cast off fairly loosely ribwise in A.
Join sleeve, side and welt seams in one continuous seam matching patts.

FLORAL AND STRIPED SWEATER
CHART 2

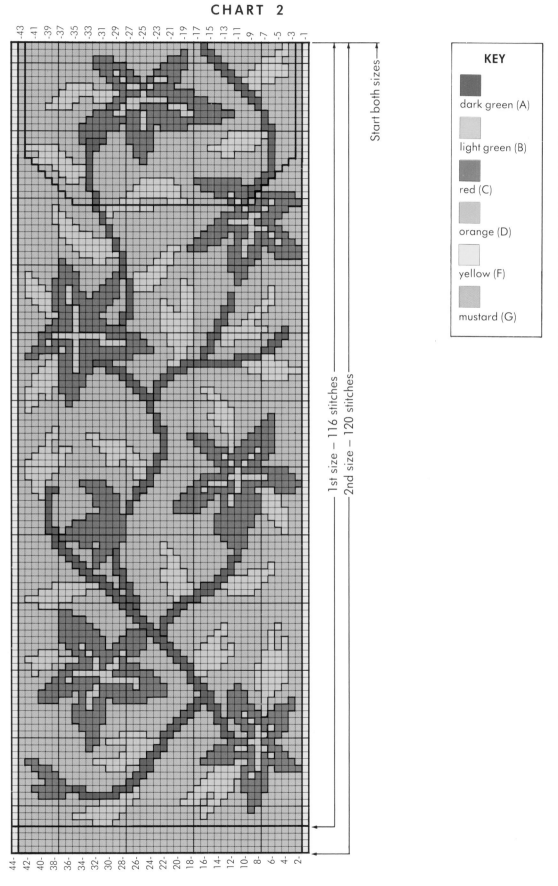

Start both sizes

1st size – 116 stitches
2nd size – 120 stitches

KEY

- dark green (A)
- light green (B)
- red (C)
- orange (D)
- yellow (F)
- mustard (G)

TURKESTAN COAT

MEASUREMENTS
To fit bust: 81-91cm/32-36in and 97-102cm/38-40in

Please see page 152 for actual measurements

VERSION 1 ★ ★ ★ ★

MATERIALS
Yarn
Any **chunky** mohair and **double-knit** weight yarns can
be used as long as they knit up to the given tension.
175(200)g/7(8)oz brown mohair (A), 50(50)g/2(2)oz
blue mohair (B), 150(150)g/6(6)oz rust mohair (C),
75(100)g/3(4)oz green mohair (D), 150(175)g/6(7)oz
yellow mohair (E), 125(150)g/5(6)oz cream mohair (F)
Borders and cuffs – DK: 100(125)g/4(5)oz brown cotton
(G), 50(50)g/2(2)oz blue wool (H), 100(100)g/4(4)oz
rust wool (I), 50(50)g/2(2)oz green wool (J), 25(25)g/
1(1)oz each of yellow wool (K) and cream wool (L)
Needles and other materials
1 pair each 4mm (US 5) and 6mm (US 9) needles
6 large hooks and eyes

TENSION
28 sts and 27 rows to 10cm/4in on 4mm (US 5) needles
over Fair Isle pattern on borders and cuffs.
18 sts and 18 rows to 10cm/4in on 6mm (US 9) needles
over main mohair pattern.

BACK
With 4mm (US 5) needles and G, cast on 152(160)sts
and starting with a K row work in st st from **border chart**
as follows:
Row 1: (RS facing) Work 8(0)sts before the dotted line,
then rep the 16-stitch patt 9(10) times across.
Row 2: Rep the 16-stitch patt 9(10) times across, work
8(0)sts beyond the dotted line.
Cont as set until the 10 rows are complete.
Next row: (RS facing, fold-line for hem) P in G.
Next row: P in G.
Now work rows 1-10 of border chart as before.**

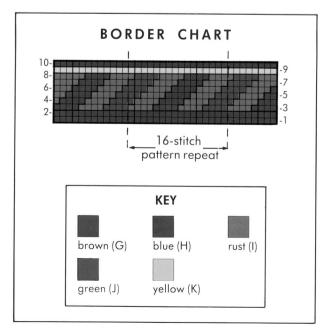

BORDER CHART

10- -9
8- -7
6- -5
4- -3
2- -1

16-stitch
pattern repeat

KEY

brown (G)	blue (H)	rust (I)
green (J)	yellow (K)	

Change to 6mm (US 9) needles and mohair yarns.
Next row: (RS facing) K in A and dec 50(52)sts evenly
across row – 102(108)sts.
Next row: P in A.
Now work in st st from **back chart**, working between
appropriate lines for size required.
Mark each end of rows 54 and 82 with a coloured
thread to indicate pocket openings.
Cont to work from chart until row 116(120) has been
worked, thus ending with a WS row.

Shape armholes
Keeping chart correct, cast off 18 sts at beg of next 2
rows – 66(72)sts.
Now cont straight following chart on these sts until row
176(180) has been worked, thus ending with a WS row.

Shape shoulders
Keeping chart correct, cast off 5(6)sts at beg of next 6
rows.
Cast off rem 36 sts, keeping colours correct as last row
worked.

LEFT FRONT
With 4mm (US 5) needles and G, cast on 76(80)sts and
starting with a K row work in st st from **border chart** as
follows:
Row 1: (RS facing) Rep the 16-stitch patt 4(5) times
across, work 12(0)sts beyond the dotted line.
Row 2: Work 12(0)sts before the dotted line, then rep
the 16-stitch patt 4(5) times across.
Cont to work border patt as now placed, and fold-line
as for back to ** – border patt matches with back at side
seam.
Change to 6mm (US 9) needles and mohair yarns.
Next row: (RS facing) K in A and dec 25(26)sts evenly
across row – 51(54)sts.
Next row: P in A.
Now work in st st from **left front chart**, working between
appropriate lines for size required.
Mark side edge only of rows 54 and 82 to indicate
pocket opening.
Cont to work from chart until row 98 has been worked.

Shape front neck
Keeping chart correct, dec 1 st at neck edge on next row
and then every foll 6th row 9 times in all, then at this
edge on every foll 4th row 8(9) times and *at the same
time*, shape armhole as for back on row 117(121) and
start shoulder shaping on row 177(181). *On 1st size
only* fasten off rem st.

RIGHT FRONT
With 4mm (US 5) needles and G, cast on 76(80)sts and
starting with a K row work in st st from **border chart** as
follows:
Row 1: (RS facing) Work 4(0)sts before the dotted line,
then rep the 16-stitch patt 4(5) times across, work 8(0)sts
beyond the dotted line.
Row 2: Work 8(0)sts before the dotted line, then rep the
16-stitch patt 4(5) times across, work 4(0)sts beyond the
dotted line.
Cont to work border patt as now placed and fold-line
as for back to ** – border patt matches with back at side
seam.
Now work as for left front, working from **right front
chart**, shaping neck as left front, but work armhole
shaping on row 118(122) and start shoulder shaping on
row 178(182).

TURKESTAN COAT BACK/FRONT CHART

KEY

- brown (A)
- blue (B)
- rust (C)
- green (D)
- yellow (E)
- cream (F)

Pocket

Pocket

Right front
1st size – 51 stitches
2nd size – 54 stitches

Left front
1st size – 51 stitches
2nd size – 54 stitches

Back
1st size – 102 stitches
2nd size – 108 stitches

TURKESTAN COAT SLEEVE AND CUFF CHART

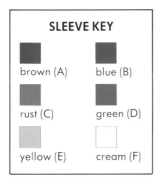

SLEEVE KEY

brown (A)   blue (B)

rust (C)   green (D)

yellow (E)   cream (F)

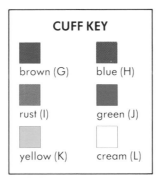

CUFF KEY

brown (G)   blue (H)

rust (I)   green (J)

yellow (K)   cream (L)

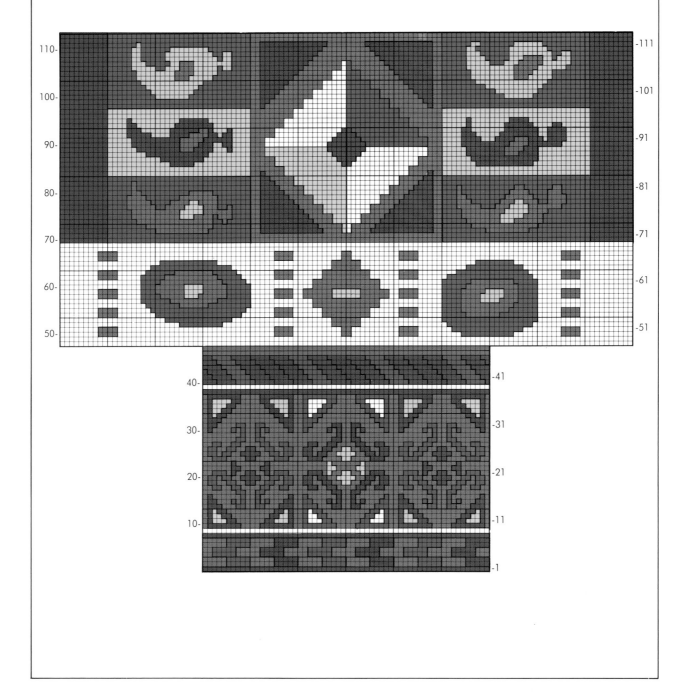

SLEEVES

Make 2. With 4mm (US 5) needles and G, cast on 60 sts and starting with a K row work in st st from **sleeve and cuff chart.**

Work rows 1-8.

Next row: (RS facing) K in K.

Next row: (Fold-line for hem) K in K.

Now starting with a K row, and starting from row 1, follow **sleeve and cuff chart** until row 47 has been worked.

Next row: (WS facing) P in L and inc 1 st in every st across row – 120 sts.

Change to 6mm (US 9) needles and mohair yarns, and cont to work straight from **sleeve chart**, placing coloured markers at each end of row 96 to indicate armhole. When chart is complete cast off fairly loosely keeping colours correct as last row worked.

TO MAKE UP

Sew in ends and press Fair Isle borders and cuffs carefully following ball band instructions. Do not press mohair sections.

Join both shoulder seams. With centre of cast-off edges of sleeves to shoulder seams, sew sleeves carefully into armholes, sewing sleeve seams above markers to cast-off sts at armhole.

Pockets
Left side of back and right side of front
Alike. With 6mm (US 9) needles and A and RS facing, pick up and K 28 sts between the coloured markers on side edge of front/back.***

Next row: (WS facing) P.

** Cont in st st and dec 1 st at *beg* of next row and at this edge on every foll alt row until 18 sts remain.

Cast off fairly loosely.**

Right side of back and left side of front
Alike. Work as for left side of back and right side of front to ***.

Now work from ** to ** (this reverses shaping).

Join underarm and side seams, and edges of pocket linings together.

Fold cuff facing in half along fold-line to inside and carefully slip stitch in position. Press.

Fold bottom edging along fold-line to inside and carefully slip stitch in position. Press.

Front bands
With 4mm (US 5) needles and G, cast on 20 sts and working in yarns G-L only in st st, work the first 10 rows of **border chart**, placing motifs to correspond with edge of bottom edging, then work rows 1-46 of **cuff chart**, working across the first 20 sts.

These 56 rows form the patt for the front bands.

Cont to rep them until band, when slightly stretched, fits up front edge and around to centre back, sewing in position as you go along.

Cast off fairly loosely.

Complete 2nd band to match.

Join centre back seam, then fold bands in half to inside and slip stitch neatly in position. Press.

To complete the garment, carefully stitch large hooks and eyes (or fur hooks) to inside of front edges to fasten coat. Alternatively a belt may be knitted using the same pattern as for front bands.

(see page 51 for illustration)

VERSION 2 ★ ★

PLAIN MOHAIR COAT WITH FAIR ISLE BORDERS

MATERIALS
Yarn

Any **chunky** mohair and **double-knit** weight yarns can be used as long as they knit up to the given tension. 700(750)g/25(27)oz of one-colour mohair yarn (used in place of yarns A-F for **Version 1**).

For borders and cuffs: as for **Version 1**.

Needles, other materials and tension as for **Version 1**.

METHOD
Work exactly as for **Version 1** but work the main body in one colour. Omit all reference to mohair pattern. Work Fair Isle border as **Version 1**. Complete as for **Version 1**.

TURKESTAN SHOULDER BAG

MEASUREMENTS
Please see page 152 for actual measurements

VERSION 1 ★ ★

MATERIALS
Yarn

Any **chunky** mohair and **double-knit** weight yarns can be used as long as they knit up to the given tension. Small amount each brown mohair (A) and blue mohair (B), 25g/1oz each rust mohair (C), green mohair (D) and yellow mohair (E), small amount cream mohair (F).

DK: 50g/2oz brown cotton (G), small amount each of blue wool (H), rust wool (I), green wool (J) and yellow wool (K)

Needles and other materials

1 pair each 4mm (US 5) and 6mm (US 9) needles
Crochet hook for fringe
Lining material

TENSION
18 sts and 18 rows to 10cm/4in on 6mm (US 9) needles over main mohair pattern.

METHOD
With 6mm (US 9) needles and D, cast on 100 sts and starting with a K row work in st st following patt for **sleeve of Turkestan coat**.

Beg patt on row 70, starting 10 sts in from right-hand side and ending 10 sts before left-hand side, therefore working over centre 100 sts of chart.

Cont to follow chart until it is complete. *On last row only* dec 4 sts evenly across – 96 sts.

Change to 4mm (US 5) needles and working in yarns G-K only, follow patt for **border of Turkestan coat**, repeating the 16-stitch patt 6 times across.

Work the 10 rows of border patt.

Next row: (RS facing – fold-line) P in G.

Next row: P in G.
Now work 10 rows in st st in J for facing.
Cast off fairly loosely in J.

TO MAKE UP
Sew in ends and press Fair Isle border carefully following ball band instructions. Do not press mohair section.
Join side edges together, then placing this seam at centre back, sew cast-on edges together. Fold facing in half along fold-line and carefully slip stitch in position to inside of bag.

Shoulder straps
Make 2. With 4mm (US 5) needles and G cast on 6 sts and work in K1, P1 rib for approx 76cm/30in (or length of strap required).
Cast off ribwise
Sew straps in position at top edge of bag.

Fringe (optional)
Cut yarns G-K into 23cm/9in lengths, approx 28 of each colour. Take 1 strand of each colour, fold in half and, using a large crochet hook, carefully pull the loop through on the front of the work, then pull ends through loop to make a tassel – repeat this all the way along the bottom edge.
If required the bag can be lined by making up a fabric bag, slipping it inside the knitted bag and folding raw edges to the inside along the top edge. Catch-stitch in position just below top facing.

VERSION 2 ★

PLAIN MOHAIR BAG WITH FAIR ISLE BORDER

MATERIALS
Yarn
Any **chunky** mohair and **double-knit** weight yarns can be used as long as they knit up to the given tension.
75g/3oz of one-colour mohair yarn (used in place of yarns A-F for **Version 1**).
Yarns G-K as for **Version 1**.
Needles, other materials and tension as for **Version 1**.

METHOD
Work exactly as for **Version 1** but work the bag in one colour. Omit all reference to mohair pattern. Work Fair Isle border as **Version 1**.
Complete as for **Version 1**.

TURKESTAN HAT

MEASUREMENTS
To fit average-size adult head

Please see page 152 for actual measurements.

VERSION 1 ★

MATERIALS
Yarn
Any **chunky** weight yarns can be used as long as they knit up to the given tension.
Small amount each blue mohair (B) and rust mohair (C), 25g/1oz green mohair (D), small amount yellow mohair (E)
Needles
1 pair each 5mm (US 7) and 6mm (US 9) needles

TENSION
18 sts and 18 rows to 10cm/4in on 6mm (US 9) needles over mohair pattern.

METHOD
With 5mm (US 7) needles and D, cast on 84 sts and work in K1, P1 rib for 6 rows.
Change to 6mm (US 9) needles and starting with a K row work in st st in D for 20 rows. (If a deeper brim on hat is required, work a few extra rows here).

Divide for top of hat
Row 1: (RS facing) ** K14E, turn and work on these sts only.
Row 2: P in E.
Row 3: In E, K1, Sl 1, K1, psso, K to last 3 sts, K2 tog, K1.
Rep rows 2 and 3 until 4 sts remain.
Next row: K2 tog twice.
Next row: P2. Slip yarn through rem sts and fasten.**
With RS facing rejoin B to rem sts.
Now rep from ** to ** as for first section but working in B. Cont to work across the rem sts in the 14-stitch segment patt as before, but work segments in colours of C, E, B and C. Do not press. Sew all segments together and join seam in hat.

BOBBLE
Cut four 25cm/10in lengths of yarn in B and attach to centre of top of hat. This can be left hanging loose as a tassel or knotted into a bobble as required. Lightly stitch hat at sides to form a pleat on each side of head.

VERSION 2 ★

WORKED IN ONE-COLOUR MOHAIR

MATERIALS
Yarn
Any **chunky** weight yarns can be used as long as they knit up to the given tension.
50g/2oz mohair yarn.
Needles and tension as for **Version 1**.

METHOD
Work exactly as for **Version 1**, but work throughout in one-colour mohair.

Turkish
Hat
Version
2.

Persian
Striped Coat
Version 2.

Turkestan Coat
Version 2

Turkish
Shoulder Bag
Version
2.

INDIA

This collection features designs inspired by regional dress in Northern India and Pakistan. Knitted in crisp, cool cotton yarn in hot, bright colours, the sweaters are perfect for holidays in the sun, hot summer days and glamorous evenings – sequins and touches of gold and silver yarn add exotic glitter.

The **Kaftan Jacket** *(page 56)* has a loose boxy shape, with strong colours standing out vividly against the black background. Gold sequins recall the mirror inserts of Indian fabrics, and textured multi-coloured lurex yarn gives extra richness and recreates the raised effect produced by the typical Indian technique of painting patterns onto coarse cotton in melted wax. Paisley motifs on the front are taken from the beautiful

Cotton Jacket clusters of beads.

Sue Bradley

With embroidery

With Sequins

Sue Bradley '87

plain!

Harem Pants

shawls of Kashmir. A chic black **Turban** —
normally, of course, a male garment — here
reinforces the Indian look.

The **Short Indian Top** *(page 60)* is based on the
midriff-baring bodices worn by Indian women
under the sari. Cool and comfortable in cotton, it
is highlighted with silver sequins, which also
appear on the matching **Bangles.** Bangles are the
essential Indian accessory — worn in large
quantities by Indians around the ankle as well as
the wrist, they complement any outfit.

The shape of the **Dolman Sweater** *(page 63)*
comes from the short silk jackets worn by the
women of Baluchistan. This version reproduces
the traditional braid decoration of the original in
jade and black Fair Isle patterns on hot pink
cotton; the vertical 'braid' stripes are decorated
with small silver metal studs, again imitating
mirrored fabric. The small slit front neck opening,
fastened with a button, is a characteristic feature
of Indian tops.

KAFTAN JACKET

MEASUREMENTS
To fit bust: 81-91cm/32-36in and 97-102cm/38-40in

Please see page 153 for actual garment measurements.

VERSION 1 ★ ★ ★

MATERIALS
Yarn
Any **double-knit** weight yarn can be used as long as it knits up to the given tension.
400(450)g/15(16)oz black cotton (A), 75(75)g/3(3)oz blue cotton (B), 50(75)g/2(3)oz each pink cotton (C) and green cotton (D), 75(75)g/3(3)oz orange cotton (E), 125(150)g/5(6)oz fancy gold slub yarn (F), 25(25)g 1(1)oz yellow cotton (G)

Needles and other materials
1 pair each 3¼mm (US 3) and 4mm (US 5) needles
24 gold sequins
7 buttons
Spare needle

TENSION
20 sts and 27 rows to 10cm/4in on 4mm (US 5) needles over st st.

LEFT FRONT
With 3¼mm (US 3) needles and A, cast on 60(64)sts and work in K1, P1 rib for 2.5cm/1in, *on 2nd size only*, dec 1 st on last row – 60(63)sts.
Change to 4mm (US 5) needles and starting with a K row, work in st st from **chart 1**, working between appropriate lines for size required.
Cont as set until the 36 rows of chart are worked, thus ending with a WS row.
Now cont in st st in A only until front measures 36(37)cm/14¼(14½)in from cast-on edge, ending with a WS row.**

Shape armhole and place chart
Next row: In A, cast off 14 sts, K until there are 8(11)sts on RH needle, now patt across the 38 sts of row 1 of **chart 2** (see page 58) – 46(49)sts.
Next row: Patt across the 38 sts of row 2 of **chart 2**, P8(11)A.
Cont as now set, working the 8(11)sts nearest armhole edge in A until row 69 of **chart 2** has been worked, thus ending at centre front edge.

Shape front neck
Next row: Cast off 8 sts, patt to end.
Keeping chart correct, dec 1 st at neck edge on every row until 27(30)sts remain.
Work 5 rows straight, thus ending at armhole edge.

Previous pages
Left *Dolman Sweater: In vibrant pink cotton, glittering with sequins, the sweater is knitted in two pieces, across back and front from cuff to cuff.*
Centre *Short Indian Top: This cool blue cotton top is worn with a matching sparkly bangle.*
Right *Kaftan Jacket: The easy-shaped black cotton jacket has colourful Fair Isle panels, highlighted with lurex yarn and sequins.*

Shape shoulder
Keeping chart correct, cast off 9(10)sts at beg of next row and foll 2 alt rows.
Place two coloured markers on side edge for pocket placement. First to come on top line of **chart 1** and second to come 13cm/5in above top line of **chart 1**.

RIGHT FRONT
Work as for left front, working between appropriate lines for size required on **chart 1**. Work to **.

Place chart
Next row: (RS facing) Patt across the 38 sts of row 1 of **chart 3**(see page 58). K to end in A.

Shape armhole
Next row: In A, cast off 14 sts, K until there are 8(11)sts on RH needle, then patt across row 2 of **chart 3** (see page 58) – 46(49)sts.
Cont as now set, working the 8(11)sts nearest armhole edge in A until row 70 of **chart 3** has been worked, thus ending at centre front edge.
Complete as for left front keeping chart correct.

BACK
With 3¼mm (US 3) needles and A, cast on 124(130)sts and work in K1, P1 rib for 2.5cm/1in.
Change to 4mm (US 5) needles and starting with a K row work in st st from **chart 1**, starting from appropriate point as indicated.
Cont as set until the 36 rows of chart are worked, thus ending with a WS row.
Now cont in st st in A only until back measures 36(37)cm/14¼(14½)in from cast-on edge, ending with a WS row.

Shape armholes
Cast off 14 sts at beg of next 2 rows – 96(102)sts.
Now cont straight in st st in A only until back measures the same as front to beg of shoulder shaping, ending with a WS row.

Shape shoulders
Cast off 9(10)sts at beg of next 6 rows.
Leave rem 42 sts on a spare needle for back neck.
Place markers at side edges, as for front, for pocket placement.

SLEEVES
Make 2. With 3¼mm (US 3) needles and A, cast on 50sts and work in K1, P1 rib for 1cm/½in.
Change to 4mm (US 5) needles and starting with a K row, work in st st from **chart 4** (see page 59).
Cont as set until the 20 rows are worked, thus ending with a WS row.
Increase row: K in A and inc 28 sts evenly across row – 78sts.
P 1 row in A.
Cont in st st in A, *at the same time*, inc 1 st at each end of next row and then every foll 3rd row until there are 112sts on the needle, ending with a WS row.

Place chart
Next row: K26A, now patt across the 60 sts of row 1 of **chart 5**, (see page 59) K26A.
The chart is now placed. Cont to follow chart, inc as set on every foll 3rd row until there are 128 sts on the needle, working inc sts into A on either side.
Now cont straight until the 52 rows of **chart 5** are complete.

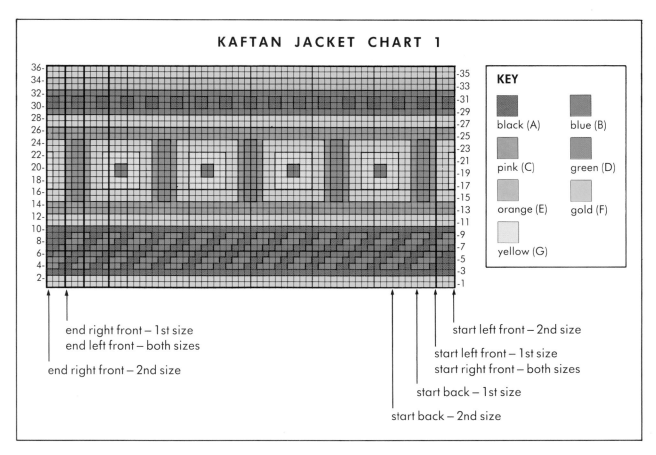

KAFTAN JACKET CHART 1

KEY

black (A)   blue (B)

pink (C)   green (D)

orange (E)   gold (F)

yellow (G)

end right front – 1st size
end left front – both sizes

end right front – 2nd size

start left front – 2nd size

start left front – 1st size
start right front – both sizes

start back – 1st size

start back – 2nd size

Cast off fairly loosely in A.
Measure down 7cm/2¾in from cast-off edges of sleeves and place coloured markers at each side edge.

TO MAKE UP
Sew in all ends and press pieces carefully following ball band instructions. Join shoulder seams. With centre of cast-off edges of sleeves to shoulder seams, sew sleeves carefully into armholes, sewing sleeve seams above markers to cast-off sts at armhole.

Pockets
Left side of back and right side of front
Alike. With 4mm (US 5) needles and A, and RS facing, pick up and K 26 sts between the coloured markers on side edge of back/front.***
Next row: (WS facing) P.
**Cont in st st and dec 1 st at *beg* of next row and at this edge on every foll alt row until 12 sts remain.
Cast off sts fairly loosely.**

Right side of back and left side of front
Alike. Work as for left side of back and right side of front to ***.
Now work from ** to ** (this reverses shaping).

Neckband
With 3¼mm (US 3) needles and A, and RS facing, pick up and K 26 sts up right front neck, K across the 42 sts at back neck and finally pick up and K 26 sts down left front neck – 94 sts.
Work in K1, P1 rib for 2.5cm/1in.
Cast off fairly loosely ribwise.

Buttonhole band
With 3¼mm (US 3) needles and A, and RS facing, pick up and K 161(163)sts evenly along right front edge and neckband.

Work in K1, P1, rib in A for 3 rows.
Buttonhole row: (RS facing) Rib 4(5), * cast off 3 sts, rib 22, rep from * to last 7(8)sts, cast off 3 sts, rib 4(5).
Next row: Rib, casting on 3 sts over cast-off sts on previous row (7 buttonholes worked in all).
Rib 3 more rows.
Cast off fairly loosely ribwise.

Button band
Work as for buttonhole band, picking up sts down left front edge and neckband, and omitting all buttonholes.

To complete
Join side seams and pocket edges, matching border pattern carefully. Join sleeve seams. Sew on buttons to correspond with buttonholes. Sew sequins on in positions marked 'X' on front and sleeve charts.

VERSION 2 ★ ★
WHITE BACKGROUND WITHOUT SEQUINS
(see page 62 for illustration)

MATERIALS
Yarn
Any **double-knit** weight yarn can be used as long as it knits up to the given tension.
400(450)g/15(16)oz white cotton (A); all other yarns the same as for **Version 1** (omit black).
Needles, other materials and tension as for **Version 1**, but omit the sequins.

METHOD
Work as for **Version 1**, using white for A (instead of black).
Do not decorate with sequins.

KAFTAN JACKET

KEY

black (A)	blue (B)	pink (C)	green (D)
orange (E)	gold (F)	yellow (G)	✕ sequins

CHART 3 (RIGHT FRONT)

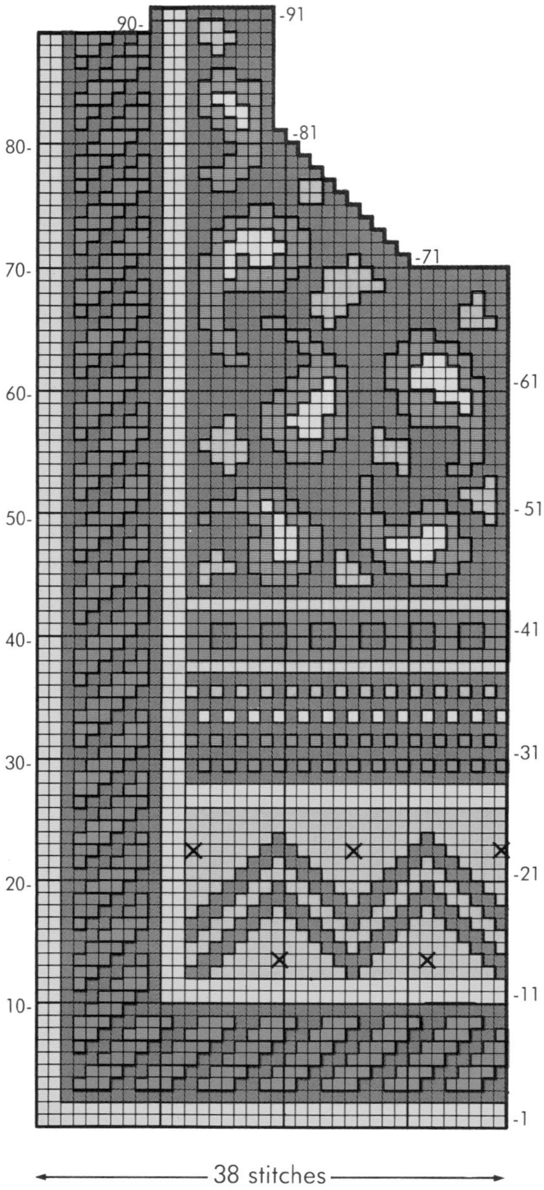

← 38 stitches →

CHART 2 (LEFT FRONT)

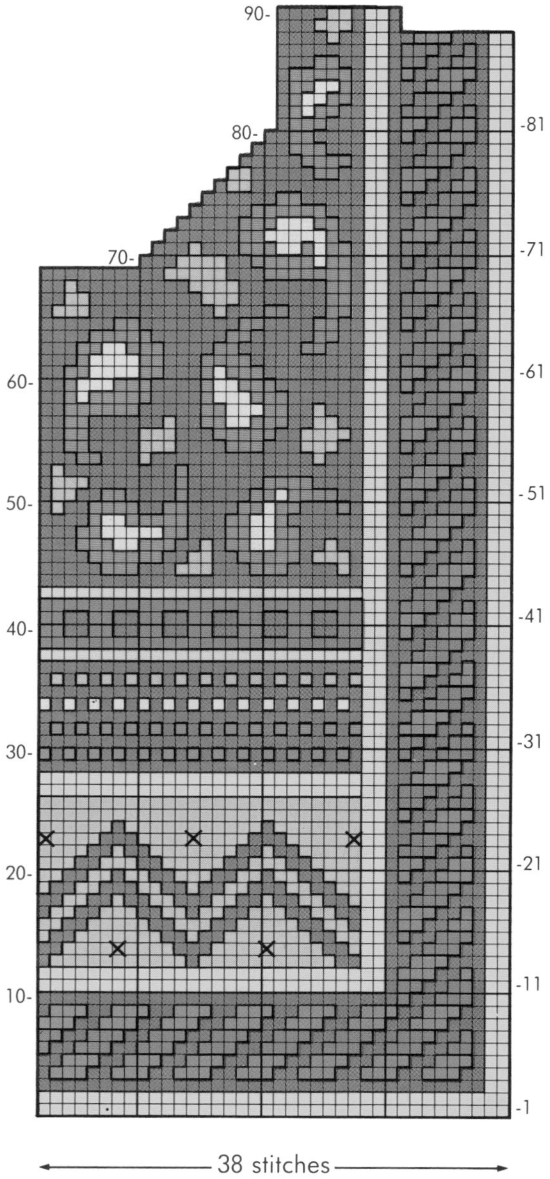

← 38 stitches →

KAFTAN JACKET

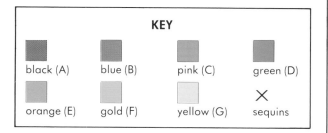

KEY

■ black (A)	■ blue (B)	■ pink (C)	■ green (D)
■ orange (E)	■ gold (F)	■ yellow (G)	✕ sequins

CHART 4 (CUFF)

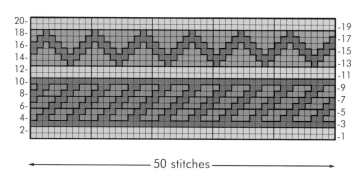

◄─── 50 stitches ───►

CHART 5 (SLEEVE)

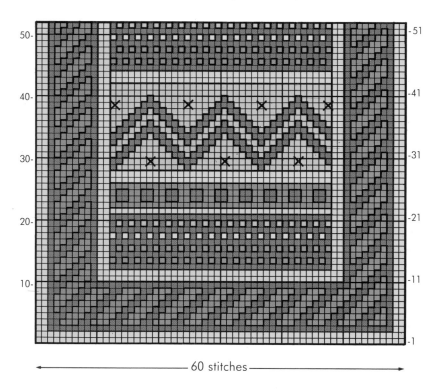

◄─── 60 stitches ───►

59

SHORT INDIAN TOP

MEASUREMENTS

To fit bust: 76-81cm/30-32in, 81-91cm/32-36in and 91-97cm/36-38in

Please see page 154 for actual garment measurements.

VERSION 1 ★

MATERIALS
Yarn
Any **double-knit** weight yarn can be used as long as it knits up to the given tension.
275(300:325)g/10(11:12)oz blue cotton (A), 25(25:50)g/1(1:2)oz black cotton (B)
Needles and other materials
1 pair each 3¼mm (US 3) and 4mm (US 5) needles
Approx 74 round silver sequins
Spare needle

TENSION
20 sts and 27 rows to 10cm/4in on 4mm (US 5) needles over st st.

BACK
With 3¼mm (US 3) needles and B, cast on 74(80:86)sts and work in K1, P1 rib in the following colour sequence:
Work 1 row in B, 4 rows in A, 2 rows in B (7 rib rows worked in all).
Increase row: (WS facing) P in A and inc 20 sts evenly across row – 94(100:106)sts.
Change to 4mm (US 5) needles and starting with a K row, work in st st in A only until back measures 12(14:16)cm/4¾(5½:6¼)in from cast-on edge, ending with a WS row.

Shape armholes
Cast off 8 sts at beg of next 2 rows – 78(84:90)sts.
Now dec 1 st at beg of foll 6 rows – 72(78:84)sts.
Work straight until back measures 33(35:37)cm/13(13¾:14½)in from the cast-on edge, ending with a WS row.

Shape shoulders
Cast off 5(6:7)sts at beg of next 4 rows.
Cast off rem 52(54:56)sts.

FRONT
Work as for back until front measures 18(20:22)cm/7(7¾:8¾)in from cast-on edge, ending with a WS row (armhole shaping complete).

Shape front neck
Next row: K20(23:26), cast off centre 32 sts, K to end of row and cont on this last set of 20(23:26)sts only, leaving rem sts on a spare needle.
** Dec 1 st at neck edge on every row until 10(12:14)sts remain.
Now cont straight until front measures the same as back to beg of shoulder shaping, ending at armhole edge.

Shape shoulder
Cast off 5(6:7)sts at beg of next row and foll alt row.
With WS facing rejoin yarn to rem sts at neck edge and work as for first side from ** to end.

SLEEVES
Make 2. With 3¼mm (US 3) needles and B, cast on 60 sts and work in single rib and colour sequence as for back welt for 7 rows.
Increase row: (WS facing) P in A and inc 20 sts evenly across row – 80 sts.
Change to 4mm (US 5) needles and starting with a K row, work in st st in A only, inc 1 st at beg of every row until there are 100 sts on the needle (sleeve now measures 10cm/4in from cast-on edge ending with a WS row).

Shape top
Cast off 8 sts at beg of next 2 rows – 84 sts.
Now dec 1 st at beg of next 28 rows.
Cast off rem 56 sts.

TO MAKE UP
Sew in all ends. Press carefully according to ball band instructions. Join left shoulder seam.

Neck ribbing
With 3¼mm (US 3) needles and A and RS facing, pick up and K 50 sts across back neck, 38 sts down left front neck, 26 sts from centre front and finally 38 sts up right front neck – 152 sts.
P 1 row in B.
Now work in K1, P1 rib in the following colour sequence:
Work 1 row in B, 4 rows in A, 1 row in B.
Cast off ribwise in B.

To complete
Join right shoulder and neck ribbing seam. With centre of cast-off edges of sleeves to shoulder seams, sew sleeves carefully into armholes, gathering top to fit. Join side and sleeve seams, matching borders. Sew sequins on ribs at regular intervals around neck, cuffs and bottom edging.

VERSION 2 ★

ONE COLOUR, DECORATED WITH SEQUINS OR BEADS
(see page 62 for illustration)

MATERIALS
Yarn
Any **double-knit** weight yarn can be used as long as it knits up to the given tension.
300(325:350)g/11(12:13)oz pink cotton
Needles and other materials
1 pair each 3¼mm (US 3) and 4mm (US 5) needles
Approx 150 sequins or beads dotted over garment as required
Spare needle

TENSION
As for **Version 1**.

METHOD
Work as for **Version 1**, but work in one colour throughout including ribs. Decorate with sequins or beads dotted all over front, back and sleeves.

BANGLE

MEASUREMENTS
To fit average adult wrist

Please see page 154 for actual garment measurements.

VERSION 1 ★

MATERIALS
Yarn
Any **double-knit** weight yarn can be used as long as it knits up to the given tension.
25g/1oz black cotton (A), small amounts blue cotton (B), pink cotton (C) and turquoise cotton (D)
Needles and other materials
1 pair 4mm (US 5) needles
Approx 14 silver sequins or studs
Washable stuffing

TENSION
20 sts and 27 rows to 10cm/4in on 4mm (US 5) needles over st st.

METHOD
With 4mm (US 5) needles and A, cast on 20 sts and starting with a K row work straight in st st from **chart**, repeating the 6 rows until bangle is required length to fit around wrist, when slightly stretched, ending with a 6th patt row (approx 24cm/9½in).
Cast off fairly loosely.

TO COMPLETE
Sew in ends. Press piece carefully following ball band instructions. Sew on sequins on alternate sides between the zigzag pattern.
Stitch cast-on and cast-off edges carefully together. Cut filling material to correct length and place inside knitting, fold knitting around filling and stitch long edges together neatly on outside of work.
Alternatively the work may be stitched, long edges together first.
Then turn right side out, stuff and sew short edges together from outside.

VERSION 2 ★
(see page 53 for illustration)

MATERIALS
Yarn
Any **double-knit** weight yarn can be used as long as it knits up to the given tension.
Small amounts black cotton (A), green cotton (B), pink cotton (C), gold lurex (D)
Needles and other materials
1 pair 4mm (US 5) needles
Approx 9 clear rhinestones

TENSION
As for **Version 1**.

METHOD
With 4mm (US 5) needles and A, cast on 10 sts and starting with a K row work straight in st st from **chart**, repeating the 8 rows until bangle is required length to fit

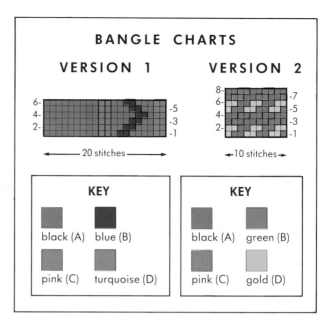

around wrist, when slightly stretched, ending with an 8th patt row, (approx 24cm/9½in). Cast off fairly loosely.

TO COMPLETE
Sew in ends. Press piece carefully following ball band instructions. Stitch cast-on and cast-off edges carefully together. Fold knitting in half and stitch long edges neatly together on outside of work.
Sew rhinestones in the centre of the black diagonals.

TURBAN ★

MEASUREMENTS
To fit average adult head

Please see page 154 for actual garment measurements.

MATERIALS
Yarn
Any **double-knit** weight yarn can be used as long as it knits up to the given tension.
50g/2oz black cotton (A), small amount fancy gold slub yarn (B)
Needles
1 pair 4mm (US 5) needles

TENSION
20 sts and 27 rows to 10cm/4in on 4mm (US 5) needles over st st.

METHOD
With 4mm (US 5) needles and A, cast on 32 sts and starting with a K row work straight in st st until piece fits around head, when slightly stretched, approx 60cm/23¾in. Cast off fairly loosely.

TO COMPLETE
Press piece carefully following ball band instructions. Join cast-on and cast-off edges together. Now gather up this seam into centre and wrap the gold yarn B around and around the seam for about 2cm/¾in. Fasten off.

Dolman Sweater
Version 2.

Kaftan Jacket
Version
2.

Short
Indian
Top
Version
2.

DOLMAN SWEATER

MEASUREMENTS
To fit bust: 81-91cm/32-36in and 91-102cm/38-40in

Please see page 155 for actual garment measurements.

VERSION 1 ★ ★ ★

MATERIALS
Yarn

Any **double-knit** weight yarn can be used as long as it knits up to the given tension.
325(350)g/12(13)oz black cotton (A), 100(125)g/4(5)oz green cotton (B), 250(250)g/9(9)oz pink cotton (C)

Needles and other materials

1 pair each 3¼mm (US 3) and 4mm (US 5) needles
One circular 3¼mm (US 3) needle
Approx 39 large silver sequins
Approx 160 small silver sequins or beads
1 silver button
Crochet hook

TENSION
20 sts and 27 rows to 10cm/4in on 4mm (US 5) needles over st st.

BACK AND SLEEVES
(Worked sideways from right cuff to left cuff.)
With 3¼mm (US 3) needles and A, cast on 30(36)sts and work in K1, P1 rib for 5cm/2in.
Increase row: Rib and inc 10 sts evenly across row – 40(46)sts.
Change to 4mm (US 5) needles and starting with a K row work in st st from **chart** (see pages 64-65), working between appropriate lines for size required.
Inc 1 st at side edge, as shown, on 3rd row and then at this edge on every foll alt row until there are 73(77)sts on the needle, working inc sts into the patt – 67th(63rd) patt row completed.
Row 68(64): (WS facing) Cast on 31(33)sts in C, patt to end of row – 104(110)sts.
Now cont straight following chart across all sts until row 189(193) has been worked.
Row 190(194): (WS facing) In C, cast off 31(33)sts, patt to end of row – 73(77)sts.
Cont to work from chart and dec 1 st at side edge as shown until 40(46)sts remain – 256th patt row completed.
Decrease row: (RS facing) K in A, dec 10 sts evenly across row – 30(36)sts.
Change to 3¼mm (US 3) needles and work in K1, P1 rib for 5cm/2in.
Cast off fairly loosely ribwise.

FRONT AND SLEEVES
(Worked sideways from left cuff to right cuff.)
Work as for back until row 106 has been worked.

Shape front neck
Row 107: (RS facing) In C, cast off 8 sts, patt to end of row – 96(102)sts.
Keeping patt correct, dec 1 st at neck edge on every row as shown until 84(90)sts remain.
Cont straight in patt until row 126 has been worked.

Shape front opening
Row 127: (RS facing) In A, cast off 24 sts, patt to end of row – 60(66)sts.
Row 128: Patt.
Row 129: In A, cast on 24 sts, patt to end – 84(90)sts.
Now work straight in patt until row 138 has been worked.
Now inc 1 st at neck edge, as shown, on every row until there are 96(102)sts on the needle.
Row 151: (RS facing) In C, cast on 8 sts, patt to end of row – 104(110)sts.
Now cont to work from chart to match back and complete as for back.

TO MAKE UP
Sew in ends and press pieces carefully following ball band instructions.
Now work edgings as follows:

Front neck opening edging
With 3¼mm (US 3) needles and A and RS facing, pick up and K 24 sts on each side of front neck opening – 48sts.
Work in K1, P1 rib for 1 row.
Cast off fairly loosely ribwise.

Neck edging
Join both shoulder seams carefully matching pattern.
With the 3¼mm (US 3) circular needle and A and RS facing, pick up and K 28 sts around right front neck, 42 sts across back neck and 28 sts around left front neck – 98 sts.
Work in K1, P1 rib in A for 2.5cm/1in.
Cast off fairly loosely ribwise.

Bottom edging
Carefully join left underarm and side seam.
With the 3¼mm (US 3) circular needle and A and RS facing, pick up and K 100 sts around bottom edge of front and 100 sts around bottom edge of back – 200 sts.
Work in K1, P1 rib in A for 10cm/4in.
Cast off fairly loosely ribwise.

To complete
Join right underarm and side seam. Sew on large sequins in between diamond motifs at positions marked 'X' on chart. Sew on small sequins at positions marked '●' on chart (along each Fair Isle stripe panel). Sew button to neck edge on left side of front opening. Crochet loop to correspond with button on right side of front opening.

VERSION 2 ★ ★
WITH WHITE RIBBING AND NO SEQUINS

METHOD
Work exactly as for **Version 1** but use white cotton for A (instead of black cotton). Omit all sequin decoration.

DOLMAN SWEATER CHART

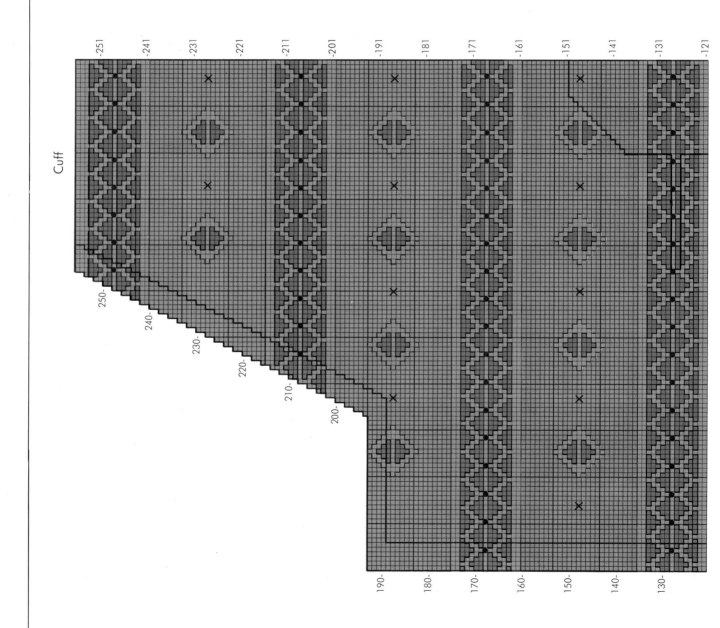

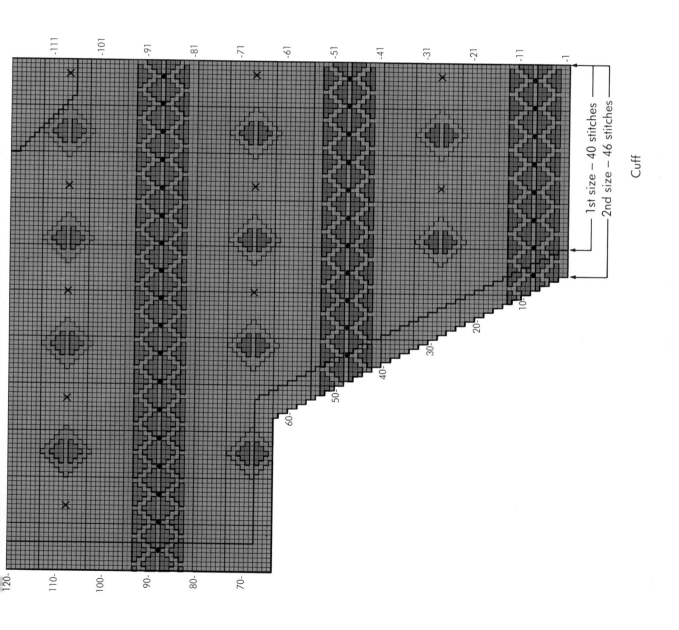

Cuff

1st size — 40 stitches
2nd size — 46 stitches

JAPAN

This chapter draws its theme from the distinctive design tradition of Japan, and in particular from Japanese textiles.

Most of the garment shapes are taken from the kimono, which is made from rectangles of fabric stitched together with little or no shaping, buttons or fastenings, held together at the hips with a wide sash, the *obi*. The simple kimono shape provides a perfect area for decoration, ideal for the display of intricate designs. Popular subjects include motifs taken from nature such as flowers and butterflies, used either in an all-over pattern or asymmetrically for more dramatic effect. The Japanese also love geometric motifs, however, and different types of pattern are often combined within the same garment.

The **Batwing Sleeve Coat** *(page 69)* borrows from the kimono its dropped sleeves and tapered body, while the broad band of checks on the hips imitates the *obi*. It is knitted in a mixture of wool tweeds, Aran and chunky cotton chenille in an austere but striking combination of colours. The

outfit is completed with matching **Gloves, Headband** and a knitted **Shoulder Bag** which recalls the *inro* – a small pouch bag usually made of lacquer which hung from the *obi* on a silk cord.

The geometric design on the **Patchwork Sweater** *(page 76)* is derived from Japanese stencil patterns, but its deep square armholes and soft shawl collar are again taken from the kimono. It is worked in double-knit wool with bright dashes of shiny cotton/rayon.

Another stencil design has inspired the **Butterfly and Bamboo Sweater** *(page 79),* but this time a naturalistic one: against a black background, bamboo stems are outlined in white and scattered with emerald green leaves; across them fly brightly coloured butterflies highlighted in gold. This sweater goes across the Japan Sea to China for features such as its wide raglan shape and mandarin-style collar.

The **Striped Symbol Sweater** *(page 82)* is a simply shaped crew neck with drop shoulders but with an interesting double collar and an exciting mixture of textured and shiny yarns. The pattern is made up from bands of alternating stencil and character motifs divided by raised stripes in a rich violet tweed, the colour reminiscent of the indigo dyes traditionally used in Japanese peasant dress.

BATWING
SLEEVE COAT ★ ★ ★

MEASUREMENTS
To fit bust: 76-81cm/30-32in, 81-91cm/32-36in and 91-102cm/36-40in

Please see page 156 for actual garment measurements.

MATERIALS
Yarn
Any **Aran-weight** yarn can be used as long as it knits up to the given tension.
725(775:825)g/26(28:29)oz black Aran (A), 275 (300:300)g/10(11:11)oz cream Aran (B), 150(175:175)g/6(7:7)oz grey tweed (C), 200(225:225)g/8(8:8)oz brown chenille (D)

Needles and other materials
1 pair each 5mm (US 7) and 4½mm (US 6) needles
1 circular 4½mm (US 6) needle
6 buttons
Spare needle
2 snap fasteners

TENSION
17 sts and 24 rows to 10cm/4in on 5mm (US 7) needles over st st using yarn A.

BACK
With 4½mm (US 6) needles and A, cast on 70(76:82)sts and work in K1, P1 rib for 2.5cm/1in.
Change to 5mm (US 7) needles and starting with a K row work in st st, inc 1 st at both ends of 6th row and then every foll 5th row until there are 94(100:106)sts on the needle. Work 1 row, thus ending with a WS row.
Change to D. Starting with a K row work 4 rows in st st.

Place chequerboard pattern
1st size only
Row 1: (RS facing) K2B, *K5A, K5B, rep from * to last 2 sts, K2A.
Row 2: P2A, *P5B, P5A, rep from * to last 2 sts, P2B.
Rep last 2 rows twice more.
Row 7: K2A, *K5B, K5A, rep from * to last 2 sts, K2B.
Row 8: P2B, *P5A, P5B, rep from * to last 2 sts, P2A.
Rep last 2 rows twice more.

2nd size only
Row 1: (RS facing) *K5A, K5B, rep from * to end.
Row 2: *P5B, P5A, rep from * to end.
Rep last 2 rows twice more.
Row 7: *K5B, K5A, rep from * to end.
Row 8: *P5A, P5B, rep from * to end.
Rep last 2 rows twice more.

3rd size only
Row 1: (RS facing) K3A, *K5B, K5A, rep from * to last 3 sts, K3B.
Row 2: P3B, *P5A, P5B, rep from * to last 3 sts, P3A.
Rep last 2 rows twice more.
Row 7: K3B, *K5A, K5B, rep from * to last 3 sts, K3A.

Batwing Sleeve Coat: This dramatic full-length coat, knitted in wool, tweed and chenille yarns, has wide kimono sleeves and features eye-catching Japanese symbol motifs, also used on the headband, gloves and shoulder bag.

Row 8: P3A, *P5B, P5A, rep from * to last 3 sts, P3B.
Rep last 2 rows twice more.

All sizes
Rep the last 12 rows twice more (36 rows of chequerboard patt worked in all – thus ending with a WS row).
Change to D. Starting with a K row work 4 rows in st st. Mark both ends of last row with coloured thread to show armholes.
Change to A and starting with a K row, work 14(18:22) rows in st st.

Place chart 1
Next row: (RS facing) K3(6:9)A, now work across the 88 sts of row 1 on **chart 1**, (see page 70 for all charts) K3(6:9)A. The chart is now placed.
Cont to follow chart until row 110 has been worked, thus ending with a WS row. Now cont in A only.

Shape shoulders
Cast off 10(11:12)sts at beg of next 6 rows.
Leave rem 34 sts on a spare needle for back neck.

RIGHT FRONT
With 4½mm (US 6) needles and C, cast on 46(48:52)sts and work in K1, P1 rib for 2.5cm/1in; on last row for *1st and 3rd sizes only*, dec 1 st – 45(48:51)sts.
Change to 5mm (US 7) needles and starting with a K row work in st st, inc 1 st at **side** edge on 6th row and then at this edge on every foll 5th row until there are 57(60:63)sts on the needle.
Work 1 row, thus ending with a WS row.
Change to D. Starting with a K row work 4 rows in st st**.

Place chequerboard pattern
Row 1: (RS facing) *K5A, K5B, rep from * to last 7(0:3)sts, K5(0:3)A, K2(0:0)B. The patt is now placed.
Cont to work in chequerboard patt, as back, until 36 rows in all have been worked ending with a WS row.
Change to D. Starting with a K row, work 4 rows in st st. Mark side edge of last row with coloured thread to show armhole.
Change to C and starting with a K row, work 14(18:22) rows in st st.

Place chart 2
Next row: (RS facing) K10(12:14)C, now work across the 36 sts of row 1 on **chart 2**, K11(12:13)C.
The chart is now placed.
Cont to follow chart until row 60 has been worked.
Now cont in C only for a further 36 rows, thus ending with a WS row.

Shape front neck
Cast off 20 sts at beg of next row. Work 1 row.
Now dec 1 st at neck edge on next row and every foll alt row 7 times in all – 30(33:36)sts, thus ending at side edge.

Shape shoulder
Cast off 10(11:12)sts at beg of next row and foll 2 alt rows.

LEFT FRONT
Work as for right front to ** but using A instead of C.

Place chequerboard pattern
Row 1: (RS facing) K2(0:0)A, K5(0:3)B, *K5A, K5B, rep from * to end. The patt is now placed.

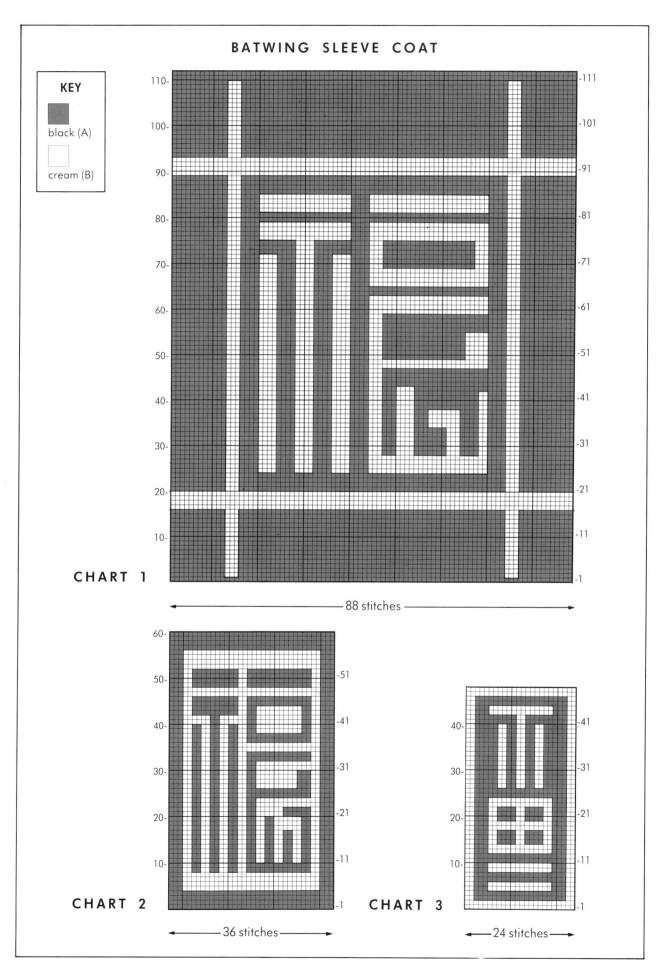

BATWING SLEEVE COAT

KEY

black (A)

cream (B)

CHART 1

88 stitches

CHART 2

36 stitches

CHART 3

24 stitches

Cont to work in chequerboard patt, as back, until 36 rows in all have been worked ending with a WS row.
Change to D. Starting with a K row, work 4 rows in st st. Mark side edge of last row with coloured thread to show armhole.
Change to A and starting with a K row, work 56(60:64) rows in st st.

Place chart 3
Next row: (RS facing) K4(6:8)A, then work across the 24 sts of row 1 on **chart 3**, K29(30:31)A.
The chart is now placed.
Cont to follow chart until row 48 has been worked.
Now cont in A only for a further 7 rows, thus ending with a RS row.

Shape front neck
Work as for right front.

SLEEVES
Make 2. With 4½mm (US 6) needles and A, cast on 40 sts and work 1·5cm/½in in K1, P1 rib.
Change to 5mm (US 7) needles and work in chequerboard patt as follows:
Row 1: (RS facing) *K5A, K5B, rep from * to end.
Row 2: *P5B, P5A, rep from * to end.
The patt is now set. Cont in chequerboard patt, as back, until 18 rows in all of this patt have been worked.
Next row: (RS facing) K in D.
Next row: P in D.
Next row: K in D and inc 26(32:38)sts evenly across row – 66(72:78)sts.
Next row: P.
Now starting with a K row cont in st st and inc 1 st at each end of 2nd and 3rd rows. Cont to inc over this 3-row interval until sleeve measures 16cm/6¼in from cast-on edge, ending with a WS row.
Now keeping incs as set, introduce A at either side of sleeve.
When there are 4 sts in A on either side, introduce C, and thereafter work all inc sts into C.
Keeping vertical stripes as now set, cont to inc until there are 180(186:194)sts on the needle.
Now work a few rows straight until sleeve measures 47(48:50)cm/18½(19:19½)in from cast-on edge ending with a WS row.
Cast off fairly loosely in colours as set.

TO MAKE UP
Sew in ends and press pieces carefully following ball band instructions. Join both shoulder seams.

Armhole ribs
Alike. With the 4½mm (US 6) circular needle and B and RS facing, pick up and K116(120:124)sts from marker for armhole to shoulder seam, and then 116(120:124)sts from shoulder seam to other marker for armhole – 232(240:248)sts.
Work in K1, P1 rib in *rows* for 4cm/1½in.
Cast off fairly loosely ribwise.

Join cast-off edge of sleeve to armhole edge *underneath* the armhole rib, so that the cast-off edge of the armhole rib remains loose from the garment. Join underarm and side seams, matching checks carefully. Stitch edges of armhole ribs together under the arm.

Right front band
With the 4½mm (US 6) circular needle and A and RS facing, pick up and K210(214:218)sts evenly along edge of right front.
Work in K1, P1 rib in *rows* for 5 rows.
Buttonhole row: (RS facing) Rib 21(25:29), * cast off 3, rib 33, rep from * 5 times in all, cast off 3, rib to end.
Next row: Rib, casting on 3 sts over cast-off sts on previous row (6 buttonholes worked in all).
Work another 5 rows of rib.
Cast off fairly loosely ribwise.

Left front band
Work as for right front band but omit buttonholes.

Collar
With 4½mm (US 6) needles and A and with RS facing, pick up and K43 sts from edge of right front band, around neck to shoulder seam, K across the 34 sts at back neck and finally pick up and K43 sts from shoulder seam to edge of left front band – 120 sts.
P 1 row in A.
Change to 5mm (US 7) needles and work in same chequerboard pattern as for cuffs, work 12 rows of pattern, then with RS facing K 1 row in A.
Next row: K in A for fold-line.
Now work 12 rows in patt as before.
Work 2 rows in st st in A.
Cast off fairly loosely in A.

Press collar lightly, then fold in half right sides together and stitch short ends together. Turn right side out and slip stitch collar facing to inside of neck. Press collar and sew on buttons to correspond with buttonholes approx 14cm/5½in from outer edge of ribbing band on left front. Add two snap fasteners to collar to hold in position.

GLOVES ★ ★

MEASUREMENTS
To fit average adult hand

Please see page 147 for actual garment measurements.

MATERIALS
Yarn
Any **double-knit** weight yarn can be used as long as it knits up to the given tension.
75g/3oz black (A), 25g/1oz white (B)
Needles
1 pair 3¾mm (US 4) needles
2 stitch-holders

TENSION
25 sts and 32 rows to 10cm/4in on 3¾mm (US 4) needles over st st.

RIGHT GLOVE
With 3¾mm (US 4) needles and A, cast on 48 sts and work in double rib as follows:
Row 1: (RS facing) *K2, P2, rep from * to end.
Rep this row 3 times more.
Change to B and work 2 rows in rib as set.
Rep these 6 rows 4 times more (30 rib rows worked).
Rows 31-36: Starting with a K row, work in st st in A.
Row 37: (RS facing) K4A, K16B (this places position of

GLOVE CHART

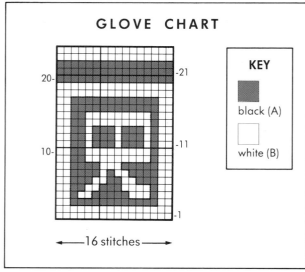

20- -21

10- -11

-1

←—16 stitches—→

KEY

■ black (A)

□ white (B)

chart for motif on back of hand), K4A, inc in next st, K1, inc in next st, K21.

Rows 38-40: Work in st st and follow chart over the 16 sts as set.

Now complete as for right **Scandinavian Glove** (see page 21), working from row 41 to end.

LEFT GLOVE

Rows 1-36: Work as for right glove.

Row 37: (RS facing) In A, K21, inc in next st, K1, inc in next st, K4A, K16B, K4A (this places position of chart).

Rows 38-40: Work in st st and follow chart over the 16 sts as set.

Now complete as for left **Scandinavian Glove** working from row 41 to end.

TO MAKE UP

Work as for **Scandinavian Gloves**.

HEADBAND CHART

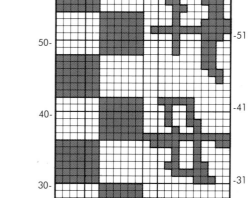

60-

50- -51

40- -41

30- -31

20- -21

10- -11

-1

←—24 stitches—→

KEY

■ black (A)   □ white (B)

HEADBAND ★

MEASUREMENTS

Please see page 156 for actual measurements.

MATERIALS

Yarn

Any **double-knit** weight yarn can be used as long as it knits up to the given tension.

25g/1oz black (A), 25g/1oz white (B)

Needles

1 pair 4mm (US 5) needles

TENSION

24 sts and 28 rows to 10cm/4in on 4mm (US 5) needles over st st.

NOTE

The headband is reversible and knitted in one piece.

METHOD

With 4mm (US 5) needles and B, cast on 24 sts and starting with a K row work in st st from **chart** repeating the 58 rows of motif section and the 60 rows of chequerboard section until band is required length to fit around head.

Cast off fairly loosely.

TO COMPLETE

Sew in ends and press band carefully following ball band instructions. Stitch cast-on and cast-off edges carefully together. Stitch long edges together, carefully stab stitching on right side of work.

Press completed band.

The band may be worn wtih either the motif side or the check pattern on the outside and can be knitted in many different colour combinations or even plain.

SHOULDER BAG ★ ★

MEASUREMENTS
Please see page 156 for actual measurements.

MATERIALS
Yarn
Any **double-knit** weight yarn can be used as long as it knits up to the given tension.
75g/3oz black (A), 50g/2oz white (B), small amount of gold thread worked double (C)
Needles and other materials
1 pair 4mm (US 5) needles
1 large button
Approx 2½m/3yds black cord trim
Approx 20×80cm/8×31½in lining material

TENSION
24 sts and 28 rows to 10cm/4in on 4mm (US 5) needles over st st.

NOTE
Yarn C must be used *double* throughout.

METHOD
Knitted in one piece. With 4mm (US 5) needles and A, cast on 40 sts and work in g st (every row K) in the following stripe sequence:
4 rows A, then 2 rows B.
Rep these 6 rows twice more, then work 4 rows in A (22 rows of g st worked in all).
Now work in st st and chequerboard patt as follows:
Row 1: (RS facing) *K4B, K4A, rep from * to end.
Row 2: *P4A, P4B, rep from * to end.
Rep last 2 rows once more.
Row 5: *K4A, K4B, rep from * to end.
Row 6: *P4B, P4A, rep from * to end.
Rep last 2 rows once more.
These 8 rows form the chequerboard patt.

Now starting with row 1 (K row), work in st st from **chart** until the 36 rows have been completed, thus ending with a WS row.
Now work rows 1-8 of chequerboard patt once more.
** Now rep the 22 rows of striped g st at beg of work.
Now work rows 1-8 of chequerboard patt twice more.**
Work from ** to ** twice more, then work the 22 rows of striped g st again. Cast off fairly loosely in A.
Sew in all ends and press carefully following ball band instructions.

TO MAKE UP
With right sides together, fold the cast-off edge to top of g st band *above* chart patt. Matching patts and leaving flap with chart free, sew side edges carefully together.

Front edgings
Alike. With 4mm (US 5) needles and A and RS facing, pick up and K 58 sts evenly along one side of flap.
K 1 row in A. Cast off fairly loosely in A.

Lining
Fold lining in same way as for bag and stitch side edges. With wrong sides of bag and lining together, place lining inside bag.
Turn all raw edges towards knitted surface and carefully slip stitch in place making sure stitches do not show on right side of bag.
Stab stitch through knitting and lining at point where flap folds, so as to hold lining in position.

Shoulder strap
Fold cord in half to find centre point. Pin the cord in position on the bag along the side edges (starting from the top at fold-line of flap) and along the bottom edge. Leave a top loop big enough to form the shoulder strap and the ends long enough to form a bow at the bottom. Carefully sew the cord in place. Tie the ends into a bow at bottom edge and fray the ends.

At centre of lower edge of flap work a button loop. Sew a button on the bag to correspond with the loop.

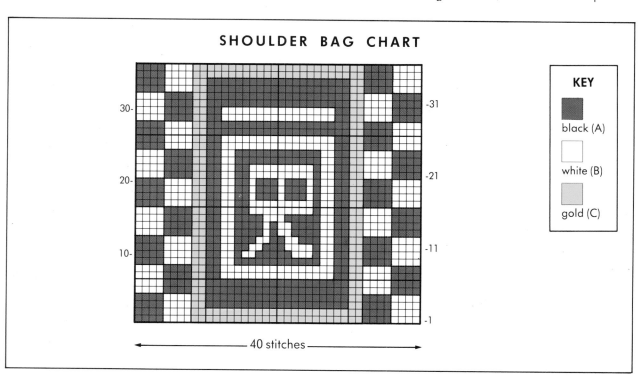

SHOULDER BAG CHART

KEY

black (A)

white (B)

gold (C)

40 stitches

PATCHWORK SWEATER

MEASUREMENTS
To fit bust: 81-87cm/32-34in, 91cm/36in and 97-102cm/38-40in

Please see page 157 for actual measurements

VERSION 1 ★ ★ ★

MATERIALS
Yarn
Any **double-knit** weight yarn can be used as long as it knits up to the given tension.
350(375:400)g/13(14:15)oz black (A), 125(125:150)g/5(5:6)oz cream (B), 25(25:50)g/1(1:2)oz each of yellow (C), pink (D), and blue (E), 125(150:150)g/5(6:6)oz brown (F)
Needles
1 pair each 3¼mm (US 3) and 4mm (US 5) needles
Spare needle

TENSION
24 sts and 28 rows to 10cm/4in on 4mm (US 5) needles over st st.

BACK
With 3¼mm (US 3) needles and A, cast on 96(100:104) sts and work in double rib as follows:
Row 1: (RS facing) *K2, P2, rep from * to end.
Rep this row 3 times more.
Change to B and work 2 rows in rib as set.
Rep these 6 rows 4 times more, then rib 1 more row in A (31 rib rows worked in all).
Increase row: Rib in A and inc 22(24:26)sts evenly across row – 118(124:130)sts.
Change to 4mm (US 5) needles and starting with row 1 (K row) work in st st from **back/front chart**, working between appropriate lines for size required.
Work straight following chart until row 42(46:50) has been worked.

Shape armholes
Keeping chart correct, cast off 16 sts at beg of next 2 rows – 86(92:98)sts.
Now cont straight until row 144(148:152) has been worked.

Shape shoulders
Keeping chart correct, cast off 8(9:10)sts at beg of next 6 rows. Cast off rem 38 sts fairly loosely for back neck.

FRONT
Work as for back until row 100(104:108) has been worked.

Previous pages
Left *Striped Symbol Sweater: A classic wool sweater with an unusual double collar has bands of stencil motifs, characters and raised stripes in tweed yarn.*
Centre *Butterfly and Bamboo Sweater: Brilliantly-coloured butterflies flutter over bamboo shoots on this exotic wool sweater sparkling with gold lurex.*
Right *Patchwork Sweater: Inspired by the kimono, this striking design has loose dolman sleeves and a shawl collar; its bold graphic patterns are typical of Japanese textiles.*

Shape front neck
Next row: (RS facing) Patt 24(27:30) sts, cast off centre 38 sts, patt to end of row and work on this last set of 24(27:30)sts only, leaving rem sts on a spare needle.
Cont straight until row 145(149:153) has been worked, thus ending at armhole edge.

Shape shoulder
Keeping chart correct, cast off 8(9:10)sts at beg of next row and foll 2 alt rows.
With WS facing rejoin yarn to neck edge of rem sts and cont in patt until row 144(148:152) has been worked, thus ending at armhole edge.
Shape shoulder as for first side.

SLEEVES
Make 2. With 3¼mm (US 3) needles and A, cast on 52 sts and work in double rib as for back welt in the same stripe sequence until 31 rib rows have been worked.
Increase row: Rib in A and inc 20 sts evenly across row – 72 sts.
Change to 4mm (US 5) needles and starting with row 1 (K row) work in st st from **sleeve chart** (see page 78) inc 1 st at both ends of 3rd row and then every foll alt row until there are 168 sts on the needle.
Now cont straight until row 116(116:122) has been worked. Cast off all sts fairly loosely.
Measure down 6·5cm/2½in from cast-off edge of sleeves and place coloured markers at each side edge.

TO MAKE UP
Sew in ends and press pieces carefully following ball band instructions. Join both shoulder seams. With centre of cast-off edges of sleeves to shoulder seams and matching horizontal stripe on front and back as indicated on chart, sew sleeves carefully into armholes, sewing sleeve seams above markers to cast-off sts at armhole.
Join side and sleeve seams.

Collar (reversible)
With 3¼mm (US 3) needles and A, cast on 56 sts and work in double rib and 6 row stripe patt as for back welt, until collar fits from centre front cast-off sts, around neck and finishes at centre front, slightly stretched, ending with 4 rib rows in A.
Cast off fairly loosely ribwise in A.
Sew cast-on and cast-off edges, crossing right over left, to centre front cast-off sts, and sew remainder of collar around neck edge. Collar can now be turned to inside to form a neat neck, or to outside to form a shawl collar.

VERSION 2 ★ ★ ★

PATCHWORK DOUBLE-BREASTED CARDIGAN

(see pages 84-85 for illustration)

MATERIALS
Yarn
Any **double-knit** weight yarn can be used as long as it knits up to the given tension.
400(425:450)g/15(15:16)oz black (A), 175(175:200)g/7(7:8)oz cream (B), amounts of C, D, E, and F as for
Version 1
Needles and tension as for **Version 1**
8 buttons

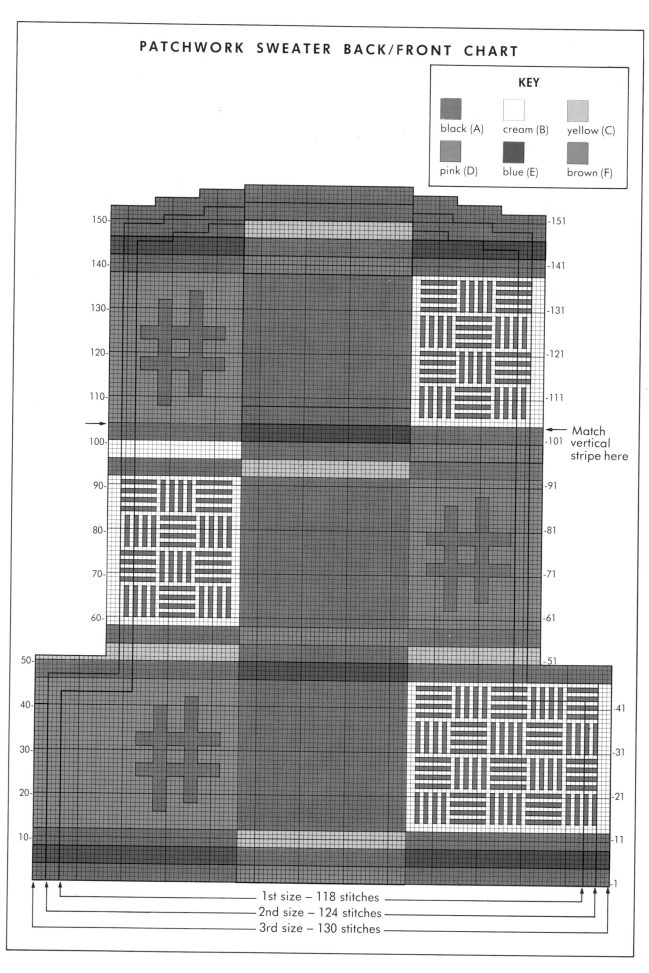

PATCHWORK SWEATER BACK/FRONT CHART

KEY

black (A)   cream (B)   yellow (C)

pink (D)   blue (E)   brown (F)

← Match vertical stripe here

1st size – 118 stitches

2nd size – 124 stitches

3rd size – 130 stitches

77

PATCHWORK SWEATER SLEEVE CHART

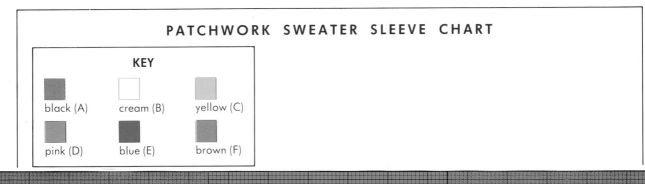

KEY

- black (A)
- cream (B)
- yellow (C)
- pink (D)
- blue (E)
- brown (F)

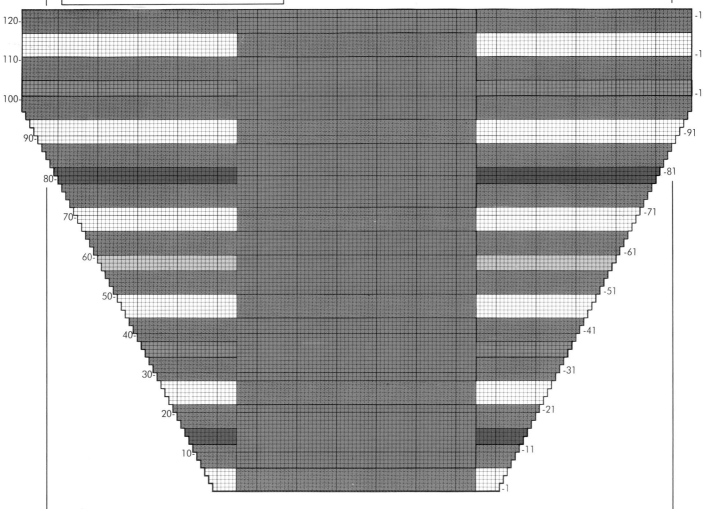

BACK AND SLEEVES
Work as for **Version 1**.

LEFT FRONT
With 3¼mm (US 3) needles and A, cast on 32(32:36)sts and work in double rib and stripe patt as for back welt of **Version 1** for 31 rib rows.

Increase row: Rib in A and inc 8(11:10)sts evenly across row – 40(43:46)sts.

Change to 4mm (US 5) needles and work from *right-hand side* of **back/front chart**, working the *first* 40 (43:46)sts of the row.

Cont on these sts only following armhole and shoulder shapings as for left-hand side of front of **Version 1**.

RIGHT FRONT
Work as for left front, but work across the *left-hand side* of **back/front chart**, working the *last* 40(43:46)sts.

RIBBED FRONT BAND
With 3¼mm (US 3) needles and A, cast on 56 sts and work in double rib and 6 row stripe patt as for back welt for 2·5cm/1in.

Buttonhole row: (RS facing) Keeping stripe sequence correct, rib 8, cast off 4 sts, rib 32, cast off 4 sts, rib 8.

Next row: Rib, casting on 4 sts over cast-off sts on previous row.

Now work a further 3 sets of buttonholes at 10cm/4in intervals (8 buttonholes worked in all).

Cont in rib until band, when slightly stretched, fits around front neck edge, ending with 4 rib rows in A.

Cast off fairly loosely ribwise in A.

TO MAKE UP
Work as for **Version 1**, except for front band, which is carefully stitched around front edges. Sew on buttons to correspond with buttonholes.

BUTTERFLY AND BAMBOO SWEATER

MEASUREMENTS
To fit bust: 81-91cm/32-36in and 91-102cm/36-40in

Please see page 158 for actual garment measurements.

VERSION 1 ★ ★ ★

MATERIALS
Yarn

Any **double-knit** weight yarn can be used as long as it knits up to the given tension.
575(600)g/21(21)oz black (A), 125g/5oz white (B), 25g/1oz deep green (C), 50g/2oz emerald green (D), 25g/1oz each of blue (E), red (F), purple (G), yellow (H), gold lurex worked double (I)

Needles

1 pair each 3¼mm (US 3) and 4mm (US 5) needles
1 circular 3¼mm (US 3) needle
Spare needle

TENSION
24 sts and 28 rows to 10cm/4in on 4mm (US 5) needles over st st.

NOTE
Yarn I must be used *double* throughout.

BACK
With 3¼mm (US 3) needles and A, cast on 132(140)sts and work in double rib as follows:
Row 1: (RS facing) *K2, P2, rep from * to end.
Rep this row 3 times more.
Change to B and work 2 rows in rib as set.
Rep these 6 rows once more (12 rib rows worked in all).
Change to 4mm (US 5) needles and starting with row 1 (K row), work in st st from **back/front chart** (see page 80) working between appropriate lines for size required.
Work straight following chart until row 100 has been worked.

Shape raglan armholes
Keeping chart correct, dec 1 st at both ends of next 5 rows – 122(130)sts.
Now dec 1 st at both ends of every foll alt row until 34(36)sts remain – row 194(200) completed.
Cast off fairly loosely.

FRONT
Work as for back noting that chart for front starts as row 31 (K row) (this makes front shorter than the back).
Work raglan armholes as for back until row 174(180) has been worked – 54(56)sts.

Shape front neck
Next row: (RS facing) Work 2 tog, patt until there are 19(20)sts on RH needle, turn and work on this first set of sts only, leaving rem sts on a spare needle.
** Keeping raglan shaping correct, dec 1 st at neck edge on every row 10(11) times – 4 sts.
Now keeping neck edge straight, cont to dec at raglan edge until all sts are worked. Fasten off.
With RS facing rejoin yarn to rem sts, cast off centre 14

sts, work to last 2 sts, work 2 tog.
Now work as for first side from ** to end.

SLEEVES
Make 2. With 3¼mm (US 3) needles and A, cast on 52(60)sts and work in double rib as for back welt, but work 4 repeats of the 6 row stripe patt making a total of 24 rib rows worked in all, and inc 20 sts evenly across last row only – 72(80)sts.
Change to 4mm (US 5) needles and starting with row 1 (K row), work in st st from **sleeve chart** (see page 81), working between appropriate lines for size required, working inc rows as indicated at each end of 3rd row, and then every foll alt row until there are 122(130)sts on the needle.
Now cont straight until row 60 has been worked.

Shape raglan top
Cont to follow chart, working raglan decs at each end of row 61 and then rows as indicated until row 154(160) has been worked.
Cast off rem 6(8)sts.

RAGLAN RIBS
4 alike (these are worked along the top shaped edges of the sleeves).
With 3¼mm (US 3) needles and A and RS facing, pick up and K88(96)sts evenly along one side of shaped raglan sleeve edge and work in double rib in following stripe sequence:
Work 2 rows in B, work 4 rows in A.
Rep these 6 rows once more.
Work 2 rows in B.
Cast off fairly loosely ribwise in A.

POCKETS
Make 2. With 4mm (US 5) needles and A, cast on 3 sts, and starting with a K row, work in st st, inc 1 st at beg of every K row until there are 26 sts on the needle.
Now cont straight until pocket measures 25cm/10in from cast-on edge.
Now dec 1 st at beg of every K row until 3 sts remain. Cast off.
Press pockets. Fold in half with right sides together and join shaped edges, leaving straight edge open.

TO MAKE UP
Press pieces carefully following ball band instructions, and sew in all ends. Join all raglan seams together.

Collar
With the 3¼mm (US 3) circular needle and RS facing and A, and starting at centre front, pick up and K 22 sts from centre front to sleeve, 22 sts across raglan ribs and sleeve top, 32 sts across back neck, 22 sts across raglan ribs and sleeve top, and finally 22 sts to centre front (mark centre front with a coloured thread) – 120 sts.
Work in *rounds* of double rib for 2 rounds.
Now work backwards and forwards in *rows* of double rib, leaving opening at centre front to split collar for mandarin effect.
Work a further 2 rows in A, then work 2 rows in B and 4 rows in A.
Rep last 6 rows twice more. Cast off fairly loosely ribwise in A.

To complete
Join underarm and side seams, but leave an opening

BUTTERFLY AND BAMBOO SWEATER BACK/FRONT CHART

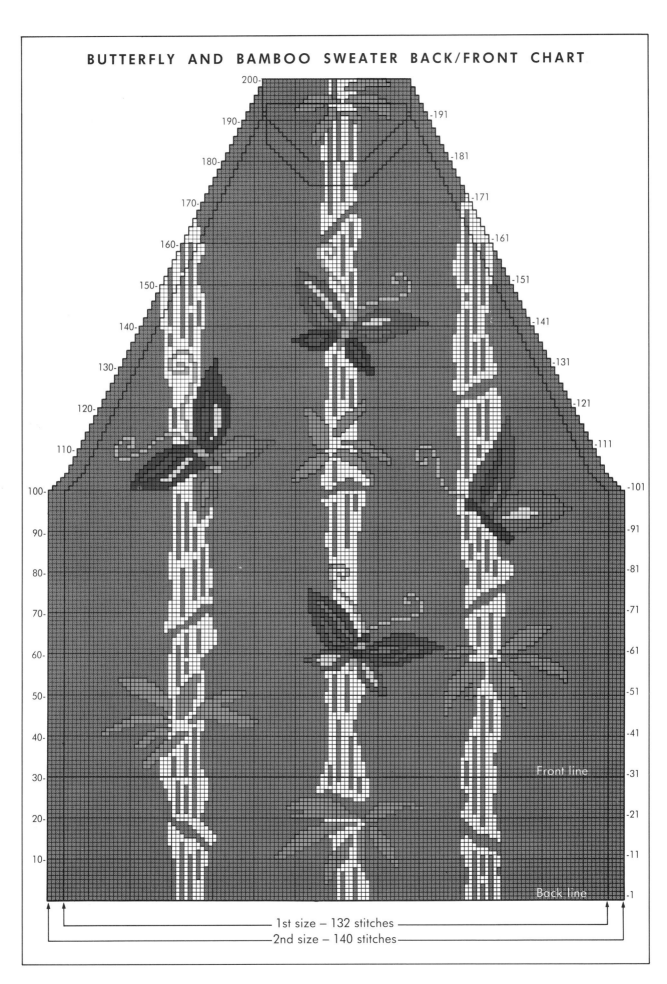

1st size — 132 stitches
2nd size — 140 stitches

SLEEVE CHART

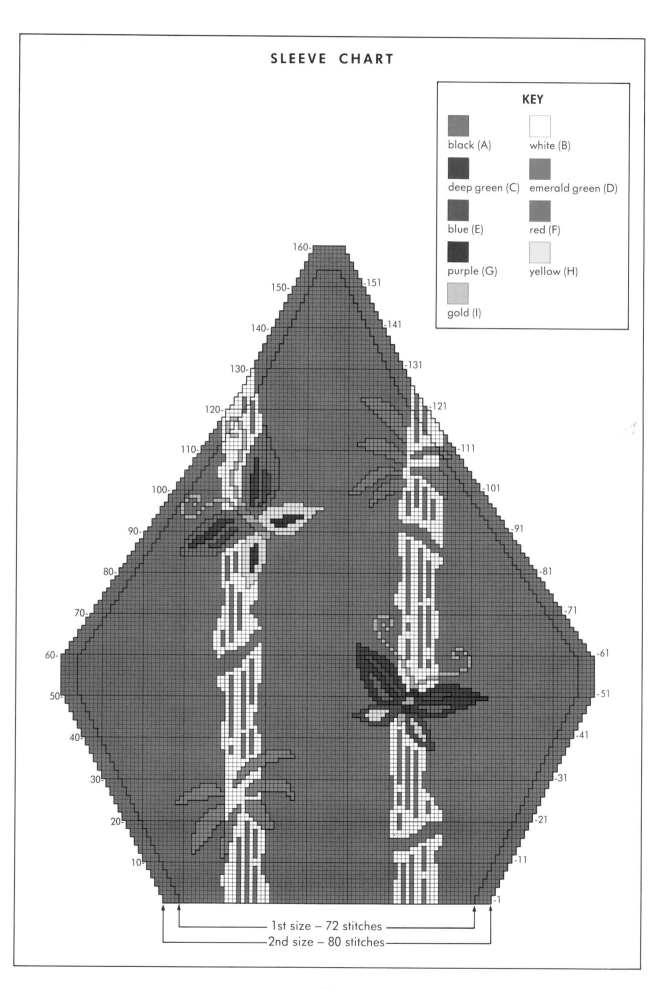

KEY

black (A)	white (B)
deep green (C)	emerald green (D)
blue (E)	red (F)
purple (G)	yellow (H)
gold (I)	

1st size – 72 stitches
2nd size – 80 stitches

for insertion of pockets starting 8cm/3in up from bottom edge on *front*.
Stitch pockets into side seams, stab stitch around pocket edges to hold pocket linings neatly in place.

Side back edgings
Alike. With 3¼mm (US 3) needles and A and RS facing, pick up and K 30 sts along side edge of back to beg of front. Work in K1, P1 rib 1 row A, 2 rows B and cast off fairly loosely ribwise in A.
Catch stitch ends neatly to bottom of front.

VERSION 2 ★ ★ ★
AS VERSION 1, BUT WITHOUT SHIRT-TAIL
(see pages 84-85 for illustrations of Versions 2 and 3)

METHOD
This is worked exactly as for **Version 1**, but the front is knitted the same length as the back (both front and back starting on row 1 of chart).
Omit side back edgings.

VERSION 3 ★ ★
WITH BLUE-STRIPED RIBBING AND BUTTERFLY AND LEAF MOTIFS ONLY

MATERIALS
Yarn
Any **double-knit** weight yarn can be used as long as it knits up to the given tension.
600(625)g/21(22)oz black (A), 25g/1oz deep green (C), 50g/2oz emerald green (D), 100g/4oz blue (E), 25g/1oz each of red (F), purple (G), yellow (H), gold thread worked double (I)
Needles and tension as for **Version 1**.

METHOD
Work as for **Version 1** but on all ribs work E instead of B.
When following chart, omit all vertical bamboo motifs (ie everything worked in B) and work the butterfly and leaf motifs only.

VERSION 4 ★ ★
AS FOR VERSION 3, BUT WITHOUT SHIRT-TAIL

METHOD
This is worked exactly as for **Version 3**, but the front is knitted the same length as the back (both front and back starting on row 1 of chart).
Omit side back edgings.

STRIPED SYMBOL SWEATER ★ ★

MEASUREMENTS
To fit bust: 76-81cm/30-32in, 81-91cm/32-36in and 91-102cm/36-40in

Please see page 158 for actual garment measurements.

MATERIALS
Yarn
Any **Aran-weight** yarn can be used as long as it knits up to the given tension.
300(325:350)g/11(12:13)oz black Aran (A), 175 (200:200)g/7(8:8)oz cream Aran (B), 200(225:250)g/ 8(8:9)oz blue tweed (C), 150(150:175)g/6(6:7)oz gold thread – 3 strands used together (D)
Needles
1 pair each 4½mm (US 6) and 5½mm (US 8) needles
1 circular 4½mm (US 6) needle

TENSION
18 sts and 20½ rows to 10cm/4in on 5½mm (US 8) needles over pattern.

NOTE
Yarn D is knitted with *3 strands* used together.

BACK
With 4½mm (US 6) needles and A, cast on 62(70:78)sts and work in K1, P1 rib for 8cm/3in.
Increase row: Rib and inc 26 sts evenly across row – 88(96:104)sts.
Change to 5½mm (US 8) needles and work from **chart** as follows, noting that all rows worked in C are to be K rows, so as to form ridges:
Row 1: (RS facing) Rep the 16-stitch patt across row to last 8(0:8)sts, work 8(0:8)sts beyond the dotted line.
Row 2: Work 8(0:8)sts before the dotted line, then rep the 16-stitch patt to end of row.
Cont to work from chart as now set, repeating the 38 rows until back measures 59(61:63)cm/23¼(24:24¾)in from cast-on edge, ending with a WS row.

Shape shoulders
Keeping patt correct, cast off 9(10:11)sts at beg of next 4 rows.
Cast off 7(9:11)sts at beg of foll 2 rows.
Cast off rem 38 sts.

FRONT
Work as for back until front measures approx 51(53:55)cm/20(21:21¾)in from cast-on edge, ending with a WS row. (If a ridge row has just been worked, work 2 extra rows, as the ridge row will become distorted when shaping.)

Shape front neck
Next row: Patt 34(38:42)sts, cast off centre 20 sts, patt to end of row and cont on this last set of 34(38:42)sts only.
** Keeping patt correct, dec 1 st at neck edge on every row until 25(29:33)sts remain.
Now cont straight in patt until front measures the same as back to beg of shoulder shaping, ending at side edge and on same patt row.

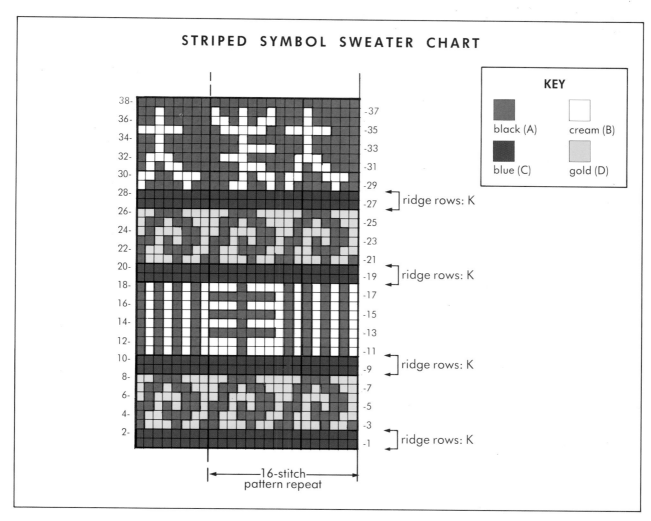

STRIPED SYMBOL SWEATER CHART

KEY

black (A)   cream (B)

blue (C)   gold (D)

ridge rows: K

ridge rows: K

ridge rows: K

ridge rows: K

16-stitch
pattern repeat

Shape shoulder

Keeping patt correct, cast off 9(10:11)sts at beg of next row and foll alt row.

Work 1 row.

Cast off rem 7(9:11)sts.

With WS facing rejoin yarn to neck edge of rem sts and work as for first side from ** to end.

SLEEVES

Make 2. With 4½mm (US 6) needles and A, cast on 40 sts and work in K1, P1 rib for 10cm/4in.

Increase row: Rib and inc 24 sts evenly across row – 64 sts.

Change to 5½mm (US 8) needles and work from **chart**, noting that all rows worked in C are to be K rows, so as to form ridges. Rep the 16-stitch patt 4 times across row.

Cont to rep the 38 rows of chart, *at the same time* inc 1 st at each and of 2nd row and then every foll 3rd row until there are 104 sts on the needle, working inc sts into the patt on either side.

Now work a few rows straight in patt until sleeve measures approx 42(44:46)cm/16½(17¼:18)in from cast-on edge, ending with a WS row and a complete motif worked.

Cast off fairly loosely in A.

TO MAKE UP

Sew in ends and press pieces carefully following ball band instructions. Join both shoulder seams.

Collar

With the 4½mm (US 6) circular needle and A and RS facing, pick up and K 38 sts from back neck, 14 sts down left front neck, 20 sts from centre front and finally 14 sts up left front neck – 86 sts.

With RS facing work straight in *rounds* of K until collar measures 8cm/3in.

Cast off using a 5½mm (US 8) needle to give a looser edge (collar will automatically roll onto right side of garment).

Inner collar

With the 4½mm (US 6) circular needle and C and RS facing, pick up and K sts exactly as for collar, picking them up along inside of collar just worked, along same pick-up row. Complete as for collar.

To complete

With centre of cast-off edges of sleeves to shoulder seams, sew sleeves carefully in position reaching down 29cm/11¼in on both back and front from shoulders. Join side and sleeve seams, matching patterns carefully.

Butterfly and Bamboo Version 2

Back View of Japanese Coat

Without Shirt-tail.

Butterfly Bamboo Version 3

Patchwork Sweater as Jacket Version 2

Headband

Gloves

AUSTRALASIA

The earthy colours of the garments in this chapter recall Ayers Rock and hot desert sands, while their bold patterns derive from the paintings of Australian aborigines and from the wood carvings of South Pacific islanders.

The **Aboriginal Bark Painting Jacket** *(page 90)* takes its images from sacred paintings applied to eucalyptus bark with pigments made from ground ochre, charcoal and clay. The paintings depicted mythical 'dreamings', stories of supernatural beings, ancestors of the Aborigines, who travelled across the land in the distant 'dreamtime'. The story told on this jacket concerns the hunter Gurrumirringu, killed by a snake at a sacred watering hole. The jacket, worked in double-knit cottons, has a very wide, loose shape.

The **Trailing Leaf Sweater** *(page 93)* was also inspired by bark painting. Its motif, representing

the leaves of a sacred tree, is used as an all-over Fair Isle pattern in repeat. Again it is knitted in cottons, with elbow-length sleeves and an unusual square neckline; however it could just as easily be made with long sleeves and in wool as a warm winter sweater.

The **Wood Carving Sweater** *(page 94)* takes its motifs from the intricate work of Polynesian woodcarvers, in Tahiti in particular. These beautiful carvings are traditionally applied to almost every type of object, from canoe paddles to drums, bowls and ladles, in stock patterns often so conventionalized as to appear almost abstract. One of the most popular designs is the stylized row of linked figures which I have used here. The sweater is knitted in a mixture of flecked cotton and tweed wool yarns and the straight-necked shape is very simple to make, with the back and front being identical.

I have also designed some basic **Striped Skirts** in easy stocking stitch to be worn with these garments *(page 96)*. The stripes could be worked in any number of alternative colour combinations.

ABORIGINAL BARK PAINTING JACKET

MEASUREMENTS
To fit bust: 81-91cm/32-36in and 97-102cm/38-40in

Please see page 159 for actual measurements.

VERSION 1 ★ ★ ★

MATERIALS
Yarn

Any **double-knit** weight yarn can be used as long as it knits up to the given tension.
600(650)g/21(23)oz light brown cotton (A), 175(200)g/7(8)oz black (B), 50(75)g/2(3)oz each yellow (C) and rust (D), 125(125)g/5(5)oz white cotton (E)

Needles and other materials

1 pair each 3¼mm (US 3) and 4mm (US 5) needles
6 buttons

TENSION
22 sts and 27 rows to 10cm/4in on 4mm (US 5) needles over main pattern.

BOBBLE EDGE PATTERN
(Worked over a multiple of 3 sts plus 2)
Row 1: (RS facing) *K2B, in D make bobble as follows: K1, P1, K1, P1, into next st, then slip 2nd, 3rd and 4th sts over 1st st (referred to as MB), rep from * to last 2 sts, K2B.
Row 2: P in B.
Rows 3 and 4: K in B (thus forming ridge).
Now rep rows 1 – 4 but using E in place of D.
Now rep rows 1 – 4 but using C in place of D.
Now rep rows 1 – ,4.
These 16 rows complete the bobble edge (4 rows of bobbles in sequence of D, E, C and D).

BACK
With 3¼mm (US 3) needles and B, cast on 125(134)sts and work 6 rows in g st (K every row).
Change to 4mm (US 5) needles and work the 16 rows of bobble-edge pattern, on last row inc 1 st *on 1st size only* – 126(134)sts.
Now starting with a K row, work in st st from **back chart**, working between appropriate lines for size required.
Cont as set for 8 rows.

Shape pockets
Rows 9 and 10: Cast on 29 sts at beg of next 2 rows – 184(192)sts.

Previous pages
Left *Aboriginal Bark Painting Jacket: Double-knit cotton yarns in strong earthy colours create a dramatic jacket with bold graphic Aboriginal images.*
Centre *Wood Carving Sweater: A subtle repeat pattern of linked dancing figures is worked in flecked cotton and tweed wool.*
Right *Trailing Leaf Sweater: Short-sleeved and square-necked, this sweater, in double-knit wool and cotton, uses black, rust and sandy yellow to evoke the heat of the stark Australian desert.*

Now cont straight until row 22 has been worked.
Cast off 2 sts at beg of next 28 rows, and then 1 st at beg of foll 2 rows – 126(134)sts.
Now cont straight until row 150(154) has been worked, thus ending with a WS row.

Shape shoulders
Cast off 10(11)sts at beg of next 8 rows.
Cast off rem 46 sts.

LEFT FRONT
With 3¼mm (US 3) needles and B, cast on 59(62)sts and work 6 rows in g st (K every row).
Change to 4mm (US 5) needles and work the 16 rows of bobble-edge pattern, on last row inc 1 st *on 2nd size only* – 59(63)sts.
Now starting with a K row, work in st st from **left front chart**, working between appropriate lines for size required, and shaping pocket at side edge as for back.
Cont straight until row 133(137) of chart has been worked, thus ending at centre front edge.

Shape front neck
Cast off 8 sts at beg (neck edge) on next row. Now dec 1 st at this edge on every row until 40(44)sts remain.
Cont straight until row 150(154) has been worked, thus ending at side edge.

Shape shoulder
Cast off 10(11)sts at beg of next row and foll 3 alt rows.

RIGHT FRONT
Work as for left front, but following **right front chart**, and shaping pocket at side edge as for back.
Start front neck shaping on row 133(137) of chart and shoulder shaping on row 152(156) of chart.

SLEEVES
Make 2. With 3¼mm (US 3) needles and B, cast on 56 sts and work 6 rows in g st (K every row).
Change to 4mm (US 5) needles and work the 16 rows of bobble edge pattern.
Increase row: In B, K and inc 24 sts evenly across row – 80 sts.
P1 row in B.
Now starting with a K row, work from **sleeve chart** (see page 92) in st st, and *at the same time*, inc 1 st at each end of 3rd row and then every foll 4th row until there are 120 sts on the needle.
Now cont straight until row 94(100) has been worked.
Cast off fairly loosely using A.

TO MAKE UP
Sew in ends and press pieces carefully following ball band instructions. Join shoulder seams. With centre of cast-off edges of sleeves to shoulder seams, sew sleeves carefully in position, reaching down to same depth on front and back. Join side and sleeve seams and edges of pockets. Push pockets to inside and carefully stab stitch around pocket opening to hold pocket in position inside garment.

Neckband
With 3¼mm (US 3) needles and B and RS facing, pick up and K 30 sts around right front neck, 44 sts across back neck and finally 30 sts around left front neck – 104 sts.

ABORIGINAL BARK PAINTING JACKET BACK/FRONTS CHART

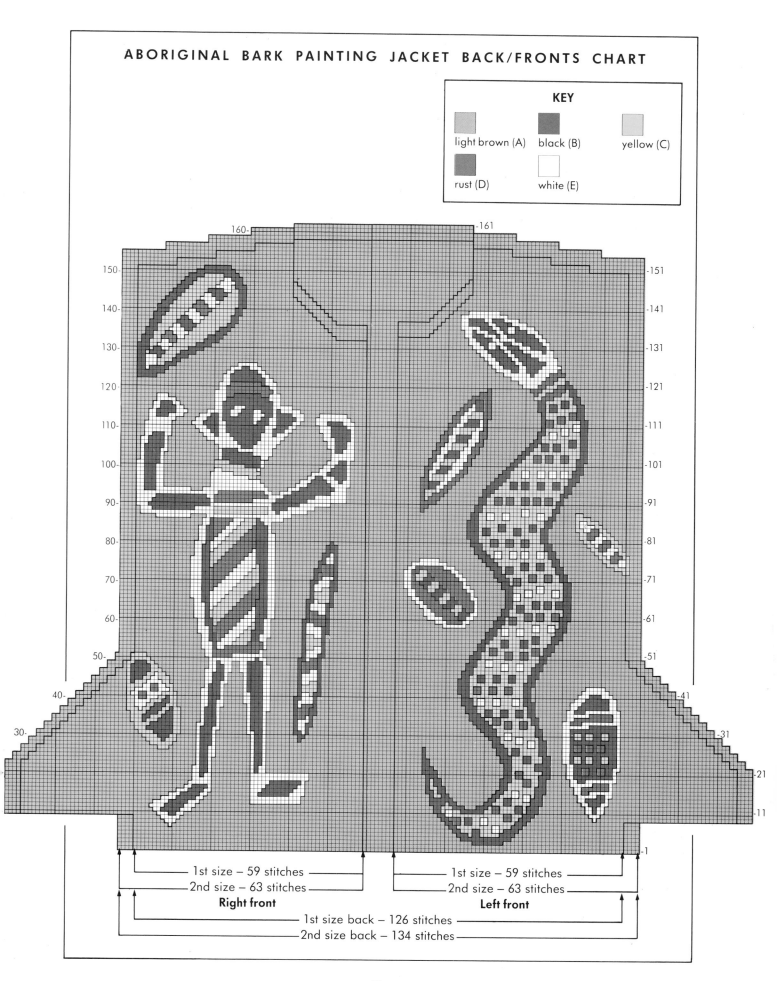

KEY

light brown (A)　black (B)　yellow (C)

rust (D)　white (E)

1st size – 59 stitches

2nd size – 63 stitches

Right front

1st size – 59 stitches

2nd size – 63 stitches

Left front

1st size back – 126 stitches

2nd size back – 134 stitches

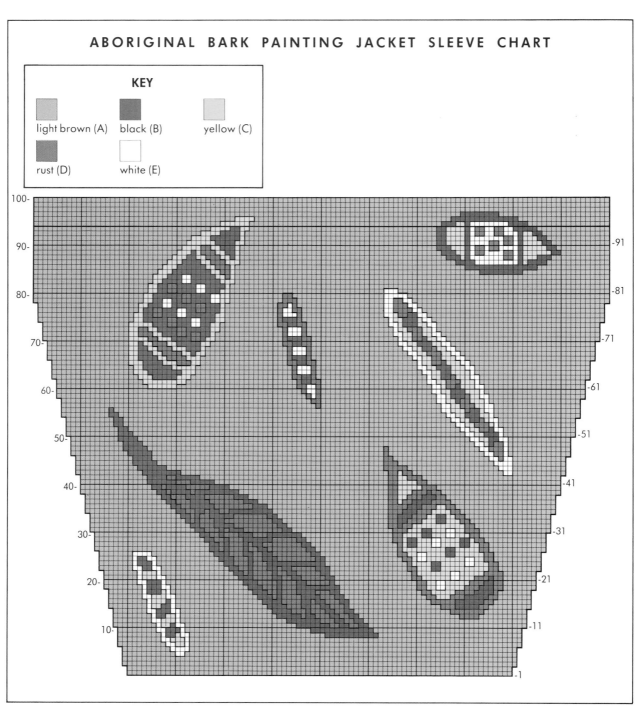

ABORIGINAL BARK PAINTING JACKET SLEEVE CHART

KEY

light brown (A) black (B) yellow (C)

rust (D) white (E)

P1 row in B.
Change to 4mm (US 5) needles and work the 16 rows of bobble-edge pattern.
Cast off using B.

Right front band
With 3¼mm (US 3) needles and B and RS facing, pick up and K 152(156)sts evenly up right front edge and neckband, and work in K1, P1, rib for 3 rows.
Buttonhole row: (RS facing) Rib 4(6), * cast off 4 sts, rib 24, rep from * 4 times more, cast off 4 sts, rib to end.
Next row: Rib, casting on 4 sts over cast-off sts on previous row (6 buttonholes made).
Rib 3 more rows. Cast off loosely ribwise.

Left front band
Work as for right front band, but omit buttonholes.
Sew on buttons to correspond with buttonholes.

VERSION 2 ★ ★ ★

ON BLACK BACKGROUND
(see page 97 for illustration)

MATERIALS
Yarn
Any **double-knit** weight yarn can be used as long as it knits up to the given tension.
600(650)g/21(23)oz black cotton (A), 175(200)g/7(8)oz light brown (B), other amounts and colours as for **Version 1**.
Needles, other materials and tension as for **Version 1**.

METHOD
Work as for **Version 1**, noting that background is black and borders are light brown.

TRAILING LEAF SWEATER

MEASUREMENTS
To fit bust: 81-91cm/32-36in and 97-102cm/38-40in

Please see page 160 for actual measurements.

VERSION 1 ★ ★

MATERIALS
Yarn
Any **double-knit** weight yarn can be used as long as it knits up to the given tension.
325(375)g/12(14)oz black cotton (A), 125(125)g/5(5)oz cream (B), 50(75)g/2(3)oz yellow (C), 125(150)g/5(6)oz rust (D)
Needles
1 pair each 3¼mm (US 3) and 4mm (US 5) needles
3¼mm (US 3) circular needle

TENSION
25 sts and 26 rows to 10cm/4in on 4mm (US 5) needles over Fair Isle pattern.

FRONT
With 3¼mm (US 3) needles and A, cast on 90(100)sts and work in K1, P1 rib for 8cm/3in.
Increase row: In A, rib and inc 36(35)sts evenly across row – 126(135)sts.
Change to 4mm (US 5) needles and starting with a K row, work in st st from chart, repeating the 9-stitch patt 14(15) times across and repeating the 36 rows as required.
Cont as set until 96 patt rows in all have been worked.

Shape front neck
Next row: (RS facing – row 25 of chart) Patt 36(40), cast off centre 54(55)sts, patt to end and cont on last set of 36(40)sts only.
** Cont straight in patt until front measures 61cm/24in from cast-on edge, ending at side edge.

Shape shoulder
Keeping patt correct, cast off 9(10)sts at beg of next row and foll 3 alt rows.
With WS facing rejoin yarn to rem sts, and work as for first side from ** to end.

BACK
Work as for front but omit front neck shaping, and cont straight until back measures same as front to beg of shoulder shaping, ending with a WS row and same patt row as front.

Shape shoulders
Keeping patt correct, cast off 9(10)sts at beg of next 8 rows.
Cast off rem 54(55)sts.

SLEEVES
Make 2. With 3¼mm (US 3) needles and A, cast on 60 sts and work in K1, P1 rib for 5cm/2in.
Increase row: In A, rib and inc 57 sts evenly across row – 117 sts.
Change to 4mm (US 5) needles and work from chart, repeating the 9-stitch patt 13 times across, and repeating the 36 rows as required, *at the same time*, inc 1 st at each end of every foll 4th row until there are 127 sts on the needle, working inc sts into the patt on either side.
Now cont straight until 60 patt rows in all have been worked.
Cast off fairly loosely using B.

TO MAKE UP
Sew in ends and press pieces carefully following ball band instructions. Join right shoulder seam.

Neckband
With the 3¼mm (US 3) circular needle and A and RS facing, pick up and K36 sts down left front neck, 1 corner st, 50 sts from front neck, 1 corner st, 36 sts up right front neck and finally 50 sts across back neck – 174 sts.
Work in rows of single rib as follows:
Rib until 2 sts before corner st, rib 2 tog, rib 1, rib 2 tog tbl, rep on other corner.
Work a further 7 rows in rib, dec as set. Cast off ribwise, dec as set.

To complete
Join left shoulder and neckband seam. With centre of cast-off edges of sleeves to shoulder seams, sew sleeves in position reaching down to same patt rows on front and back. Join side and sleeve seams matching patterns.

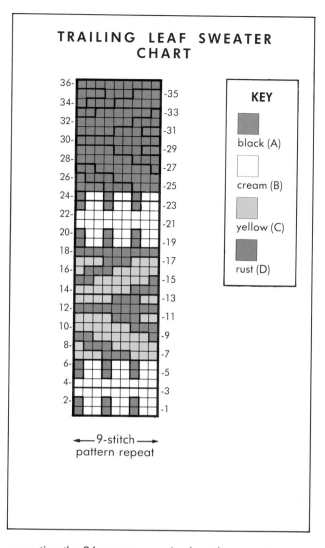

TRAILING LEAF SWEATER CHART

KEY

black (A)

cream (B)

yellow (C)

rust (D)

◄— 9-stitch —► pattern repeat

VERSION 2 ★ ★
WITH LONG SLEEVES
(see page 97 for illustration)

MATERIALS
Yarn
Any **double-knit** weight yarn can be used as long as it knits up to the given tension.
350(400)g/13(15)oz black cotton (A), 150(150)g/6(6)oz cream (B), 75(100)g/3(4)oz yellow (C), 150(175)g/6(7)oz rust (D)
Needles and tension as for **Version 1**.

METHOD
Work exactly as for **Version 1**, but inserting following instructions for sleeves.

LONG SLEEVES
Make 2. With 3¼mm (US 3) needles and A, cast on 48 sts and work in K1, P1 rib for 8cm/3in.
Increase row: Rib and inc 33 sts evenly across row — 81 sts.
Change to 4mm (US 5) needles and work from chart, repeating the 9-stitch patt 9 times across, and repeating the 36 rows as required, *at the same time*, inc 1 st at each end of every foll 4th row until there are 127 sts on the needle, working inc sts into the patt on either side.
Now cont straight until 96 patt rows in all have been worked.
Cast off fairly loosely using B.
Complete as for **Version 1**.

WOOD CARVING SWEATER

MEASUREMENTS
To fit bust: 81-87cm/32-34in, 91-97cm/36-38in and 102-107cm/40-42in

Please see page 161 for actual measurements.

VERSION 1 ★ ★

MATERIALS
Yarn
Any **double-knit** weight yarn can be used as long as it knits up to the given tension.
200(225:250)g/8(8:9)oz cream (A), 225(225:250)g/8(8:9)oz brown fleck (B), 150(175:175)g/6(7:7)oz beige fleck slub cotton mix (C), 50(50:50)g/2(2:2)oz rust (D), 75(100:100)g/3(4:4)oz light brown cotton (E)
Needles
1 pair each 3¼mm (US 3) and 4mm (US 5) needles

TENSION
25 sts and 26 rows to 10cm/4in on 4mm (US 5) needles over st st pattern.

BACK AND FRONT
Alike. With 3¼mm (US 3) needles and A, cast on 82(90:98)sts and work in double rib as follows:
Row 1: (RS facing) K2, *P2, K2, rep from * to end.
Row 2: P2, *K2, P2, rep from * to end.
Rep last 2 rows until rib measures 10cm/4in, ending with row 1.
Increase Row: In A, rib and inc 39(42:45)sts evenly across row — 121(132:143)sts.
Change to 4mm (US 5) needles and starting with a K row, work in st st and place chart as follows:
Rows 1-24: Rep the 11-stitch patt 11(12:13) times across.
Row 25: (RS facing) Work 1(2:3)st(s) before the dotted line, then rep the 10-stitch patt 12(13:14) times across.
Row 26: Rep the 10-stitch patt 12(13:14) times, work 1(2:3)st(s) beyond the dotted line.
Rows 27-40: Work as last 2 rows, working from appropriate chart rows.
Rows 41-64: Work as rows 1-24, working from appropriate chart rows.
Rows 65-80: Work as rows 25-40, working from appropriate chart rows.
These 80 rows form the patt and are repeated as required.
Cont in patt as now set until 120 patt rows in all have been worked, thus ending with a WS row.
Next row: K in A and inc 1(2:3)st(s) evenly across row — 122(134:146)sts.
Change to 3¼mm (US 3) needles and working in A, and starting with a 2nd row, work in double rib as for welt for 6(8:10)cm/2½(3:4)in.
Cast off loosely ribwise.

SLEEVES
Make 2. With 3¼mm (US 3) needles and A, cast on 62 sts and work in double rib as for back welt for 5cm/2in, ending with row 1.
Increase row: Rib and inc 37 sts evenly across row — 99 sts.

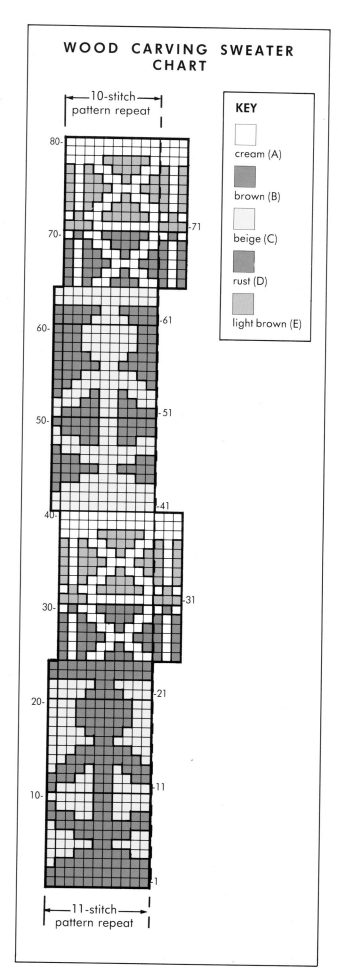

WOOD CARVING SWEATER CHART

←— 10-stitch —→
pattern repeat

KEY

☐ cream (A)

■ brown (B)

☐ beige (C)

▨ rust (D)

▨ light brown (E)

←— 11-stitch —→
pattern repeat

Change to 4mm (US 5) needles and starting with a K row, work in st st and place chart as follows:

Rows 1 and 2: Rep the 11-stitch patt 9 times across. Keeping chart as now placed, inc 1 st at each end of next row and then every foll 3rd row until there are 131 sts on the needle, working inc sts into the patt on either side and keeping patt repeats correct.

Now cont straight until 80 patt rows in all have been worked.

Cast off loosely using A.

TO MAKE UP

Sew in ends and press pieces carefully following ball band instructions. Join both shoulder seams, leaving approx 25cm/10in open in centre for neck edge. With centre of cast-off edges of sleeves to shoulder seams, sew sleeves in position, reaching down to same patt rows on front and back. Join side and sleeve seams, matching pattern carefully.

VERSION 2 ★

STRIPED IN TWO COLOURS
(see page 97 for illustration)

MATERIALS
Yarn
Any **double-knit** weight yarn can be used as long as it knits up to the given tension.
375(400:425)g/14(15:15)oz first colour (A),
325(350:375)g/12(13:14)oz second colour (B)
Needles and tension as for **Version 1**.

METHOD
Work as for **Version 1**, but instead of working from chart, work main body and sleeves in stripe sequence of 24 rows B and 16 rows A.

STRIPED SKIRT

MEASUREMENTS
To fit hips: 81cm/32in, 87cm/34in and 91cm/36in

Please see page 161 for actual garment measurements.

VERSION 1 ★

MATERIALS
Yarn
Any **double-knit** weight yarn can be used as long as it knits up to the given tension.
225(250:275)g/8(9:10)oz black (A), 50(50:75)g/2(2:3)oz rust (B)
Needles and other materials
1 pair each long 3¼mm (US 3) and long 4mm (US 5) needles *or* circular needles
Waist-length elastic (optional)

TENSION
22 sts and 27 rows to 10cm/4in on 4mm (US 5) needles over striped st st.

NOTE
Both these skirts may be made longer or shorter as required, also any combination of colours can be used, and stripes can be of any width, but if these changes are made, please adjust yarn quantities accordingly.

METHOD
With 3¼mm (US 3) needles *or* circular needle and A, cast on 180(190:200) sts and work in rows of K1, P1, rib for 8cm/3in.
Change to 4mm (US 5) needles *or* circular needle and starting with a K row work 2 rows of st st in A. Now work in the following stripe sequence of 2 rows B and 10 rows A. The last 12 rows form the stripe sequence and are repeated as required.
Cont straight until skirt measures approx 51cm/20in from cast-on edge, or length required, ending with 2 rows of B.
Now work in rows of K1, P1 rib for 4cm/1½in in A.
Cast off fairly loosely ribwise in A.

TO COMPLETE
Carefully join centre back seam matching stripes. If elasticated waist is required, fold waistband in half to inside and carefully slip stitch in position leaving a small gap. Insert waist-length elastic, secure and close gap in waistband.

VERSION 2 ★

MATERIALS
As for **Version 1**, but use cream for (A) instead of black, and brown fleck for (B) instead of rust.
Needles and tension as for **Version 1**.

METHOD
As for **Version 1**, with optional elasticated waistband.

BANGLES

MEASUREMENTS
To fit average-size adult wrist

Please see page 161 for actual garment measurement.

VERSION 1 ★
PLAIN BANGLE

MATERIALS
Yarn
Any **double-knit** weight yarn can be used as long as it knits up to the given tension.
Small amount yarn any colour
Needles and other materials
1 pair 4mm (US 5) needles
Washable stuffing (optional)

TENSION
22 sts and 28 rows to 10cm/4in on 4mm (US 5) needles over st st.

METHOD
With 4mm (US 5) needles cast on 12 sts. (For wider bangle cast on more sts as required.)
Starting with a K row work straight in st st until bangle is required length. Cast off.

TO COMPLETE
Press piece carefully following ball band instructions. Stitch cast-on and cast-off edges carefully together. Stitch long edges together neatly on inside of work. If a padded effect is required, cut filling material to correct length and place inside knitting before the long edges are joined.

VERSION 2 ★
WIDE STRIPED BANGLE

MATERIALS
As for **Version 1**, but small amounts of yarn in rust (A) and black (B). Needles and tension as for **Version 1**.

METHOD
With 4mm (US 5) needles and A, cast on 20 sts and starting with a K row work straight in st st in the following stripe sequence: 8 rows A, 8 rows B.
Rep these 16 rows until bangle is required length, ending with 8 rows B.
Cast off. Complete as for **Version 1**.

VERSION 3 ★
THIN STRIPED BANGLE

MATERIALS
As for **Version 1**, but small amounts of yarn in black (A) and cream (B). Needles and tension as for **Version 1**.

METHOD
Work exactly as for **Version 2**, but in the stripe sequence of 4 rows A, 4 rows B. Finish as for **Version 2**.

Trailing Leaf
Sweater
Version
2

Woodcarving
Sweater
Version
2.

Dark-
Painting
Jacket
Version
2

mohair

Tweed

Eskimo
Border
KNIT
SWATCH.

Fur trims

almost "parka" shape
and afghan coat

ribbons
or leather

Back

NORTH
AMERICA

The Wild West provides the theme for North America, the designs influenced by Navajo rugs, Hopi *kachina* dolls, teepees, Indian jewellery and beadwork, and by typical cowboy dress.

The **Teepee Sweater** *(page 102)* borrows its motifs from the Plains Indians familiar from cinema Westerns. Bold images of teepees and arrows, taken from a piece of Indian leatherwork embroidery, stand out on a fine-striped background. The sweater is in a light double-knit yarn in a basic crew-neck shape with drop-shoulder sleeves. To complement it I have designed knitted versions of **Indian Headbands and Earrings.**

These accessories would go equally well with the **Indian Sweater Dress** *(page 104),* which is also worked in double-knit wool, in a loose shape that is easy to make. This design takes elements from various American Indian sources. Its Fair Isle

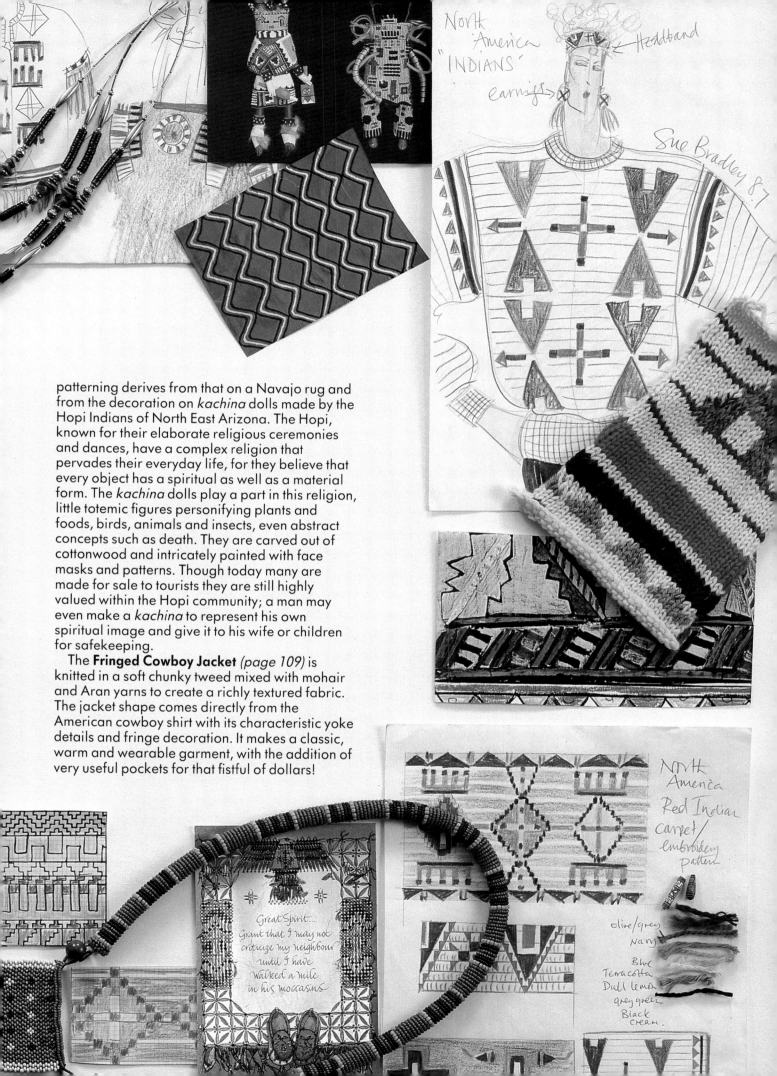

patterning derives from that on a Navajo rug and from the decoration on *kachina* dolls made by the Hopi Indians of North East Arizona. The Hopi, known for their elaborate religious ceremonies and dances, have a complex religion that pervades their everyday life, for they believe that every object has a spiritual as well as a material form. The *kachina* dolls play a part in this religion, little totemic figures personifying plants and foods, birds, animals and insects, even abstract concepts such as death. They are carved out of cottonwood and intricately painted with face masks and patterns. Though today many are made for sale to tourists they are still highly valued within the Hopi community; a man may even make a *kachina* to represent his own spiritual image and give it to his wife or children for safekeeping.

The **Fringed Cowboy Jacket** *(page 109)* is knitted in a soft chunky tweed mixed with mohair and Aran yarns to create a richly textured fabric. The jacket shape comes directly from the American cowboy shirt with its characteristic yoke details and fringe decoration. It makes a classic, warm and wearable garment, with the addition of very useful pockets for that fistful of dollars!

North 'America "INDIANS"

earrings →

← Headband

Sue Bradley 87

Great Spirit...
Grant that I may not
criticize my neighbour
until I have
walked a mile
in his moccasins

North America Red Indian carpet/ embroidery pattern

olive/grey
Navy
Blue
Terracotta
Dull lemon
grey green
Black
cream.

TEEPEE SWEATER ★ ★

MEASUREMENTS
To fit bust: 81-87cm/32-34in, 91cm/36in and 97-102cm/ 38-40in

Please see page 162 for actual measurements.

MATERIALS
Yarn
Any **double-knit** weight yarn can be used as long as it knits up to the given tension.
375(400:425)g/14(15:15)oz cream (A), 50(50:75)g/ 2(2:3)oz each of navy (B), blue cotton (C) and dark green (D), 25(50:50)g/1(2:2)oz each of grass green (E), rust (F) and black (G)
Needles
1 pair each 3¼mm (US 3) and 4mm (US 5) needles
2 spare needles

TENSION
23 sts and 28 rows to 10cm/4in on 4mm (US 5) needles over striped st st.

SPECIAL NOTE FOR THIS PATTERN
At every colour change separate balls of yarn *must* be used, and yarn *must not* be carried over wrong side of work, not even over a few sts, as this will pucker the garment.

BACK
With 3¼mm (US 3) needles and A, cast on 98(102:106)sts and work in double rib as follows:
Row 1: (RS facing) K2, *P2, K2, rep from * to end.
Row 2: P2, *K2, P2, rep from * to end.
Rep these 2 rows working in the following stripe sequence:
3 rows A, 1 row B, 3 rows A, 1 row D.
Rep these 8 rows twice more, then work 3 rows A, 1 row B and 2 rows A – 30 rib rows worked in all.
Increase row: (RS facing) In A, K and inc 24(26:28)sts evenly across row – 122(128:134) sts.
Change to 4mm (US 5) needles and P 1 row in A.
Now starting with a K row work in st st from **chart**, working between appropriate lines for size required.
Cont to follow chart, marking each end of row 69 with a coloured thread to denote beg of armholes. Cont straight until row 136(140:144) has been completed.

Previous pages
Left *Indian Sweater Dress: The intricate all-over patterning in warm, deep colours combines elements from Indian embroidery, beadwork, carpets and leatherwork for a wonderfully rich effect. The Sweater Dress, in double-knit wool and cotton, has an easy loose shape and roll neck and looks just as good worn as a dress over warm tights or as an extra-long sweater. The broad headband adds the final fashion touch.*
Right *Teepee Sweater: An easy, casual style in double-knit wool and cotton, the sweater has a crew neck, dropped shoulders and straight sleeves. Fine horizontal stripes appear on the sleeves and also form the background to brightly coloured arrow and teepee motifs on front and back. There is a matching zigzag headband.*

Shape shoulders
Keeping stripes correct, cast off 13(14:15)sts at beg of next 6 rows. Leave rem 44 sts on a spare needle.

FRONT
Work as for back until row 114(118:122) of chart has been completed.
Shape front neck
Row 115(119:123): (RS facing) Patt 50(53:56), turn, and work on this first set of sts only.
** Keeping patt correct, dec 1 st at neck edge on every row until 39(42:45)sts remain.
Cont straight until row 136(140:144) has been completed.

Shape shoulder
Keeping stripes correct, cast off 13(14:15)sts at beg of next row and foll 2 alt rows.
Return to rem sts and slip centre 22 sts onto a spare needle, with RS facing rejoin yarn to rem sts and patt to end of row.
Now work as for first side from ** to end, but starting shoulder shaping on row 138(142:146) of chart.

SLEEVES
Make 2. With 3¼mm (US 3) needles and A, cast on 46(50:54)sts and work in double rib and stripe sequence as for back welt for 30 rows.
Increase row: (RS facing) In A, K2, *K and inc into next st, rep from * to last 2 sts, K2 – 88(96:104)sts.
Change to 4mm (US 5) needles and starting with a P row work in st st in the following stripe sequence:
7 rows A, 1 row D, 7 rows A, 1 row B.
These 16 rows form the stripe sequence for the sleeves and are repeated, *at the same time*, inc 1 st at each end of every foll 4th row until there are 114(120:126)sts on the needle, working inc sts into the stripe patt.
Now cont straight in patt until sleeve measures approx 38(40·5:43)cm/15(16:17)in from cast-on edge, ending with either 1 row in D or B.
Keeping st st correct, cont in patt as follows:
Next row: *2A, 1E, 3A, rep from * to end.
Next row: *2A, 3E, 1A, rep from * to end.
Next row: *5E, 1A, rep from * to end.
Work 2 rows in E.
Work 4 rows G, 2 rows A, 6 rows F and 2 rows A.
Cast off loosely in A.

NECKBAND
Join right shoulder seam.
With 3¼mm (US 3) needles and A and RS facing, pick up and K 26 sts down left front neck, K across 22 sts at centre front, pick up and K 26 sts up right front neck and finally K across the 44 sts at back neck – 118 sts.
Starting with a 2nd row, work in double rib as for back welt, and work in stripe patt as for welt for 16 rows.
Work 1 row A.
Cast off loosely ribwise in A.

TO MAKE UP
Sew in all ends, and press pieces carefully following ball band instructions. Join left shoulder and neckband seam, reversing seam for turn-back. With centre of cast-off edges of sleeves to shoulder seams, sew sleeves in position between coloured markers. Join side and sleeve seams matching stripes. Fold neckband in half to right side and neatly stitch in position.

TEEPEE SWEATER BACK/FRONT CHART

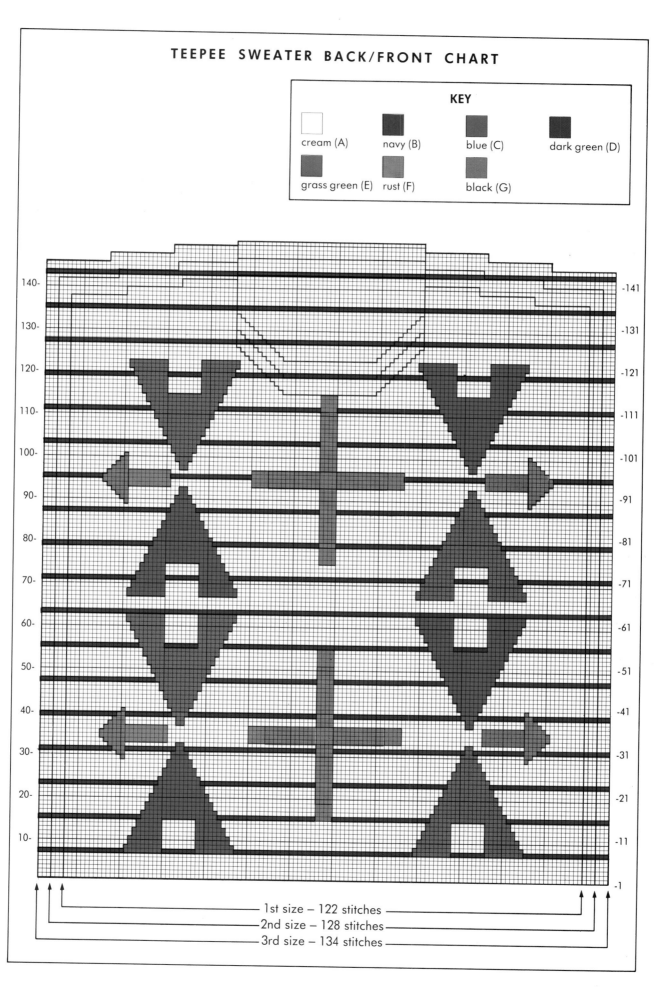

KEY

cream (A)　navy (B)　blue (C)　dark green (D)

grass green (E)　rust (F)　black (G)

1st size – 122 stitches
2nd size – 128 stitches
3rd size – 134 stitches

INDIAN
SWEATER DRESS ★ ★ ★

MEASUREMENTS
To fit bust: 81-87cm/32-34in, 91cm/36in and 97-102cm/38-40in

Please see page 162 for actual measurements.

MATERIALS
Yarn
Any **double-knit** weight yarn can be used as long as it knits up to the given tension.
350(375:400)g/13(14:15)oz brown cotton (A),
175(175:200)g/7(7:8)oz green cotton (B),
125(125:150)g/5(5:6)oz each of rust (C) and cream (D),
100(100:125)g/4(4:5)oz bright blue cotton (E),
50(75:75)g/2(3:3)oz deep blue (F), 100(125:125)g/4(5:5)oz beige cotton (G)
Needles
1 pair each 3¼mm (US 3) and 4mm (US 5) needles
2 spare needles

TENSION
25 sts and 24 rows to 10cm/4in on 4mm (US 5) needles over Fair Isle pattern.

BACK
With 3¼mm (US 3) needles and A, cast on 108(112:116)sts and work in K1, P1 rib for 7cm/2¾in.
Increase row: (RS facing) K and inc 28(28:30)sts evenly across row – 136(140:146)sts.
Change to 4mm (US 5) needles and P 1 row.
Now starting with a K row, work in st st from **chart 1** as follows:
Row 1: (RS facing) Work 0(2:5)sts before the dotted line, rep the 27-stitch patt 5 times, then work 1(3:6)st(s) beyond the dotted line.
Row 2: Work 1(3:6)st(s) before the dotted line, rep the 27-stitch patt 5 times, then work 0(2:5)sts beyond the dotted line. Cont as now set until the 22 rows of **chart 1** have been worked.
Now cont in st st and patt as follows:
Row 23: (RS facing) K1(0:1)F, *4C, 1F, rep from * to end.
Row 24: *P2F, 3C, rep from * to last 1(0:1)st, P1(0:1)F.
Row 25: K1(0:1)F, *2C, 3F, rep from * to end.
Row 26: *P4F, 1C, rep from * to last 1(0:1)st P1(0:1)F.
Row 27: K0(0:1)A, *2A, 1D, 1A, rep from * to last 0(0:1)st, K0(0:1)A.
Row 28: P0(0:1)A, *1D, 1A, 1D, 1A, rep from * to last 0(0:1)st, P0(0:1)A.
Row 29: K0(0:1)A, *1D, 3A, rep from * to last 0(0:1)st, K0(0:1)A.
Row 30: P in A.
Now work in st st from **chart 2** as follows:
Row 31: (RS facing) Work 4(6:1)st(s) before the dotted line, rep the 16-stitch patt 8(8:9) times, work 4(6:1)st(s) beyond the dotted line.
Chart 2 is now placed. Cont as set until the 12 rows are complete.
Row 43: (RS facing) K2(1:1)F, *5A, 1F, rep from * to last 2(1:1)st(s) K2(1:1)F.
Row 44: P2(1:1)F, *2F, 3A, 1F, rep from * to last 2(1:1)st(s), P2(1:1)F.
Row 45: K2(1:1)F, *2F, 1A, 3F, rep from * to last 2(1:1)st(s), K2(1:1)F.

Row 46: P in F.
Row 47: K0(0:1)G, *2G, 2D, rep from * to last 0(0:1)st, K0(0:1)G.
Row 48: P0(0:1)G, *1G, 2D, 1G, rep from * to last 0(0:1)st, P0(0:1)G.
These 48 rows form the pattern and are repeated as required.
Cont straight in patt until back measures 84(86·5:89)cm/33(34:35)in from cast-on edge, ending with a WS row.

Shape shoulders
Keeping patt correct, cast off 14(15:16)sts at beg of next 4 rows and then 15(15:16)sts at beg of foll 2 rows.
Leave rem 50 sts on a spare needle.

FRONT
Work as for back until front measures 76(78·5:81)cm/30(31:32)in from cast-on edge, ending with a WS row.

Shape front neck
Next row: Patt 58(60:63), turn, and work on this first set of sts only.
** Keeping patt correct, dec 1 st at neck edge on every row until 43(45:48)sts remain. Now cont straight until front measures same as back to beg of shoulder shaping, ending at side edge.

Shape shoulder
Cast off 14(15:16)sts at beg of next row and foll alt row. Work 1 row. Cast off rem 15(15:16)sts.
Return to rem sts and slip centre 20 sts onto a spare needle, with RS facing rejoin yarn to rem sts and patt to end of row.
Now work as for first side from ** to end.

SLEEVES
Make 2. With 3¼mm (US 3) needles and A, cast on 48 sts and work in K1, P1 rib for 7cm/2¾in.
Increase row: (RS facing) K and inc 38 sts evenly across row – 86 sts.
Change to 4mm (US 5) needles and P 1 row.
Now starting with a K row work in st st from **chart 1**, working as for *2nd size on back, at the same time*, inc 1 st at each end of every foll 4th row. When **chart 1** is complete, cont in the 48-row patt as for back, and cont to inc 1 st at each end of every 4th row as set until there are 120(124:128) sts on the needle, working inc sts into patt on either side.
Now cont straight until the 48 patt rows have been repeated twice – 96 patt rows worked. Cast off loosely.

COLLAR
Join right shoulder seam.
With 3¼mm (US 3) needles and A and RS facing, pick up and K 26 sts down left front neck, K across centre 20 sts, pick up and K 26 sts up right front neck, and finally K across the 50 sts of back neck – 122 sts.
Work in K1, P1 rib for 15cm/6in.
Cast off loosely ribwise using a 4mm (US 5) needle.

TO MAKE UP
Sew in ends and press pieces carefully following ball band instructions.
Join left shoulder and collar seam, reversing seam for turn-back.
With centre of cast-off edges of sleeves to shoulder seams, sew sleeves in position reaching down to same patt row on front and back. Join side and sleeve seams matching patts.

INDIAN SWEATER DRESS

CHART 1

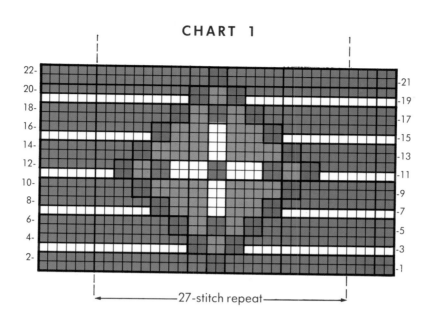

27-stitch repeat

KEY

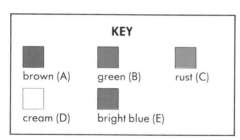

brown (A)   green (B)   rust (C)

cream (D)   bright blue (E)

CHART 2

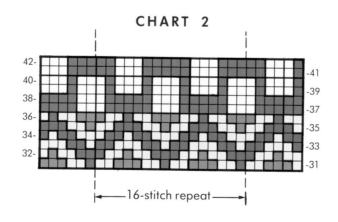

16-stitch repeat

KEY

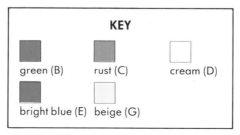

green (B)   rust (C)   cream (D)

bright blue (E)   beige (G)

HEADBANDS

MEASUREMENTS
To fit average-size adult head

Please see page 163 for actual garment measurements.

VERSION 1 ★
ZIGZAG PATTERN

MATERIALS
Yarn
Any **double-knit** weight yarn can be used as long as it knits up to the given tension.
25g/1oz rust (A), small amount blue cotton (B), 25g/1oz green (C)
Needles
1 pair 4mm (US 5) needles

TENSION
21 sts and 27 rows to 10cm/4in on 4mm (US 5) needles over main pattern.

NOTE
These bands may be worn with either the motif side or the plain side on the outside and can be knitted in many different combinations of colours or even plain.

METHOD
Knitted in one piece. With 4mm (US 5) needles and A, cast on 24 sts and starting with a K row work in st st from appropriate chart. Cont to rep the 12-row patt until band, when slightly stretched, fits around head, ending with a 12th patt row.
Cast off.

TO COMPLETE
Sew in ends and press piece carefully following ball band instructions. Stitch cast-on and cast-off edges carefully together. Stitch long edges together carefully, stab-stitching on right side of work. Press completed band.

VERSION 2 ★
TEEPEE HEADBAND

MATERIALS
Yarn
Any **double-knit** weight yarn can be used as long as it knits up to the given tension.
75g/3oz brown (A), 25g/1oz blue (B), small amount cream (C), 25g/1oz rust (D)
Needles and tension as for **Version 1**.

METHOD
Knitted in one piece. With 4mm (US 5) needles and A, cast on 36 sts and starting with a K row work in st st from appropriate chart. Cont to rep the 32-row patt until band, when slightly stretched fits around head.
Cast off.
Complete as for **Version 1**.

EARRINGS

MEASUREMENTS
Please see page 163 for actual garment measurements.

VERSION 1 ★
CROSS EARRINGS
(see page 111 for illustration)

MATERIALS
Yarn
Any **double-knit** weight yarn can be used as long as it knits up to the given tension.
Small amounts each brown (A), blue cotton (B), rust (C) and cream (D)
Needles and other materials
1 pair 4mm (US 5) needles
Earring fitments

TENSION
21 sts and 27 rows to 10cm/4in on 4mm (US 5) needles over main pattern.

METHOD
Make 2. With 4mm (US 5) needles and A, cast on 20 sts and starting with a K row work in st st from appropriate chart. When the 10 rows of chart are complete, cast off in A.

TO COMPLETE
Sew in ends and press piece carefully following ball band instructions. Fold in half along fold-line right sides together, and stitch bottom edges and side edges together. Turn to right side and stitch top edges together neatly.
Press flat. Stitch on earring clip or hook as required.

VERSION 2 ★
STRIPED EARRINGS
(see page 111 for illustration)

MATERIALS
As for **Version 1**, but small amounts each rust (A), blue (B) and cream (C)
Needles and tension as for **Version 1**.

METHOD
Make 2. Work as for **Version 1**, but work from **Version 2** chart.
Complete as for **Version 1**.

HEADBAND CHARTS

VERSION 1

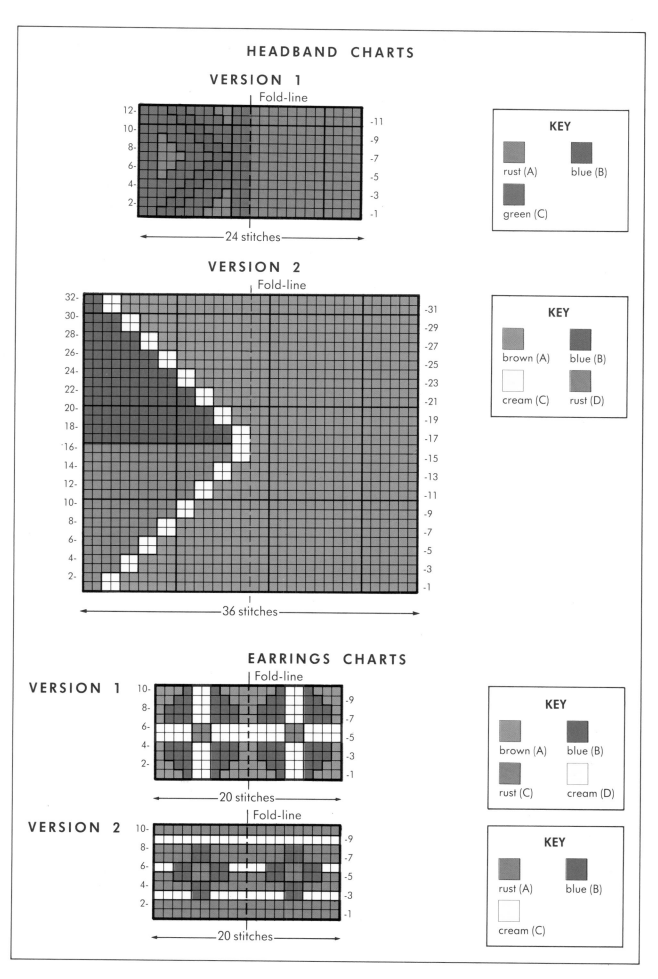

Fold-line

12-
10-
8-
6-
4-
2-

-11
-9
-7
-5
-3
-1

←—24 stitches—→

KEY

rust (A)   blue (B)

green (C)

VERSION 2

Fold-line

32-
30-
28-
26-
24-
22-
20-
18-
16-
14-
12-
10-
8-
6-
4-
2-

-31
-29
-27
-25
-23
-21
-19
-17
-15
-13
-11
-9
-7
-5
-3
-1

←————36 stitches————→

KEY

brown (A)   blue (B)

cream (C)   rust (D)

EARRINGS CHARTS

VERSION 1

Fold-line

10-
8-
6-
4-
2-

-9
-7
-5
-3
-1

←—20 stitches—→

KEY

brown (A)   blue (B)

rust (C)   cream (D)

VERSION 2

Fold-line

10-
8-
6-
4-
2-

-9
-7
-5
-3
-1

←—20 stitches—→

KEY

rust (A)   blue (B)

cream (C)

FRINGED COWBOY JACKET

MEASUREMENTS

To fit bust: 81-87cm/32-34in, 91cm/36in and 97-102cm/38-40in

Please see page 163 for actual measurements.

VERSION 1 ★ ★

MATERIALS

Yarn

Any **Aran-knit** weight yarn can be used as long as it knits up to the given tension.
650(700:750)g/23(25:26)oz brown tweed (A), 100(100:125)g/4(4:5)oz blue mohair (B), 50(75:75)g/2(3:3)oz each of green (C) and rust (D)

Needles and other materials

1 pair each 4mm (US 5) and 5mm (US 7) needles
7 wooden buttons
Crochet hook

TENSION

18 sts and 25 rows to 10cm/4in on 5mm (US 7) needles over st st.

BACK

With 4mm (US 5) needles and A, cast on 92(98:104)sts and work in K1, P1 rib for 4cm/1½in.
Change to 5mm (US 7) needles and starting with a K row work in st st from **chart 1** (back) (see page 110), working between appropriate lines for size required.
Cont as set until row 40 has been completed.
Now cont in st st in A only for a further 88 rows, mark both ends of rows 5 and 41 with a coloured thread to denote pocket openings.
Now starting with a K row work in st st from **chart 2** (back), working between appropriate lines for size required.
Cont to follow chart until the 34 rows have been completed.
Now cont straight in B only until back measures 78(80:82)cm/30¾(31½:32¼)in from cast-on edge, ending with a WS row.

Shape shoulders

Cast off 10(11:12)sts at beg of next 6 rows.
Cast off rem 32 sts.

LEFT FRONT

With 4mm (US 5) needles and A, cast on 42(46:48)sts and work in K1, P1 rib for 4cm/1½in, on *1st and 3rd sizes only* inc 1 st in middle of last row – 43(46:49)sts.
Change to 5mm (US 7) needles and starting with a K row work in st st from **chart 1** (left front), working between appropriate lines for size required.
Cont as set until row 40 has been completed.

Fringed Cowboy Jacket: This chunky jacket is knitted in a mixture of flecked tweed, mohair and Aran yarns for a warm textured effect. The shaped yoke is typical of cowboy shirts while the fringing gives a fashionable Wild West look. The border pattern motifs are taken from Indian leather embroidery.

Now cont in st st in A only for a further 88 rows, mark edge of rows 5 and 41 with a coloured thread to denote pocket opening.
Now starting with a K row work in st st from **chart 2** (left front), working between appropriate lines for size required.
Cont to follow chart until the 34 rows have been completed.
Now cont straight in B only until front measures 70(72:74)cm/27½(28¼:29)in from cast-on edge, ending at centre front edge.

Shape front neck

Cast off 8 sts at beg (neck edge) on next row. Now dec 1 st at this edge on every foll alt row until 30(33:36)sts remain.
Now work straight until front measures same as back to beg of shoulder shaping, ending at side edge.

Shape shoulder

Cast off 10(11:12)sts at beg of next row and foll 2 alt rows.

RIGHT FRONT

Work as for left front but working from charts relating to right front, and reverse all shapings.

SLEEVES

Make 2. With 4mm (US 5) needles and A, cast on 32(36:40)sts and work in K1, P1 rib for 8cm/3in.
Increase row: In A, K and inc 1 st in every 2nd st of row – 48(54:60)sts.
P1 row in A.
Change to 5mm (US 7) needles and starting with a K row work in st st, inc 1 st at each end of every foll 4th row until there are 80(86:92)sts on the needle.
Now cont straight until sleeve measures 44(46:48)cm/17¼(18:19)in from cast-on edge, ending with a WS row.
Cast off loosely.

POCKETS

Left side of back and right side of front

Alike. With 4mm (US 5) needles and A and RS facing, pick up and K 36 sts between the coloured markers on side edge of front/back.***
Next row: (WS facing) P.
** Cont in st st and dec 1 st at *beg* of next row and at this edge on every foll alt row until 22 sts remain.
Cast off fairly loosely.**

Right side of back and left side of front

Alike. Work as for left side of back and front side of front to ***.
Now work from ** to ** (this reverses shaping).

TO MAKE UP

Sew in all ends and press pieces carefully following ball band instructions. Join both shoulder seams. With centre of cast-off edges of sleeves to shoulder seams, sew sleeves in position reaching down to same depth on front and back. Join side and sleeve seams and edges of pockets together.

Right front band

With 4mm (US 5) needles and A and RS facing, pick up and K 162(166:170) sts evenly along right front edge. (Circular needle may be used to accommodate all sts.)
Work in K1, P1 rib for 3 rows.

FRINGED COWBOY JACKET

CHART 1

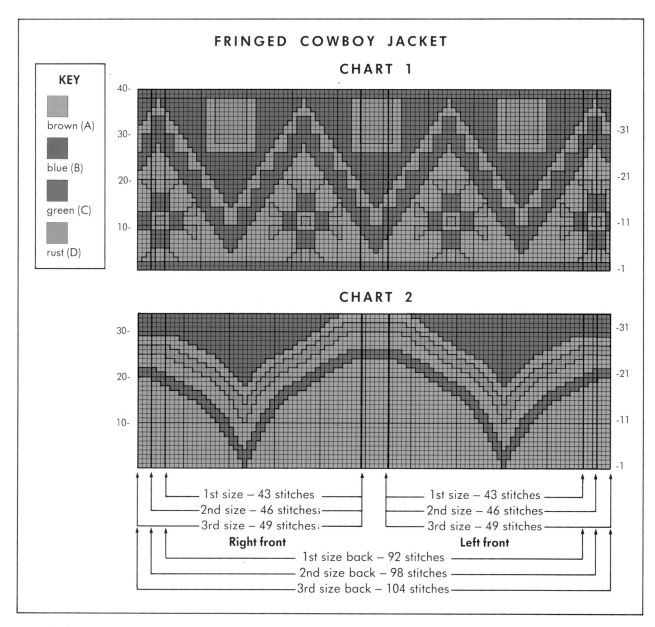

KEY

- brown (A)
- blue (B)
- green (C)
- rust (D)

CHART 2

1st size – 43 stitches
2nd size – 46 stitches
3rd size – 49 stitches

Right front

1st size – 43 stitches
2nd size – 46 stitches
3rd size – 49 stitches

Left front

1st size back – 92 stitches
2nd size back – 98 stitches
3rd size back – 104 stitches

Buttonhole row: Rib 2(4:3), * cast off 3, rib 23(23:24), rep from * 5 times more, cast off 3 sts, rib to end.
Next row: Rib, casting on 3 sts over cast-off sts on previous row (7 buttonholes worked).
Work a further 3 rows in rib.
Cast off loosely ribwise.

Left front band
Work as for right front band, but omit all buttonholes.

Collar
With 4mm (US 4) needles and A and RS facing, and starting half-way across right front band, pick up and K 28 sts to shoulder seam, 32 sts across back neck and 28 sts down other front to half-way across button band – 88 sts.
Work in K1, P1 rib for 10cm/4in.
Cast off loosely ribwise.
Sew on buttons to correspond with buttonholes.

To make fringes
These fringes are added along the underarm seams and along the shaped patterns on front and back yokes.
To make one tassel: Cut one 23cm/9in length each of

yarns A, C and D (or longer if required). Hold all three lengths together, fold in half and using a crochet hook, carefully pull the loop through on the front of the work, then pull ends through loop to make a tassel – repeat this as required along underarm seams and shaped yoke on back and fronts.

VERSION 2 ★

PLAIN CARDIGAN WITHOUT FRINGES

MATERIALS
Yarn

Any **Aran-knit** weight yarn can be used as long as it knits up to the given tension.
875(900:925)g/31(32:33)oz chosen colour
Needles and tension as for **Version 1**, but omit crochet hook.

METHOD
Work as for **Version 1**, but work throughout in one colour only and omit fringing.

Cowboy Jackets
in Plain Colour
(without Fringes)
Version 2.

SOUTH AMERICA

The fabrics of the Andes are an endless source of
inspiration for me with their rich colours, intricate
patterns and distinctive stylized motifs. The
ancient Incas were outstanding spinners and
weavers, making luxurious yarns from the coats of
llamas, alpaca and vicuna. Their textiles were
dyed in a myriad subtle shades, and the richest
were shot through with threads of gold and silver
– 'the sweat of the sun and the tears of the moon'
as they were poetically called.

The design of the **Diamond Jacket** *(page 116)* is
inspired by a repeat pattern on one of the
beautifully woven Incan belts or *chumpi* – these
are still an important item of Peruvian Indian
clothing. Bands of Fair Isle and diamond motifs
are worked in Aran wool against a background of
soft, sparkling black mohair, providing an
interesting textural contrast.

The **Motif Sweater** *(page 120)* is knitted in a rich red tweed wool in a loose, casual shape, with raglan sleeve details and a crew neck, perfect for both women and men. The motifs used, many of them also taken from *chumpi* designs, have symbolic significance. The puma symbolizes the god of the Punas (the high plains of the Andes), the double dove signifies matrimonial union, the double zigzag denotes water and the fish is thought to represent the god Viracocha who put fish into water for the use of mankind.

The **Peruvian Dolman Jacket** *(page 123)* and matching **Skirt** and **Hat** are worked mainly in a double-knit flecked black wool with pattern motifs in contrasting yarns. The rich colours are those of Incan textiles. The jacket is worked horizontally from cuff to cuff in bands of repeated motif patterns divided by textured ridges in a multi-coloured yarn flecked with gold. It has a double-breasted front band and is shaped at the waist with elastic to form a peplum. The matching skirt is made in four panels, alternately plain and patterned. The hat with ear-flaps is typical of those worn today by the Indians of the High Andes.

DIAMOND JACKET ★ ★ ★

MEASUREMENTS
To fit bust: 81-91cm/32-36in and 91-102cm/36-40in

Please see page 164 for actual garment measurements.

MATERIALS
Yarn
Any **Aran-weight** yarn or **mohair** can be used as long as it knits up to the given tension.
375(425)g/14(15)oz black sparkle mohair (A), 25(50)g/1(2)oz blue Aran (B), 50(75)g/2(3)oz rust Aran (C), 50g/2oz turquoise Aran (D), 25g/1oz yellow Aran (E), 25g/1oz indigo Aran (F), 50(75)g/2(3)oz lilac Aran (G), 50(75)g/2(3)oz black Aran (H)
Needles and other materials
1 pair each 5½mm (US 8) and 6½mm (US 10) needles
8 buttons
Shirring elastic for cuffs
Spare needle
2 safety-pins

TENSION
15 sts and 18 rows to 10cm/4in on 6½mm (US 10) needles over st st using A yarn.

BACK
With 5½mm (US 8) needles and A, cast on 84(90)sts and work in K1, P1 rib for 2·5cm/1in.
Change to 6½mm (US 10) needles and starting with a K row, work in st st from **back chart** working between appropriate lines for size required.
Cont straight as set until row 116(120) of chart has been worked.

Shape shoulders
Cast off 10(11)sts at beg of next 4 rows.
Cast off 9(10)sts at beg of foll 2 rows.
Leave rem 26 sts on a spare needle for back neck.

RIGHT FRONT
With 5½mm (US 8) needles and A, cast on 42(44)sts and work in K1, P1 rib for 2·5cm/1in, on last row inc 1 st on *2nd size only* – 42(45)sts.
Change to 6½mm (US 10) needles and starting with a K row work in st st from **right front chart** (see page 118) working between appropriate lines for size required.

Previous pages
Left *Motif Sweater: Animals, fish and magic Andean Indian symbols decorate this casual sweater knitted in rich red tweed fleck wool. The line of the raglan sleeves is emphasized by ribbed bands and there is a comfortable wide crew neck.*
Centre *Diamond Jacket: Black sparkle mohair gives an exotic look to this wonderfully warm, soft jacket. The diamond motifs and Fair Isle bands at the cuffs, tops of the sleeves and around the lower edge are knitted in plain Aran yarn to contrast with the textured mohair.*
Right *Peruvian Dolman Jacket: A dramatic outfit whose motifs come from Inca legends. The double-breasted jacket, with black flecked wool as the main yarn, is worked horizontally from cuff to cuff. The straight skirt is made in four panels – two patterned and two in plain rib – and there is a matching Peruvian-style hat.*

Cont straight as set until row 106(110) of chart has been worked.

Shape front neck
Row 107(111): (RS facing) Keeping chart correct, cast off 6 sts at beg of row.
Now dec at neck edge on every row until 29(32)sts remain. Cont straight until row 117(121) of chart has been worked.

Shape shoulder
Cast off 10(11)sts at beg of next row and foll alt row.
Cast off rem 9(10)sts.

LEFT FRONT
Work as for right front, following **right front chart** but reverse position of neck and shoulder shapings.

SLEEVES
Make 2: With 5½mm (US 8) needles and A, cast on 42 sts and work in K1, P1 rib for 2 rows.
Change to 6½mm (US 10) needles and starting with a K row work the border patt in st st from **right front chart**, 1st size, working rows 1-14.
Increase row: (RS facing) With A, K and inc 18 sts evenly across row – 60 sts.
P 1 row in A.
Now work from **sleeve chart** (see page 119) shaping as shown by inc 1 st at each end of 3rd row and then every foll 3rd row until there are 84 sts on the needle.
Cont straight following chart until row 66 has been worked. Cast off all sts fairly loosely in H.

POCKET LININGS
Make 2. With 6½mm (US 10) needles and A, cast on 22 sts and starting with a K row, cont straight in st st until lining measures 26cm/10¼in from cast-on edge.
Cast off all sts fairly loosely.

TO MAKE UP
Sew in ends. Press all pieces carefully following ball band instructions. Join both shoulder seams. With centre of cast-off edges of sleeves to shoulder seams, sew sleeves carefully in position, reaching down to same patt row on front and back. Fold pocket linings in half and stitch along side edges. Now position at appropriate places along side edges of back and front and sew cast-on and cast-off edges in place. Join side and sleeve seams, matching pattern carefully and leaving pocket edges open.

Button band
With 5½mm (US 8) needles and A, cast on 8 sts and work in K1, P1 rib until band measures up centre front when slightly stretched, sewing it in position as you work. Leave sts on a safety-pin.
Mark on this band position of 7 buttons – first to come 2·5cm/1in from bottom edge, the 7th to come 2·5cm/1in from neck edge, and remaining 5 buttons spaced between at regular intervals.

Buttonhole band
Work as for button band with the addition of buttonholes when button positions are reached.
Buttonhole row: (RS facing) Rib 3, cast off 3 sts, rib to end.
Next row: Rib, casting on 3 sts over cast-off sts on previous row.
Leave sts on a safety-pin.

DIAMOND JACKET BACK CHART
(see page 118 for key)

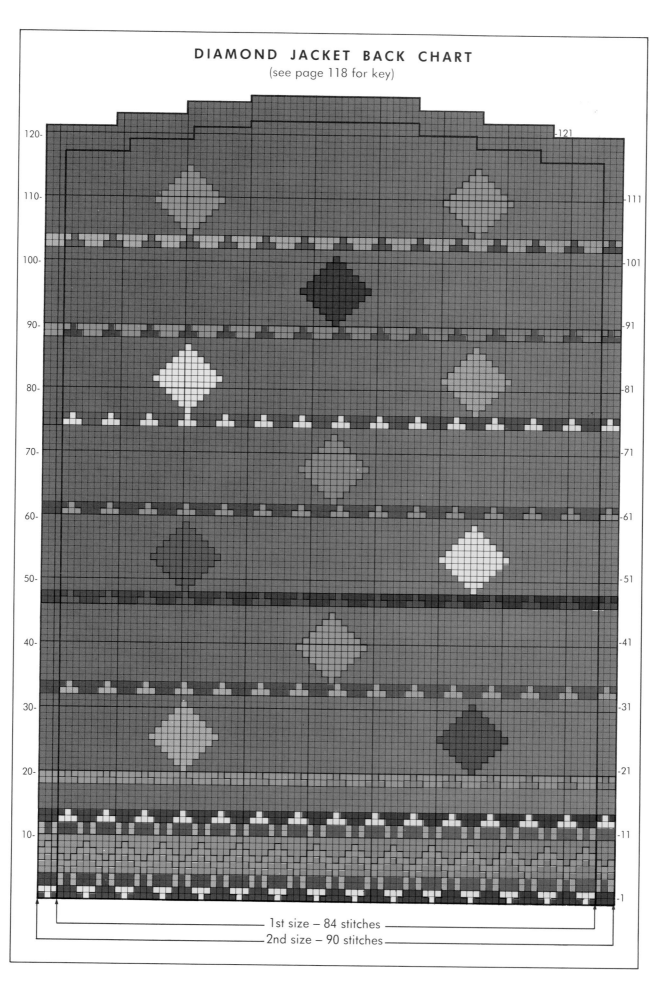

DIAMOND JACKET RIGHT FRONT CHART

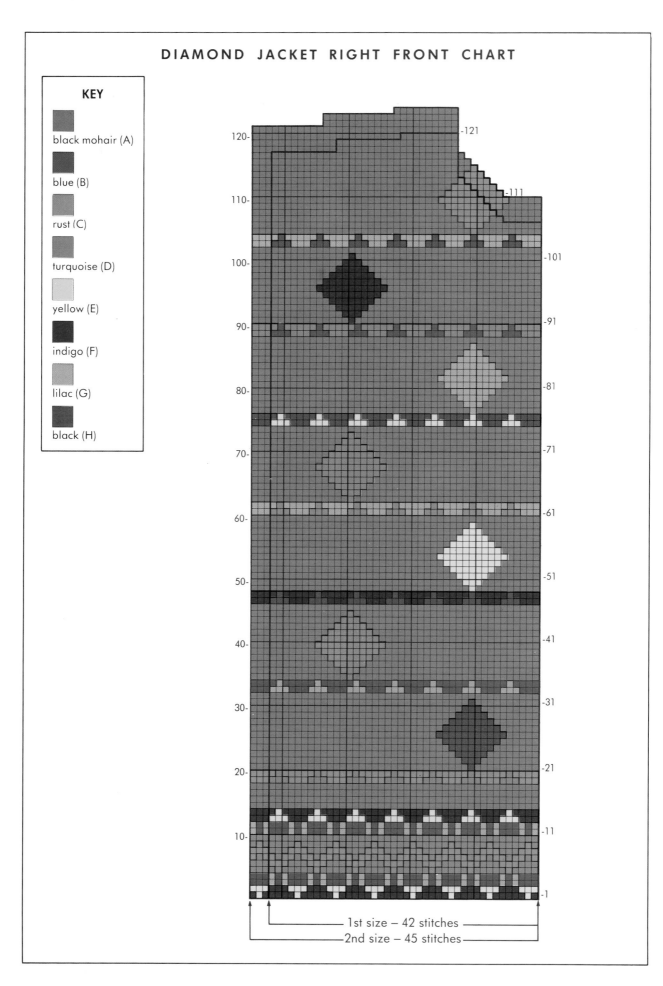

KEY

black mohair (A)

blue (B)

rust (C)

turquoise (D)

yellow (E)

indigo (F)

lilac (G)

black (H)

1st size – 42 stitches
2nd size – 45 stitches

DIAMOND JACKET SLEEVE CHART

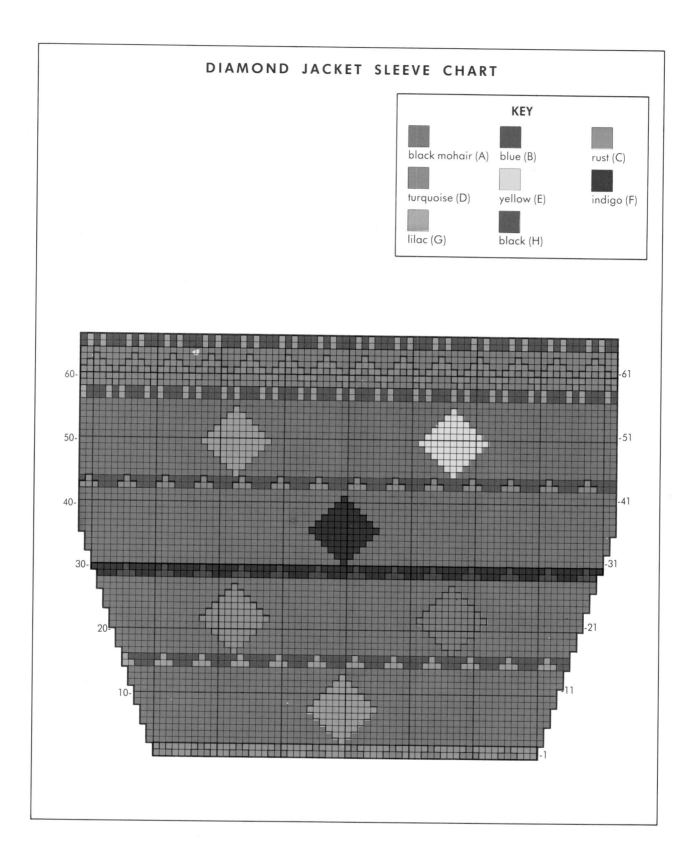

KEY

black mohair (A) blue (B) rust (C)

turquoise (D) yellow (E) indigo (F)

lilac (G) black (H)

Neckband

With 5½mm (US 8) needles and A and RS facing, rib across the 8 sts of buttonhole band, pick up and K18 sts along right front neck edge, K across the 24 sts at back neck, pick up and K18 sts along left front neck edge and finally rib across the 8 sts of button band – 76 sts.

Work in K1, P1 rib for 2·5cm/1in, ending with a WS row. Now work a buttonhole as before.

Cont in rib for a further 5cm/2in, then place another buttonhole. Work a further 2·5cm/1in in rib.

Cast off fairly loosely ribwise.

To complete

Fold neckband in half to wrong side and slip stitch loosely in position. Oversew around buttonhole. Sew on buttons to correspond with buttonholes. To give the cuffs more elasticity, thread a few rows of shirring elastic through cuffs and secure ends.

MOTIF SWEATER ★ ★ ★

MEASUREMENTS

To fit bust/chest: 81-91cm/32-36in and 91-107cm/ 36-42in

Please see page 165 for actual garment measurements.

MATERIALS

Yarn

Any **double-knit** weight yarn can be used as long as it knits up to the given tension.
600(650)g/21(23)oz red tweed (A), 50g/2oz blue (B), 50g/2oz green (C), 25g/1oz turquoise (D), 25g/1oz yellow (E), 50g/2oz purple (F), 25g/1oz black (G), 50g/2oz brown (H)

Needles

1 pair each 3¼mm (US 3) and 4mm (US 5) needles
4 spare needles

TENSION

20 sts and 27 rows to 10cm/4in on 4mm (US 5) needles over st st.

BACK

With 3¼mm (US 3) needles and A, cast on 90(96)sts and work in K1, P1 rib for 7cm/2¾in.
Increase row: Rib and inc 20 sts evenly across row – 110(116)sts.
Change to 4mm (US 5) needles and starting with a K row, work in st st from **back chart**, working between appropriate lines for size required, working decs for raglan shapings as indicated until row 146(152) has been worked.
Leave rem 24 sts on a spare needle for back neck.

FRONT

Work as for back until row 126(130) of **front chart** has been worked.

Shape front neck

Next row: (RS facing – following chart) Work 2 tog, patt until there are 13(14)sts on RH needle, turn and work on this first set of sts only leaving rem sts on a spare needle.
**Patt 1 row.
Now dec 1 st at each end of next row and 3 foll alt rows.
Now keeping neck edge straight, dec at raglan edge, following chart, until all sts are worked. Fasten off.
Return to rem sts and slip centre 16 sts onto spare

needle, with RS facing rejoin yarn to rem sts, patt to last 2 sts, work 2 tog.
Now work as for first side from ** to end.

SLEEVES

Make 2. With 3¼mm (US 3) needles and A, cast on 36(40)sts and work in K1, P1 rib for 7cm/2¾in.
Increase row: Rib and inc 28(30)sts evenly across row – 64(70)sts.
Change to 4mm (US 5) needles and starting with a K row, work in st st from **sleeve chart** (see page 122), working between appropriate lines for size required, working inc rows as indicated at each end of 4th row and then every foll 3rd row until there are 104(110)sts on the needle.
Cont to follow chart working raglan decs at each end of row 76(79) and then rows as indicated until row 162(170) has been worked.
Leave rem 10(8)sts on a spare needle.
Sew in all ends and press all pieces lightly on wrong side following ball band instructions.

RAGLAN RIBS

4 alike (these are worked along the top shaped edges of the sleeves). With 3¼mm (US 3) needles and A and RS facing, pick up and K80(84)sts evenly along one side of shaped raglan sleeve edge and work in K1, P1 rib for 4cm/1½in.
Cast off loosely ribwise.

NECKBAND

Join raglan seams leaving left back raglan open.
With 3¼mm (US 3) needles and A and RS facing, pick up and K5 sts along top edge of left raglan rib, K across the 10(8)sts at top of left sleeve, pick up and K5 sts along raglan rib, 16(18)sts down left front neck, K across the 16 centre front sts, pick up and K16(18)sts up right front neck, 5 sts at top of raglan rib, K across the 10(8)sts at top of right sleeve, pick up and K5 sts along raglan rib and finally K across the 24 sts at back neck – 112 sts.
Work in K1, P1 rib for 7cm/2¾in.
Cast off in rib using a 4mm (US 6) needle.

TO MAKE UP

Join remaining raglan seam and neckband seam. Join side and sleeve seams. Press seams. Fold neckband in half to outside and slip stitch neatly in position.

(See page 129 for alternative colourway.)

MOTIF SWEATER BACK/FRONT CHART

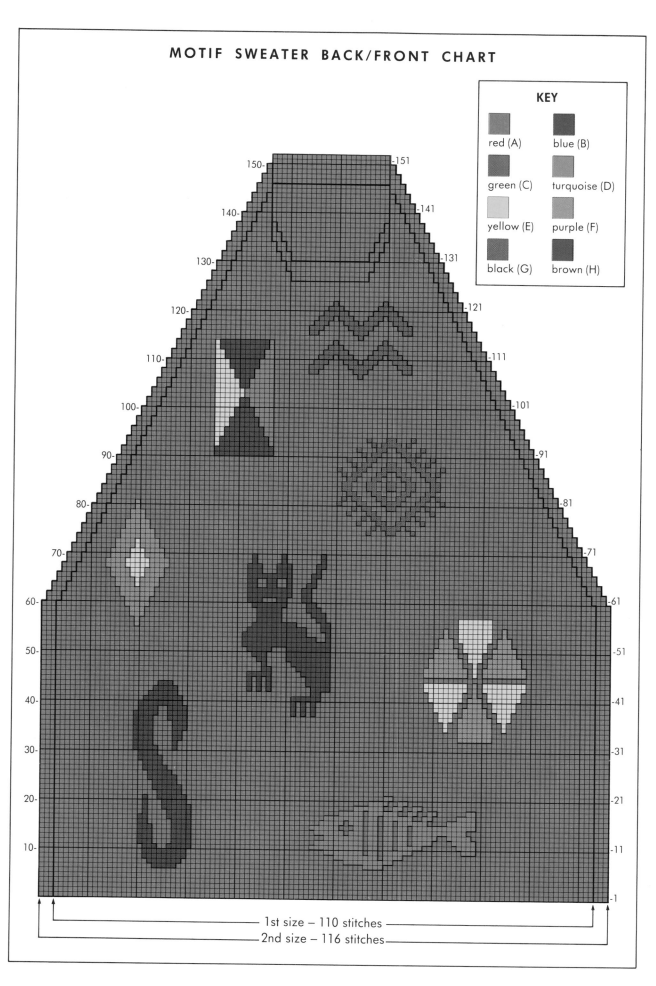

KEY

red (A)		blue (B)	
green (C)		turquoise (D)	
yellow (E)		purple (F)	
black (G)		brown (H)	

150-   -151
140-   -141
130-   -131
120-   -121
    -111
110-   -101
100-
90-   -91
80-   -81
    -71
70-
60-   -61
50-   -51
40-   -41
30-   -31
20-   -21
10-   -11
    -1

1st size – 110 stitches
2nd size – 116 stitches

MOTIF SWEATER SLEEVE CHART

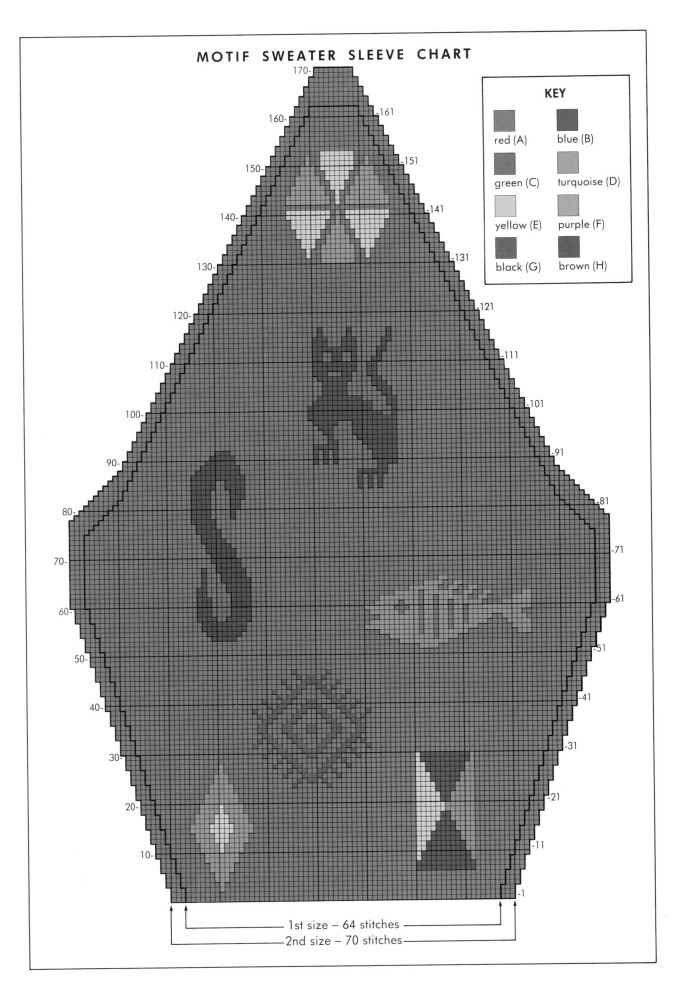

KEY

red (A) blue (B)

green (C) turquoise (D)

yellow (E) purple (F)

black (G) brown (H)

1st size – 64 stitches
2nd size – 70 stitches

PERUVIAN DOLMAN JACKET

MEASUREMENTS
To fit bust: 81-91cm/32-36in and 97-102cm/38-40in

Please see page 166 for actual garment measurements.

VERSION 1 ★ ★ ★

MATERIALS
Yarn

Any **double-knit** weight yarn can be used as long as it knits up to the given tension.
550(600)g/20(21)oz black fleck (A), 100g/4oz royal blue (B), 50(75)g/2(3)oz turquoise (C), 200(225)g/8(8)oz rust (D), 100g/4oz lilac (E), 50(75)g/2(3)oz yellow (F); for raised stripe: 100(125)g/4(5)oz **chunky** fleck tweed which includes a gold thread (G)

Needles and other materials

1 pair each 3¾mm (US 4) and 4½mm (US 6) needles
3¾mm (US 4) and 4½mm (US 6) circular needles
6 large buttons
Shirring elastic for waist

TENSION
22 sts and 24 rows to 10cm/4in on 4½mm (US 6) needles over pattern.

BACK
(Worked horizontally from right cuff to left cuff).
With 3¾mm (US 4) needles and A, cast on 24(28)sts and work in K2, P2 rib for 7cm/2¾in.
Increase row: Rib and inc 1 st in every 2nd st across row – 36(42)sts.
Change to 4½mm (US 6) needles and work from **chart** (see pages 124-125) as follows:
Row 1: (RS facing) K, using G.
Row 2: K, using G; this forms the raised stripe.
Now starting with a K row, work in st st from chart, following underarm shaping as given and working between appropriate lines for size required and noting that 'raised stripe' rows should be worked as rows 1 and 2.
Cont to inc at underarm until row 94 has been worked – 82(88)sts.
Row 95: Patt to end of row, turn, then cast on 58 sts – 140(146)sts, changing to the circular 4½mm (US 6) needle when necessary to accommodate all the sts, and cont to work in rows. Now cont straight in patt until row 240 has been worked.
Row 241: Patt to last 58 sts, cast off these sts – 82(88)sts.
Now cont to dec at underarm as chart until row 332 has been completed – 36(42)sts.
Next row: (RS facing) Using A, *K1, K2 tog, rep from * to end – 24(28)sts.
Change to 3¾mm (US 4) needles and work 7cm/2¾in in K2, P2 rib. Cast off fairly loosely ribwise.

LEFT FRONT
Work exactly as for back to row 145 of chart.
Row 146: Cast off fairly loosely in A.

RIGHT FRONT
With 4½mm (US 6) needles and A, cast on 140(146)sts

and work from row 189 of back chart.
Cont to row 332, then follow dec and cuff instructions as for back.

TO MAKE UP
Sew in ends and press pieces carefully following ball band instructions. Join shoulder seams matching pattern carefully and leaving approx 18cm/7in gap at centre for back neck. Join underarm and side seams.

Bottom edging
With the 3¾mm (US 4) circular needle and A and RS facing, pick up and K40 sts across bottom of left front edge, 120 sts across bottom of back edge and 40 sts across bottom of right front edge – 200 sts.
Work in K2, P2 rib in A for 4 rows.
Cast off fairly loosely ribwise.

Front band
With 3¾mm (US 4) needles and A, cast on 52 sts and work in K2, P2 rib for 2.5cm/1in.
Buttonhole row: Rib 8, cast off 4 sts, rib 28, cast off 4 sts, rib 8.
Next row: Rib, casting on 4 sts over cast-off sts on previous row.
** Work a further 10cm/4in in rib, then work another set of buttonholes.** Rep from ** to ** once more (6 buttonholes worked in all).
Now cont in double rib until band measures up centre front, around back neck and down other centre front, when slightly stretched. Sew it in position as you work.. Cast off fairly loosely ribwise.

To complete
Sew on buttons to correspond with buttonholes. Roll collar over to right side. To give the jacket more shape, thread a few lengths of shirring elastic through work at waist level and secure ends. Do not gather front bands.

VERSION 2 ★ ★ ★
NEUTRALS DOLMAN JACKET
(see page 129 for illustration of versions 2 and 3)

MATERIALS
Use same amounts as for **Version 1**, but in the following colour sequence: beige fleck (A), dark grey (B), white (C), brown (D), black (E), blue (F), chunky brown tweed which includes a gold thread (G).

METHOD
Work exactly as for **Version 1** in the above colour sequence but omit the shirring elastic at waist.

VERSION 3 ★ ★ ★
PASTEL DOLMAN JACKET

MATERIALS
Use same amounts as for **Version 1**, but in the following colour sequence: pale grey fleck (A), light turquoise (B), white (C), pale pink (D), pale blue (E), lemon (F), chunky pastel tweed which includes a gold thread (G).

METHOD
Work exactly as for **Version 1** in the above colour sequence.

PERUVIAN DOLMAN JACKET CHART

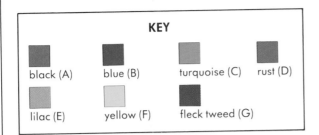

KEY

black (A)	blue (B)	turquoise (C)	rust (D)
lilac (E)	yellow (F)	fleck tweed (G)	

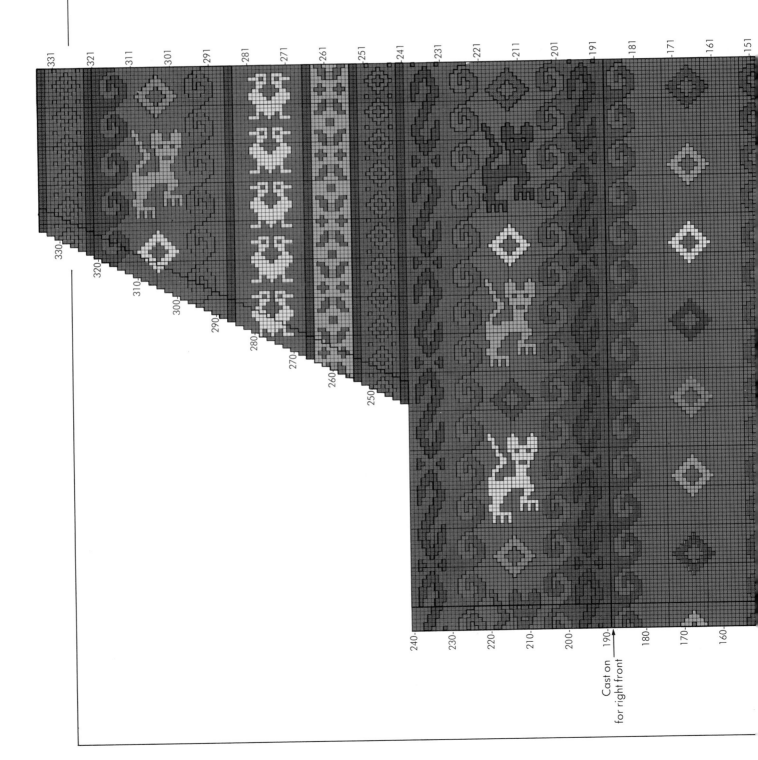

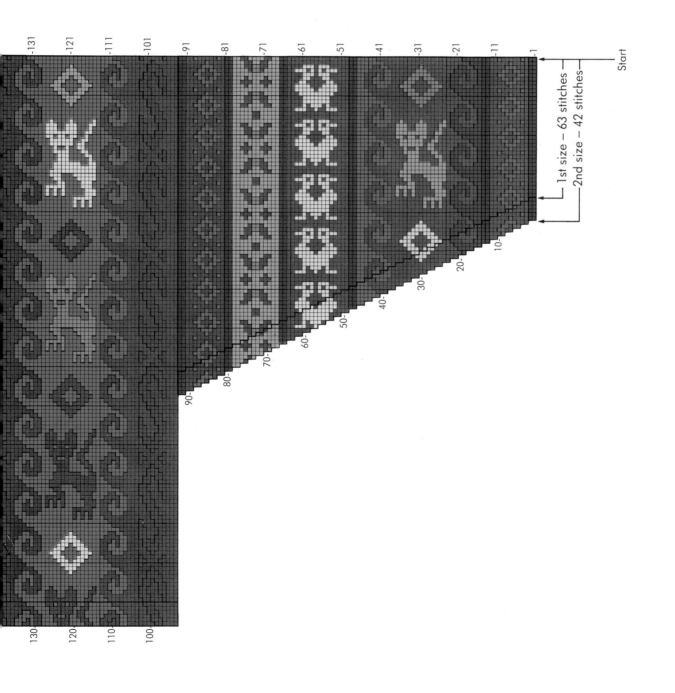

1st size — 63 stitches
2nd size — 42 stitches

Start

PERUVIAN SKIRT

MEASUREMENTS
To fit hips: 81-91cm/32-36in and 97-102cm/38-40in

Please see page 167 for actual garment measurements.

VERSION 1 ★ ★ ★

MATERIALS
Yarn
Any **double-knit** weight yarn can be used as long as it knits up to the given tension.
400(450)g/15(16)oz black fleck (A), 25g/1oz royal blue (B), 25g/1oz turquoise (C), 75g/3oz rust (D), 25g/1oz lilac (E), 25g/1oz yellow (F)
Needles and other materials
1 pair each 3¾mm (US 4) and 4½mm (US 6) needles
3¾mm (US 4) circular needle
Waist length of 2.5cm/1in wide elastic

TENSION
22 sts and 24 rows to 10cm/4in on 4½mm (US 6) needles over pattern.

NOTE
The skirt is worked in four separate pieces.

1st MOTIF PANEL
With 3¾mm (US 4) needles and A, cast on 33 sts and work in single rib as follows:
Row 1: (RS facing) K1, *P1, K1, rep from * to end.
Row 2: P1, *K1, P1, rep from * to end.
Rep last 2 rows once more (4 rib rows worked).
Change to 4½mm (US 6) needles and starting with a K row work in st st from **chart**, noting the colour sequence for **1st motif panel.**
Cont straight until row 166 has been worked. Leave sts on a length of yarn.

2nd MOTIF PANEL
Work exactly as for **1st motif panel**, but follow the colour sequence for **2nd motif panel.**

RIBBED PANELS
Make 2. With 4½mm (US 6) needles and A, cast on 68(72)sts and work in K2, P2 rib until panel measures the same length as motif panels.
Leave sts on a length of yarn.

TO MAKE UP
Sew in all ends and press the motif panels only according to ball band instructions. Stitch all the panels together alternating motif and rib panels, leaving one seam open.

Waistband
Slip all the waist sts onto the 3¾mm (US 4) circular needle – 202(210)sts – and work backwards and forwards in rows.
Row 1: (WS facing) P in A.
Row 2: K in A and dec 80 sts evenly across row – 122(130)sts.
Work in K1, P1 rib for 7cm/2¾in.
Cast off loosely in A using a 4½mm (US 6) needle.

To complete
Join remaining side and waistband seam. Fold waistband in half to inside and slip stitch loosely down, leaving a gap for insertion of elastic. Thread elastic into waistband, adjust to fit and secure ends. Close gap in waistband.

VERSION 2 ★ ★ ★
NEUTRALS SKIRT
(see page 129 for illustration of versions 2 and 3)

MATERIALS
Use same amounts as for **Version 1**, but in the following colour sequence: beige fleck (A), dark grey (B), white (C), brown (D), black (E), blue (F).

METHOD
Work exactly as for **Version 1** in the above colour sequence.

VERSION 3 ★ ★ ★
PASTEL SKIRT

MATERIALS
Use same amounts as for **Version 1**, but in the following colour sequence: pale grey fleck (A), light turquoise (B), white (C), pale pink (D), pale blue (E), lemon (F).

METHOD
Work exactly as for **Version 1** in the above colour sequence.

PERUVIAN HAT

MEASUREMENTS
To fit: average-size adult head

Please see page 167 for actual garment measurements.

VERSION 1 ★ ★ ★

MATERIALS
Yarn
Any **double-knit** weight yarn can be used as long as it knits up to the given tension.
75g/3oz black fleck (A), 25g/1oz each of turquoise (C), rust (D), lilac (E), yellow (F); for raised stripe: 25g/1oz **chunky** fleck tweed which includes a gold thread (G)
Needles
1 pair each 3¾mm (US 4) and 4½mm (US 6) needles.

TENSION
22 sts and 24 rows to 10cm/4in on 4½mm (US 6) needles over pattern.

NOTE
The earflaps are optional.

METHOD
With 3¾mm (US 4) needles and A, cast on 120 sts and

PERUVIAN SKIRT MOTIF CHART

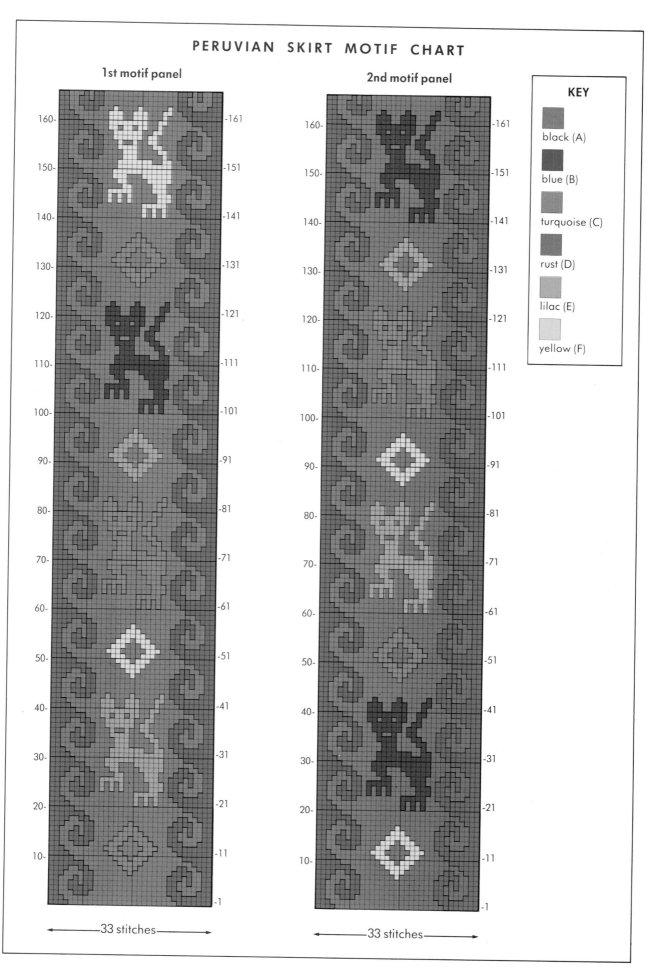

1st motif panel

2nd motif panel

KEY

black (A)

blue (B)

turquoise (C)

rust (D)

lilac (E)

yellow (F)

33 stitches

33 stitches

work in K2, P2 rib for 4 rows, dec 1 st in middle of last row – 119 sts.
Change to 4½mm (US 6) needles and work as follows:
Row 1: (RS facing) K, using G.
Row 2: K, using G; this forms the raised stripe.
Now starting with a K row, work in st st from **chart 1**, rep the 17 st patt across row, noting that 'raised stripe' row should be worked as rows 1 and 2.
Cont as set until row 16 has been worked.
Row 17: K in A, and dec 31 sts evenly across row – 88 sts.
Now work from chart, rep the 8 st patt across row.
Cont as set until row 25 has been worked.
Row 26: P in A, and dec 26 sts evenly across row – 62 sts.
Row 27: (RS facing) *K1A, K1F, rep from * to end.
Row 28: *P1A, P1F, rep from * to end.
Row 29: *K1A, K1D, rep from * to end.
Row 30: *P1A, P1D, rep from * to end.
Row 31: K in A and dec 14 sts evenly across row – 48 sts.
Row 32: P in A.
Row 33: *K1A, K1C, rep from * to end.
Row 34: *P1A, P1C, rep from * to end.
Row 35: *K1A, K1E, rep from * to end.
Row 36: *P1A, P1E, rep from * to end.
Row 37: In A, K2 tog across row – 24 sts.
Now cont in A only and work 3 rows in st st.
Next row: K2 tog across row – 12 sts.
Work 1 row.
Next row: K2 tog across row – 6 sts.
Slip yarn through rem sts leaving a long end. Pull tight and fasten off.

TO MAKE UP
Sew in ends. Press carefully following ball band instructions. Join back seam matching pattern.

EARFLAPS (optional)
Alike. With 3¾mm (US 4) needles, A and RS facing and seam at centre back, pick up and K21 sts evenly at required position at side of hat for earflap (approx 7cm/2¾in) away from back seam).
Change to 4½mm (US 6) needles and work 3 rows in moss st in A.
Next row: (RS facing) Moss st 3 sts in A, now work across the 1st row of **chart 2**, moss st last 3 sts in A.
Cont as now set, working from chart and sts at each side in moss st in A, until the 31 rows of chart are complete.
Work 3 rows in moss st in A.
Cast off in A.

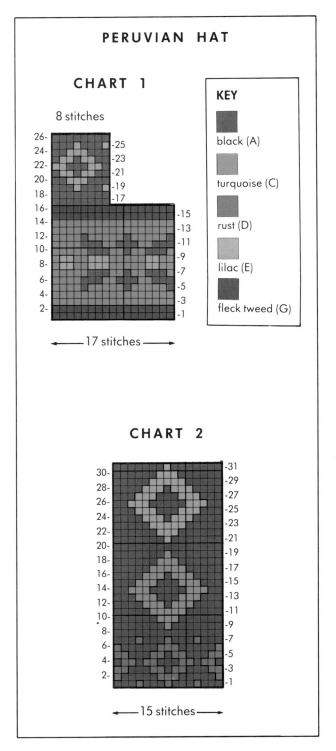

VERSION 2 ★ ★ ★
NEUTRALS HAT

MATERIALS
Use same amounts as for **Version 1**, but in the following colour sequence: beige fleck (A), white (C), brown (D), black (E), blue (F), chunky brown tweed which includes a gold thread (G).

METHOD
Work exactly as for **Version 1** in the above colour sequence, noting that earflaps are optional.

VERSION 3 ★ ★ ★
PASTEL HAT

MATERIALS
Use same amounts as for **Version 1**, but in the following colour sequence: pale grey fleck (A), white (C), pale pink (D), pale blue (E), lemon (F), chunky pastel tweed which includes a gold thread (G).

METHOD
Work exactly as for **Version 1** in the above colour sequence, noting that earflaps are optional.

Peruvian Hat
Version
2 →

Peruvian Dolman
Jacket Version
3→
Version
2
↙

Motif
Sweater
on
Black
↙

Motif Sweater
on Blue
↓

AFRICA

For the African section I have chosen to base all my designs on the wonderful beadwork of the Yoruba people of Western Nigeria, which presents a wealth of uniquely African colours and patterns.

Though it may look like an ancient tradition, the beadwork was developed only as a result of the flood of seed beads brought by nineteenth-century traders from Europe — tiny round beads of regular size in an almost limitless palette of luminous colours. These so appealed to the Yoruba that they became the basis of a new art form, used to make crowns, bags, belts, staffs, footrests, shoes, fans and numerous ceremonial objects, some so treasured that they might be worn only by kings. Beadwork also took on religious significance; in particular the faces depicted on many of the beaded bags and dance panels worn on festive occasions were considered to be images of the spirit residing within the wearer.

The **Yoruba Sweater** *(page 134)* takes its intricate all-over diamond and beadwork pattern from a ritual dance panel worn by a high priestess. It is knitted in cotton, in an easy wide T-shirt shape with three-quarter-length sleeves. There is a **Hat** to go with it, in complementary colours and inspired by the beadwork crowns of Yoruba kings.

The **Diamond Slipover** *(page 138)* has a pattern of abstract shapes, diamonds and blocks of colour inspired by statuettes known as *ibeji* – twin figures in beaded garments thought to be 'spirit children' and to bring good fortune to parents. This sweater, which is also knitted in cotton, may be worn on its own as a cool summer top or over something else in cooler weather.

The final garment is the chunky, double-breasted **Mask Jacket** *(page 140)* in double-knit cotton. It is decorated with a bold design of vertical panels of mask-like faces, diamonds and zigzags in an unusual combination of colours, some of which are echoed in the accompanying **Hat.**

YORUBA SWEATER

MEASUREMENTS
To fit bust: 81-91cm/32-36in and 97-102cm/38-40in

Please see page 168 for actual garment measurements.

VERSION 1 ★ ★

MATERIALS
Yarn

Any **double-knit** weight yarn can be used as long as it knits up to the given tension.
225(250)g/8(9)oz each navy cotton (A) and brown cotton (B), 50(75)g/2(3)oz yellow ochre mohair (C), 25(50)g/1(2)oz pale yellow cotton (D), 25(25)g/1(1)oz royal blue cotton (E), 50(50)g/2(2)oz turquoise cotton (F), 100(100)g/4(4)oz grey-blue cotton (G), 75(100)g/3(4)oz cream cotton (H)

Needles

1 pair each 3¼mm (US 3) and 4mm (US 5) needles
2 spare needles

TENSION
21 sts and 27 rows to 10cm/4in on 4mm (US 5) needles over main pattern.

BACK
With 3¼mm (US 3) needles and A, cast on 128(136)sts and work in K1, P1, rib for 4cm/1½in.
Change to 4mm (US 5) needles and starting with a K row work in st st from **back chart**, working between appropriate lines for size required.
Work straight following chart, marking both ends of row 80(86) with coloured threads to indicate armholes.
When row 144(150) has been worked, thus ending with a WS row, cont as follows:

Shape shoulders
Keeping chart correct, cast off 11(12)sts at beg of next 8 rows. Leave rem 40 sts on a spare needle.

FRONT
Work as for back until row 124(130) has been worked, thus ending with a WS row.

Shape front neck
Next row: Patt 54(58), turn and work on this first set of sts only.
** Keeping chart correct, dec 1 st at neck edge on every row until 44(48)sts remain.
Now cont straight until front measures same as back to beg of shoulder shaping, ending at side edge.

Shape shoulder
Keeping chart correct, cast off 11(12)sts at beg of next row and 3 foll alt rows.
Return to rem sts and slip centre 20 sts onto a spare needle, with RS facing rejoin yarn to rem sts and patt to end of row. Now work as for first side from ** to end.

Previous pages
Left *Yoruba Sweater: Nigerian beadwork inspires the pattern of this cotton sweater and matching cap.*
Centre *Diamond Slipover: Sharp abstract shapes are knitted in crisp cotton for a cool sleeveless top.*
Right *Mask Jacket: Striking mask-like faces and geometric motifs stand out boldly on this cotton jacket.*

SLEEVES
Make 2. With 3¼mm (US 3) needles and A, cast on 60 sts and work in K1, P1 rib for 4cm/1½in.
Increase row: Rib and inc 20 sts evenly across row – 80 sts.
Change to 4mm (US 5) needles and starting with a K row work in st st from **sleeve chart** (centre of back chart), working between appropriate lines for size required, *at the same time* inc 1 st at both ends of every foll 5th row as shown until there are 100 sts on the needle, working inc sts into chart as shown. Now cont straight until row 74(80) has been worked, thus ending with a WS row.
Cast off fairly loosely.

NECKBAND
Join right shoulder seam.
With 3¼mm (US 3) needles and A and RS facing, pick up and K 24 sts down left front neck, K across centre front sts, pick up and K 24 sts up right front neck and finally K across centre back sts – 108 sts.
Work in K1, P1 rib for 2·5cm/1in.
Cast off fairly loosely ribwise.

TO MAKE UP
Sew in ends and press pieces carefully following ball band instructions. Join left shoulder seams and neckband seam. With centre of cast-off edges of sleeves to shoulder seams, and positioning between coloured markers, sew sleeves carefully in place. Join side and sleeve seams, matching pattern where possible.

VERSION 2 ★ ★
SLEEVELESS
(see page 137 for illustration)

MATERIALS
Yarn

Any **double-knit** weight yarn can be used as long as it knits up to the given tension.
150(175)g/6(7)oz each navy cotton (A) and brown cotton (B), 50(50)g/2(2)oz yellow ochre mohair (C), 25(25)g/1(1)oz each of pale yellow cotton (D) and royal blue cotton (E), 50(50)g/2(2)oz turquoise cotton (F), 100(100)g/4(4)oz grey-blue cotton (G), 75(100)g/3(4)oz cream cotton (H)
Needles and tension as for **Version 1**.

BACK AND FRONT
Work as for **Version 1**.
Omit sleeves but work neckband as **Version 1**.

ARMHOLE BORDERS
Alike. Sew in ends and press pieces carefully following ball band instructions.
Join left shoulder and neckband seam.
With 3¼mm (US 3) needles and A and RS facing, pick up and K 120 sts evenly between coloured markers on one side edge.
Work in K1, P1 rib for 2·5cm/1in.
Cast off fairly loosely ribwise.

TO MAKE UP
Join side and armhole border seams, matching pattern where possible.

YORUBA SWEATER BACK/FRONT/SLEEVE CHART

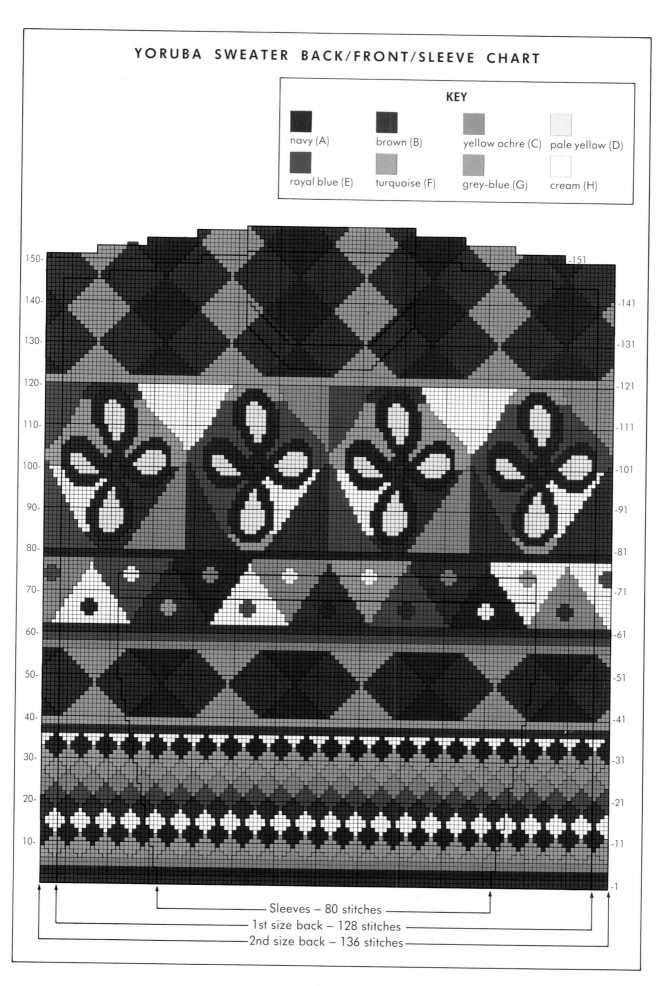

KEY

navy (A)
brown (B)
yellow ochre (C)
pale yellow (D)
royal blue (E)
turquoise (F)
grey-blue (G)
cream (H)

Sleeves – 80 stitches
1st size back – 128 stitches
2nd size back – 136 stitches

YORUBA HAT ★ ★

MEASUREMENTS
To fit average size adult head

Please see page 168 for actual garment measurements.

MATERIALS
Yarn
Any **double-knit** weight yarn can be used as long as it knits up to the given tension.
50g/2 oz brown cotton (A), small amounts of the following: navy cotton (B), turquoise cotton (C), blue cotton (D), yellow wool (E)
Needles and other materials
1 pair 4mm (US 5) needles
Approx 56×15cm/22×6in iron-on interfacing
Lining fabric to match (optional)

TENSION
21 sts and 28 rows to 10cm/4in on 4mm (US 5) needles over st st.

BRIM
With 4mm (US 5) needles and A, cast on 24 sts and starting with a K row work in st st from **chart** repeating the 30 rows of chart until piece is required length to fit around head easily.
Cast off fairly loosely in last colour worked.

TO MAKE UP
Sew in all ends. Press carefully according to ball band instructions. Cut the interfacing to fit and then carefully iron on to the wrong side of the knitted piece to stiffen it.

Top of hat
With 4mm (US 5) needles and A, cast on 12 sts and starting with a K row work in st st shaping as follows:
Cast on 2 sts at beg of next 2 rows – 16 sts.
Now cast on 4 sts at beg of foll 2 rows – 24 sts.
Cast on 2 sts at beg of every row until there are 36 sts on the needle.
Inc 1 st at beg of every row until there are 48 sts on the needle.
Work 12 rows straight.
Now reverse shapings by dec 1 st at beg of every row until 36 sts remain. Now cast off 2 sts at beg of every row until 24 sts remain.
Cast off 4 sts at beg of next 2 rows – 16 sts.
Cast off 2 sts at beg of foll 2 rows. Cast off rem 12 sts.
Press piece carefully.

To complete
Stitch short edges of brim together. Now carefully stitch top of hat to brim. Stab stitch completely around top edge of hat to form a raised rim.
If a lining is required, make up lining to match hat, and carefully stitch it inside hat.

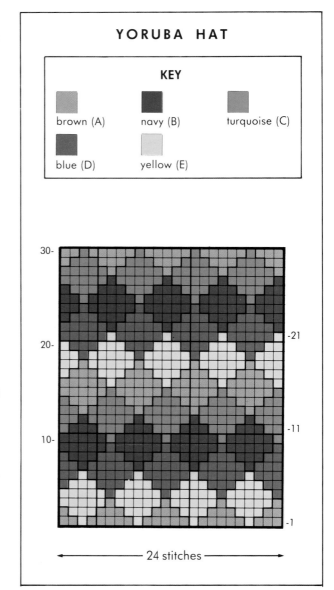

YORUBA HAT

KEY

brown (A) navy (B) turquoise (C)
blue (D) yellow (E)

30-
20-
10-
-21
-11
-1

← 24 stitches →

Back View
of MaskJacket

Yoruba Beadwork
Sweater
Version
2.

DIAMOND SLIPOVER ★ ★

MEASUREMENTS
To fit bust: 81-87cm/32-34in, 91-97cm/36-38in and 102-107cm/40-42in

Please see page 168 for actual garment measurements.

MATERIALS
Yarn
Any **double-knit** weight yarn can be used as long as it knits up to the given tension.
125(150:150)g/5(6:6)oz dark brown cotton (A), 25(25:50)g/1(1:2)oz beige cotton (B), 50(50:75)g/2(2:3)oz royal blue cotton (C), 75(100:100)g/3(4:4)oz navy blue cotton (D), 125(150:150)g/5(6:6)oz rust cotton (E), 75(75:100)g/3(3:4)oz duck-egg blue cotton (F), 25(50:50)g/1(1:2)oz cream cotton (G).
Needles and other materials
1 pair each 3¼mm (US 3) and 4mm (US 5) needles
3¼mm (US 3) circular needle
Spare needle
Safety-pin

TENSION
21 sts and 27 rows to 10cm/4in on 4mm (US 5) needles over main pattern.

BACK
With 3¼mm (US 3) needles and A, cast on 108(112:120)sts and work in K2, P2, rib for 4cm/1½in, on *2nd size only* inc 2 sts on last row – 108(114:120)sts. Change to 4mm (US 5) needles and starting with a K row work in st st from **back chart**, working between appropriate lines for size required. Work straight following chart, marking both ends of row 79(83:87) with coloured threads to indicate armholes. When row 142(146:150) has been worked, thus ending with a WS row, cont as follows:

Shape shoulders
Keeping chart correct, cast off 11(12:13)sts at beg of next 6 rows.
Leave rem 42 sts on a spare needle.

FRONT
Work as for back until row 72(76:80) has been worked.

Shape front neck
Next row: (RS facing) Patt 53(56:59), slip centre 2 sts onto a safety-pin, and patt to end of row and cont on this last set of 53(56:59)sts only.
**Keeping chart correct, dec 1 st at neck edge on next alt row, then on every foll 3rd row until 47(50:53)sts remain, then at this edge on every foll 4th row until 33(36:39)sts remain, as indicated on chart, *at the same time*, mark armholes with coloured threads as for back and start shoulder shaping when front measures same as back to beg of shoulder shaping, ending at side edge.

Shape shoulder
Keeping chart correct cast off 11(12:13)sts at beg of next row and 2 foll alt rows.
With WS facing rejoin yarn to rem sts and work as for first side from ** to end.

NECKBAND
Join right shoulder seam.
With the 3¼mm (US 3) circular needle and A and RS facing, pick up and K 68 sts down left front neck, K centre 2 sts, pick up and K 68 sts up right front neck and finally K across centre back sts – 180 sts.
Work in *rows* of K2, P2. Rib for 1 row.

Next row: (RS facing) Rib to 2 sts before centre 2 sts, then P2 tog, K2, P2 tog tbl cont in rib to end.
Cont as now set, dec 1 st either side of centre 2 sts, until neckband measures 2·5cm/1in.
Cast off ribwise, dec on this row as before.

TO MAKE UP
Sew in all ends. Press carefully according to ball band instructions. Join left shoulder and neckband seam.

Armbands
Alike. With 3¼mm (US 3) needles and A and RS facing, pick up and K 120 sts evenly between coloured markers on one side edge. Work in K2, P2, rib for 2·5cm/1in.
Cast off fairly loosely ribwise.
Join side and armband seams, matching pattern carefully.

HAT ★ ★

MEASUREMENTS
To fit average size adult head

Please see page 169 for actual garment measurements.

MATERIALS
Yarn
Any **double-knit** weight yarn can be used as long as it knits up to the given tension.
50g/2 oz brown cotton (A), small amount of blue cotton (B), 50g/2oz taupe cotton (C), small amount each of cream wool (D) and rust wool (E)
Needles and other materials
1 pair 4mm (US 5) needles
Approx 56×15cm/22×6in iron-on interfacing
Lining fabric to match (optional)

TENSION
21 sts and 28 rows to 10cm/4in on 4mm (US 5) needles over st st.

BAND
With 4mm (US 5) needles and A, cast on 16 sts and starting with a K row work in st st from **chart** for band of hat (see page 140), repeating the 12 rows until piece is required length to fit around head easily.
Cast off fairly loosely.

TO MAKE UP
Sew in ends and press piece carefully following ball band instructions.
Cut the interfacing to fit and then carefully iron on to the wrong side of the knitted piece to stiffen it.

Top
Make 4 – identical segments. With 4mm (US 5) needles

DIAMOND SLIPOVER BACK/FRONT CHART

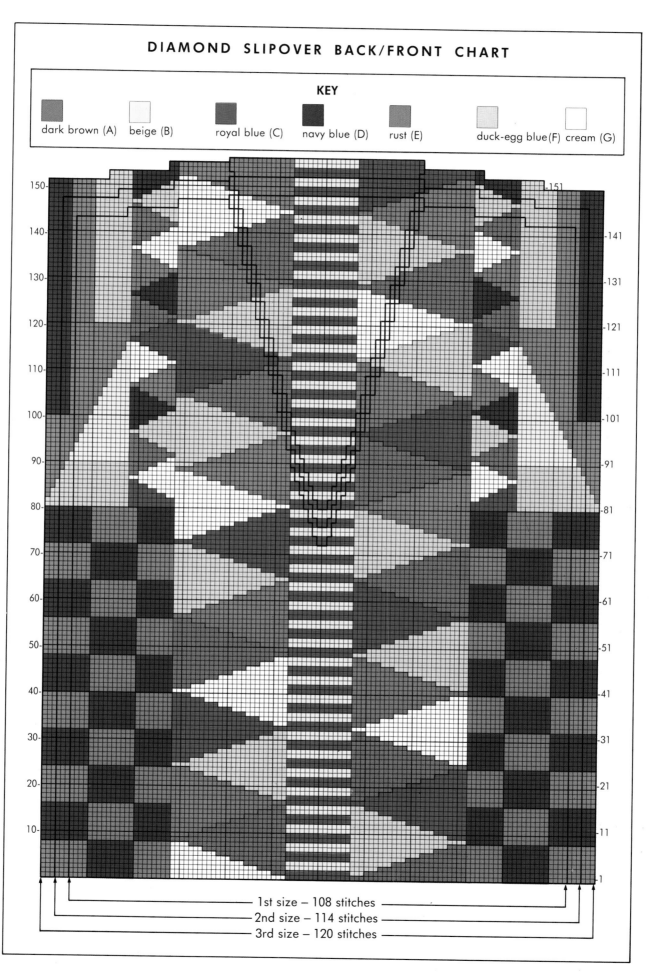

KEY

dark brown (A) beige (B) royal blue (C) navy blue (D) rust (E) duck-egg blue(F) cream (G)

1st size – 108 stitches
2nd size – 114 stitches
3rd size – 120 stitches

HAT CHART

KEY

brown (A)   blue (B)   taupe (C)

cream (D)   rust (E)

BAND CHART

10-

-11

-1

←—16 stitches—→

TOP CHART

40-

-41

30-

-31

20-

-21

10-

-11

-1

←————32 stitches————→

and D, cast on 32 sts and starting with a K row work in st st from chart for top of hat, shaping as shown. When chart is complete, K2 tog in C and fasten off.

To complete
Press the four segments carefully. Matching stripes carefully, join all shaped edges of segments together leaving one side edge free. Now attach band to bottom edge of segments. Join final seam and short edges of band together. Wrap yarn D tightly around tip of hat to form a point.
If required hat can be lined, by making up a lining to match hat and carefully stitching it inside hat.

MASK JACKET ★ ★

MEASUREMENTS
To fit bust: 81-91cm/32-36in and 97-102cm/38-40in

Please see page 169 for actual garment measurements.

MATERIALS
Yarn
Any **double-knit** weight yarn can be used as long as it knits up to the given tension.
400(425)g/15(15)oz navy cotton (A), 150(175)g/6(7)oz brown cotton (B), 100(100)g/4(4)oz beige cotton (C), 100(125)g/4(5)oz royal blue cotton (D), 75(100)g/3(4)oz yellow ochre wool (E), 25(25)g/1(1)oz cream cotton (F), 50(50)g/2(2)oz rust wool (G), 50(75)g/2(3)oz grey-blue cotton (H), 50(50)g/2(2)oz turquoise cotton (I)
Needles and other materials
1 pair each 3¼mm (US 3) and 4mm (US 5) needles
6 buttons

TENSION
21 sts and 27 rows to 10cm/4in on 4mm (US 5) needles over main pattern.

BACK
With 3¼mm (US 3) needles and A, cast on 128(136)sts and work in K1, P1 rib for 5cm/2in.
Change to 4mm (US 5) needles and starting with a K row, work in st st from **back chart**, working between appropriate lines for size required. Work straight following chart, marking both ends of row 81(85) with coloured threads to indicate armholes. When row 152(158) has been worked, thus ending with a WS row, cont as follows:

Shape shoulders
Keeping chart correct, cast off 11(12)sts at beg of next 4 rows, and 12(13)sts at beg of foll 4 rows. Cast off rem 36 sts.

LEFT FRONT
With 3¼mm (US 3) needles and A, cast on 46(50)sts and work in K1, P1 rib for 5cm/2in.
Change to 4mm (US 5) needles and starting with a K row work in st st from **left front chart**, working between appropriate lines for size required (**NB** left front chart follows *first* 46(50)sts of back chart).
Work straight following chart marking side edge of row 81(85) with coloured threads to indicate armhole. When row 152(158) has been worked, thus ending with a WS row, cont as follows:

Shape shoulder
Keeping chart correct, cast off 11(12)sts at beg of next row and foll alt row.
Now cast off 12(13)sts at beg of foll 2 alt rows.

RIGHT FRONT
Work as for left front, but following **right front chart** (**NB** right front chart follows *last* 46(50)sts of back chart). Start shoulder shaping on row 154(160) of chart.

SLEEVES
Make 2. With 3¼mm (US 3) needles and A, cast on 40(48)sts and work in K1, P1 rib for 10cm/4in.

MASK JACKET BACK/FRONTS CHART

(see page 142 for key)

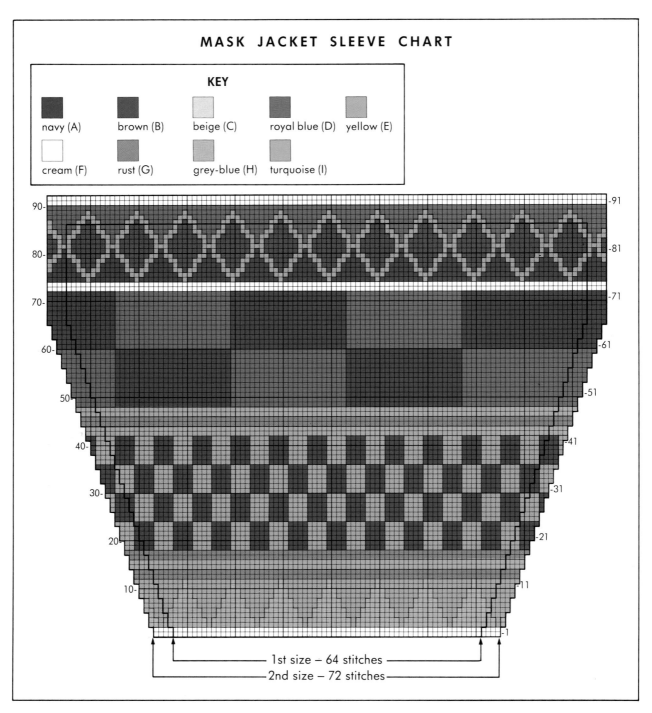

MASK JACKET SLEEVE CHART

KEY

navy (A) brown (B) beige (C) royal blue (D) yellow (E)

cream (F) rust (G) grey-blue (H) turquoise (I)

1st size – 64 stitches
2nd size – 72 stitches

Increase row: Rib and inc 24 sts evenly across row – 64(72)sts.

Change to 4mm (US 5) needles and starting with a K row work in st st from **sleeve chart**, working between appropriate lines for size required, *at same time* inc 1 st at both ends of every foll 3rd row as shown until there are 108(116)sts on the needle, working inc sts into chart as shown.

Now cont straight until row 86(92) has been worked, thus ending with a WS row. Cast off fairly loosely.

TO MAKE UP

Sew in ends and press pieces carefully following ball band instructions. Join shoulder seams. With centre of cast-off edges of sleeves to shoulder seams, and positioning between coloured markers, sew sleeves carefully in place. Join side and sleeve seams.

Front band

With 3¼mm (US 3) needles and A, cast on 48 sts and work in K1, P1 rib for 2·5cm/1in.

* Next row: (RS facing) Rib 8, cast off 4 sts, rib 24, cast off 4 sts, rib 8.

Next row: Rib, casting on 4 sts over cast-off sts on previous row.

Work in rib for a further 10cm/4in.*

Now rep from * to * once more, and then work the 2 buttonhole rows again (3 sets of buttonholes completed).

Now cont straight in rib until band, when slightly stretched, fits up front edge, around back neck and down other front edge, sewing in position as you go along. Cast off fairly loosely ribwise.

Sew on buttons to correspond with buttonholes. Roll collar onto right side.

MEASUREMENTS

The diagrams indicate approximate shape of pattern pieces for each garment.
Shaded areas indicate ribbed sections

PEARLY KING WAISTCOAT
(p 10)

- **A** 16cm/6¼in
- **B** 10(12)cm/4(4¾)in
- **C** 2.5cm/1in
- **D** 28cm/11in
- **E** 21.5(23)cm/8½(9)in
- **F** 2cm/¾in
- **G** 50(53)cm/19¾(21)in
- **H** 33(34.5)cm/13(13½)in
- **I** 19cm/7½in
- **J** 12cm/4¾in
- **K** 8cm/3in
- **L** 16(18)cm/6¼(7)in
- **M** 26(28)cm/10¼(11)in
- **N** 41(44)cm/16(17¼)in
- **O** 4cm/1½in
- **P** 41cm/16in
- **Q** 6.5cm/2½in

PEARLY KING BERET
(p 14)

- **A** 62cm/24½in
- **B** 2.5cm/1in
- **C** 80cm/31½in
- **D** 3.5cm/1½in
- **E** 9cm/3½in
- **F** 13.3cm/5¼in

PEARLY KING TIE
(p 14)

- **A** 97cm/38in
- **B** 43cm/17in
- **C** 4cm/1½in

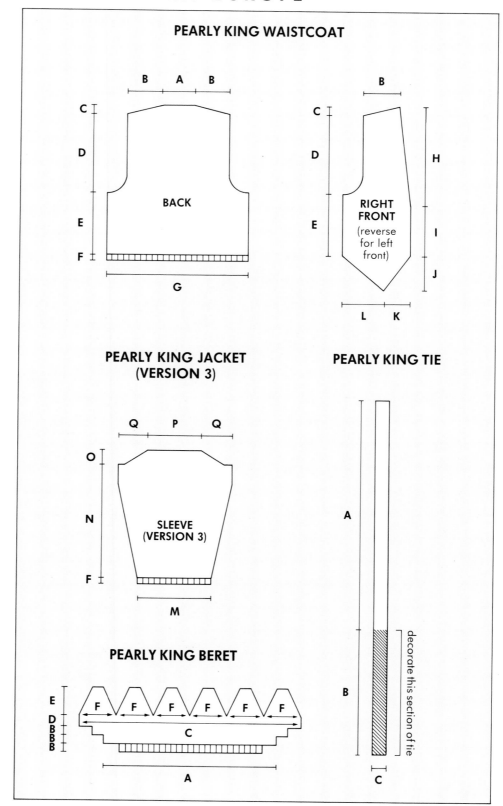

NORTHERN EUROPE

PEARLY KING WAISTCOAT

BACK

RIGHT FRONT
(reverse for left front)

PEARLY KING JACKET
(VERSION 3)

SLEEVE
(VERSION 3)

PEARLY KING TIE

decorate this section of tie

PEARLY KING BERET

FAIR ISLE SMOCK SWEATER (p 16)

A   15(18)cm/6(7)in
B   15.5(18.5)cm/6¼(7¼)in
C   3cm/1¼in
D   30(32)cm/11¾(12½)in
E   42(44)cm/16½(17¼)in
F   2cm/¾in
G   46(55)cm/18(21¾)in
H   12(14)cm/4¾(5½)in
I   21cm/8¼in
J   14(18)cm/5½(7)in
K   9cm/3½in
L   26cm/10¼in
M   14cm/5½in
N   52(56)cm/20½(22)in
O   46(51)cm/18(20)in
P   5cm/2in

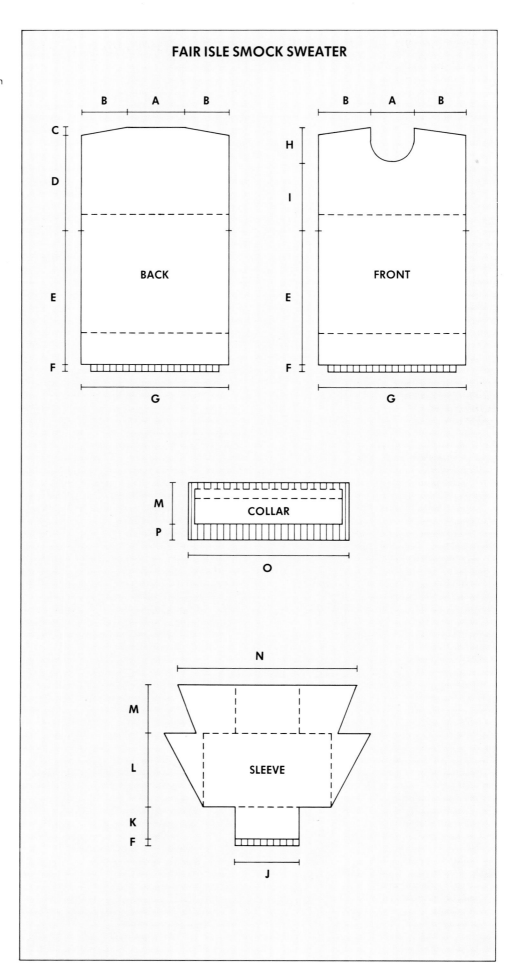

FAIR ISLE SMOCK SWEATER

SCANDINAVIAN SWEATER (p 19)

A 20cm/8in
B 16.5(18)cm/6½(7)in
C 2.5cm/1in
D 55(57)cm/21¾(22½)in
E 10cm/4in
F 53(56)cm/21(22)in
G 7.5cm/3in
H 50(52)cm/19¾(20½)in
I 62(65)cm/24½(25½)in
J 38(41)cm/15(16)in
K 36(40)cm/14¼(15¾)in

GLOVES SCANDINAVIAN (p 21) + JAPAN (p 71)
(both the same)

A 9cm/3½in
B 10cm/4in
C 12cm/4¾in
D 5.5cm/2¼in
E 6cm/2½in
F 7cm/2¾in
G 14cm/5½in

SCANDINAVIAN BOBBLE HAT (p 22)

A 10cm/4in
B 14cm/5½in
C 2cm/¾in
D 53cm/21in

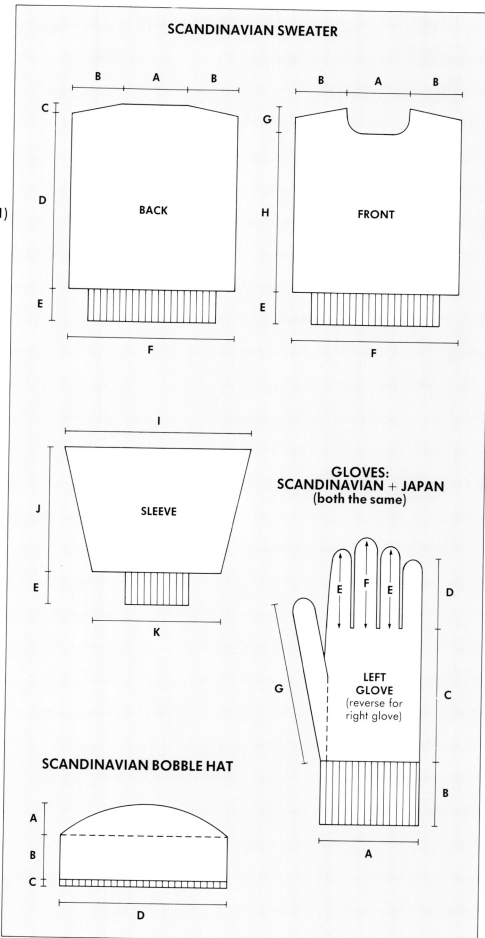

SCANDINAVIAN SWEATER

BACK

FRONT

SLEEVE

GLOVES: SCANDINAVIAN + JAPAN (both the same)

LEFT GLOVE (reverse for right glove)

SCANDINAVIAN BOBBLE HAT

EASTERN EUROPE

FLORAL AND LACE CARDIGAN (p 28)

A 20(21)cm/8(8¼)in
B 15.5(18)cm/6¼(7)in
C 2cm/¾in
D 66cm/26in
E 51(57)cm/20(22½)in
F 26(29cm/10¼(11½)in
G 60cm/23½in
H 8cm/3¼in
I 10.5(11)cm/4¼(4½)ins
J 19cm/7½in
K 6cm/2½in
L 33(40)cm/13(15¾)in
M 57cm/22½in

PEASANT SHIRT (p 30)

A 19cm/7½in
B 16.5(18:19.5)cm/
   6½(7:7¾)in
C 2cm/¾in
D 58.5(60.5:62.5)cm/
   23(24:24¾)in
E 2.5cm/1in
F 52(55:58)cm/20½
   (21¾:23)in
G 14cm/5½in
H 29.5(31.5:33.5)cm/
   (11½(12½:13¼)in
I 21cm/8¼in
J 10cm/4in
K 24cm/9½in
L 48cm/19in
M 11cm/4¼in
N 30(32:34)cm/
   11¾(12½:13½)in
O 70cm/27½in

FLORAL AND LACE CARDIGAN

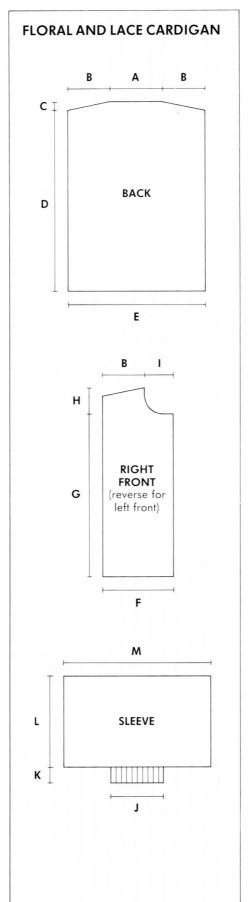

PEASANT SHIRT

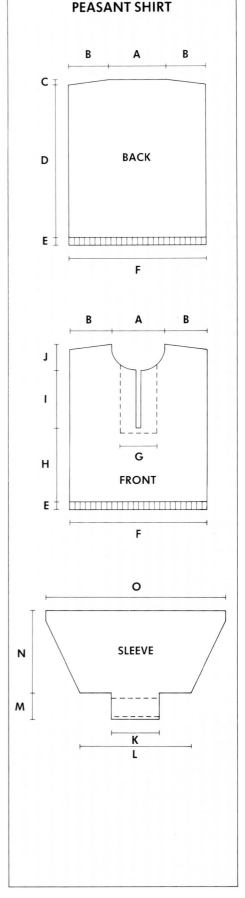

148

FLORAL COSSACK JACKET (p 32)

A 17cm/6¾in
B 8.5(9.5)cm/3½(3¾)in
C 2cm/¾in
D 28cm/11in
E 8(9)cm/3(3½)in
F 45(47)cm/17¾(18½)in
G 34(36)cm/13¼(14¼)in
H 21(22)cm/8¼(8¾)in
I 15(16)cm/6(6¼)in
J 23cm/9in
K 7cm/2¾in
L 6.5cm/2½in
M 24cm/9½in
N 152cm/60in
O 35(38)cm/13¾(15)in
P 52(54)cm/20½(21¼)in
Q 21cm/8¼in
R 15(17)cm/6(6¾)in

COSSACK HAT (p 35)

A 14cm/5½in
B 56cm/22in
C 20cm/8in
D 19cm/7½in

FLORAL GLOVES (p 36)

A 9cm/3½in
B 2.5cm/1in
C 4cm/1½in
D 12cm/4¾in
E 5.5cm/2¼in
F 6cm/2½in
G 7cm/2¾in
H 14cm/5½in

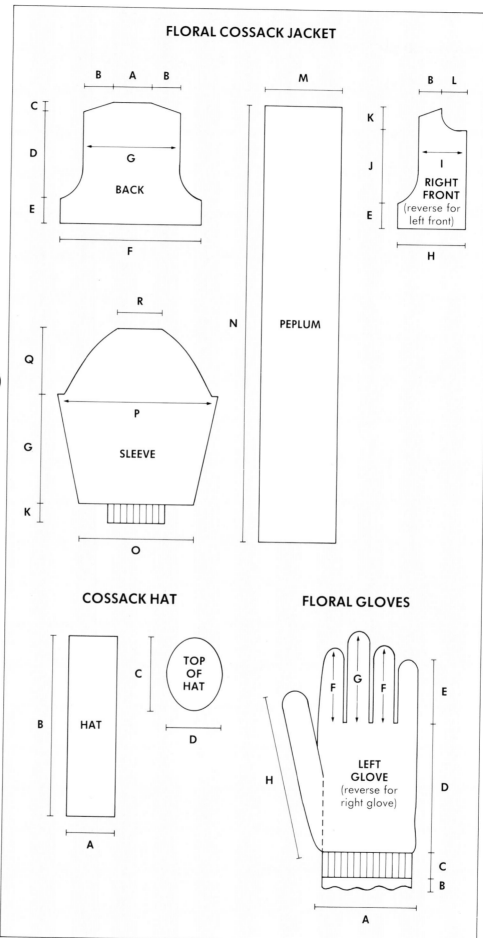

FLORAL COSSACK JACKET

BACK

RIGHT FRONT
(reverse for left front)

PEPLUM

SLEEVE

COSSACK HAT

HAT

TOP OF HAT

FLORAL GLOVES

LEFT GLOVE
(reverse for right glove)

PERSIAN STRIPED COAT (p 42)

- **A** 65(70)cm/25½(27½)in
- **B** 8cm/3in
- **C** 20(21)cm/8(8¼)in
- **D** 1.5(2)cm/½(¾)in
- **E** 8.5(9.25)cm/3¼(3¾)in
- **F** 16(17)cm/6¼(6¾)in
- **G** 7.5(8)cm/2¾(3)in
- **H** 25(26)cm/10(10¼)in
- **I** 53(56)cm/21(22)in
- **J** 47(51)cm/18½(20)in
- **K** 57(61)cm/22½(24)in
- **L** 40(42)cm/16(16½)in
- **M** 52(59)cm/20½(23¼)in
- **N** 153cm/60in
- **O** 14(15)cm/5½(6)in
- **P** 108(115.5)cm/42½ (45½)in

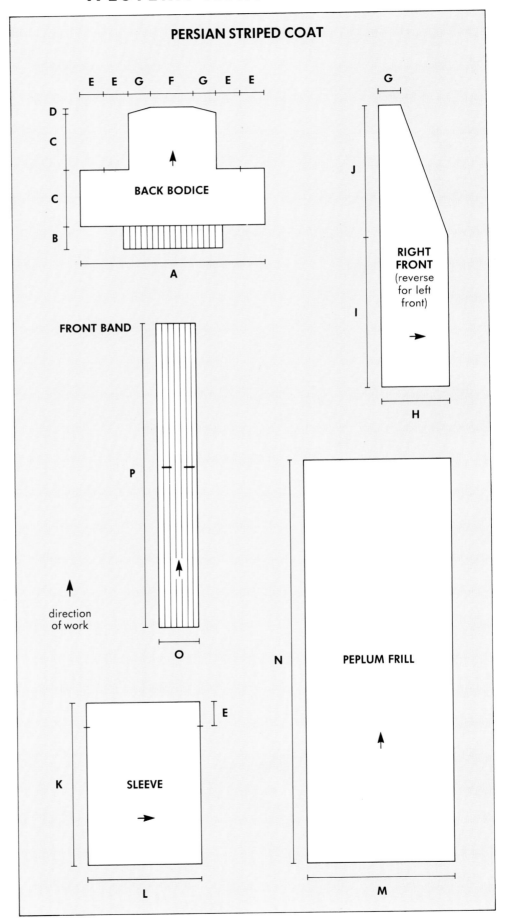

PERSIAN STRIPED COAT

BACK BODICE

RIGHT FRONT (reverse for left front)

FRONT BAND

direction of work

SLEEVE

PEPLUM FRILL

FLORAL AND STRIPED SWEATER (p 43)

A 10cm/4in
B 41(40)cm/16(15¾)in
C 16(17)cm/6¼(6¾)in
D 16cm/6¼in
E 20(22)cm/8(8¾)in
F 16.5(16)cm/6½(6¼)in
G 14(14.25)cm/5½(5¾)in
H 48(50)cm/19(19¾)in
I 15cm/6in
J 10.5cm/4¼in

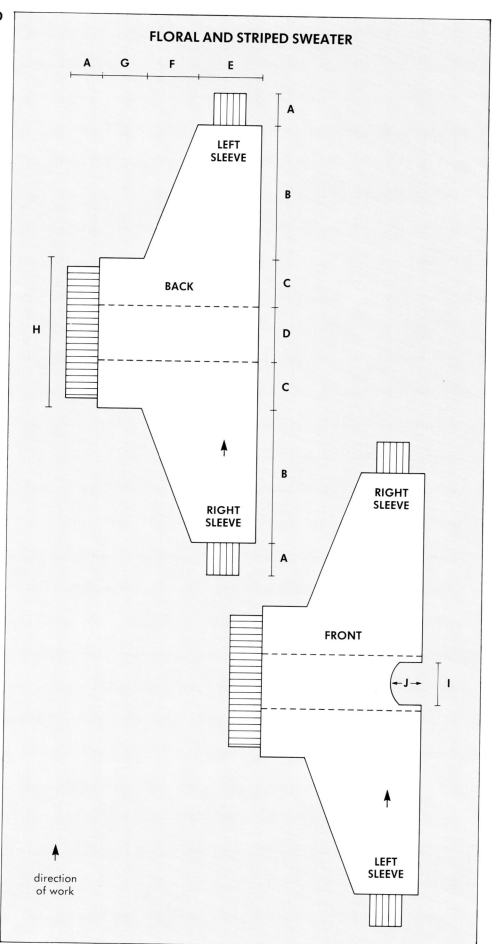

FLORAL AND STRIPED SWEATER

A G F E

LEFT SLEEVE

BACK

A

B

C

D

C

B

A

H

RIGHT SLEEVE

RIGHT SLEEVE

FRONT

J I

LEFT SLEEVE

direction of work

TURKESTAN COAT
(p 46)

A 57(60)cm/22½(23¾)in
B 4cm/1½in
C 30cm/11¾in
D 16cm/6¼in
E 19(21)cm/7½(8¼)in
F 33cm/13in
G 10cm/4in
H 3cm/1¼in
I 20cm/8cm
J 8.5(10)cm/3¼(4)in
K 28(30)cm/11(11¾)in
L 54cm/21¼in
M 47cm/18½in
N 24cm/9½in
O 14cm/5½in
P 27cm/10¾in
Q 66cm/26in
R 115cm/45¼in

TURKESTAN
SHOULDER BAG (p 49)

A 56cm/22in
B 24cm/9½in
C 4cm/1½in
D 2cm/1¾in
E 76cm/30in

TURKESTAN
HAT (p 50)

A 47cm/18½in
B 2cm/1¾in
C 11cm/4¼in
D 6cm/2¼in
E 7.75cm/3in

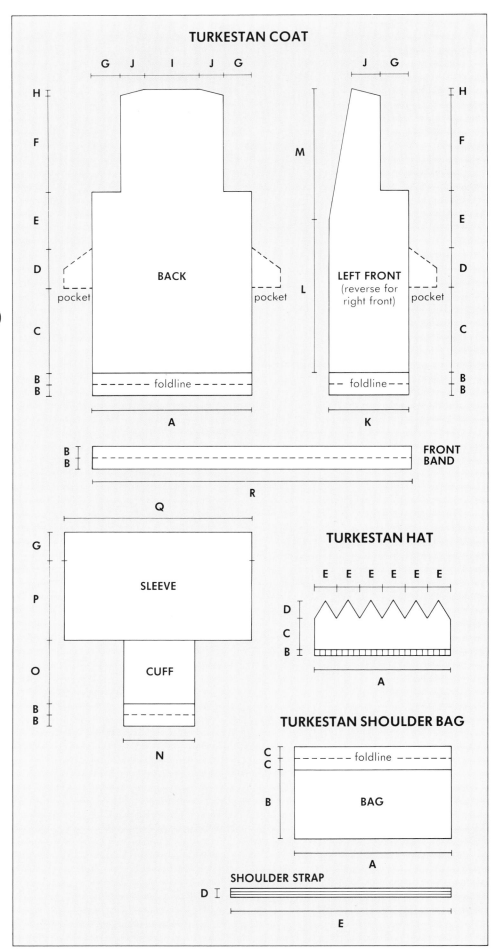

TURKESTAN COAT

BACK

LEFT FRONT
(reverse for
right front)

pocket

foldline

FRONT
BAND

SLEEVE

CUFF

TURKESTAN HAT

TURKESTAN SHOULDER BAG

foldline

BAG

SHOULDER STRAP

INDIA

KAFTAN JACKET (p 56)

A 9.5cm/3¾in
B 13.5(15)cm/5¼(6)in
C 8cm/3¾in
D 59(60)cm/23¼(23¾)in
E 2.5cm/1in
F 30(31.5)cm/11¾(12½)in
G 13cm/5in
H 7.5(8.5)cm/3(3¼)in
I 32cm/12½in
J 21cm/8¼in
K 62(65)cm/24½(25½)in
L 7cm/2¾in
M 39cm/15¼in
N 1cm/½in
O 31cm/12¼in
P 64cm/25¼in

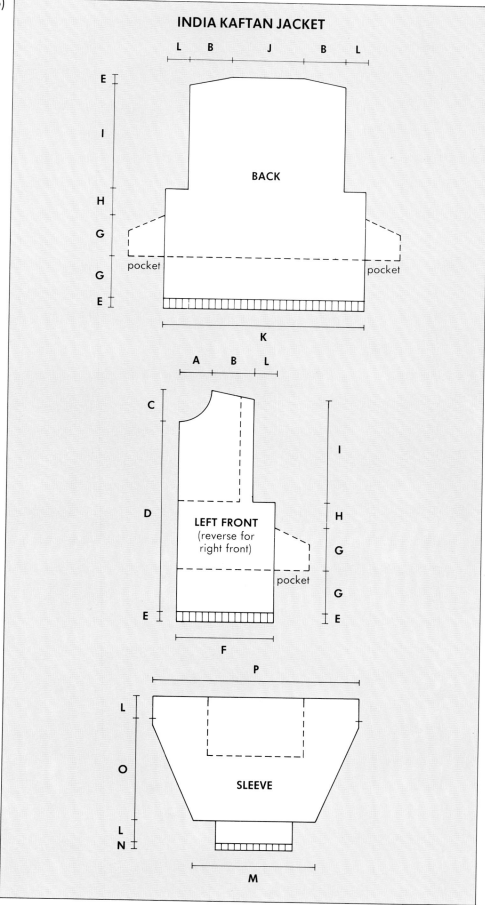

INDIA KAFTAN JACKET

BACK

LEFT FRONT
(reverse for
right front)

SLEEVE

SHORT INDIAN TOP
(p 60)

A 26(27:28)cm/
   10¼(10½:11)in
B 5(6:7)cm/2(2¼:2¾)in
C 1.5cm/½in
D 21cm/8¼in
E 9(11:13)cm/3½(4¼:5)in
F 3cm/1¼in
G 36(39:42)cm/14¼
   (15¼:16½)in
H 47(50:53)cm/18½
   (19¾:21)in
I 6cm/2½in
J 16.5cm/6½in
K 40cm/15¾in
L 7cm/2¾in
M 11cm/4¼in
N 28cm/11in
O 50cm/19¾in

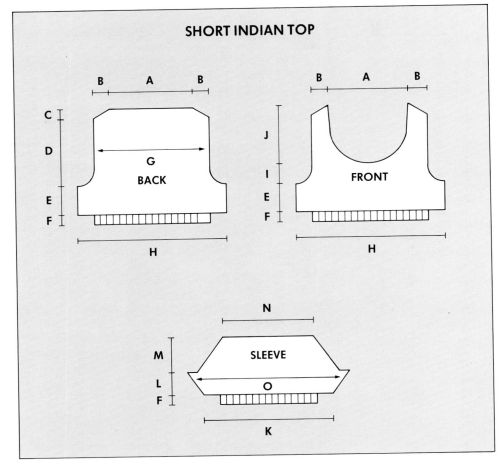

SHORT INDIAN TOP

BACK

FRONT

SLEEVE

BANGLE (p 61)

A 24cm/9½in
B 5cm/2in

TURBAN (p 61)

A 16in/6¼in
B 60cm/23¾in

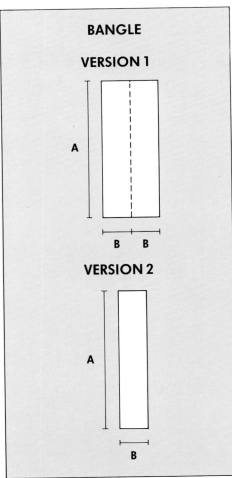

BANGLE

VERSION 1

VERSION 2

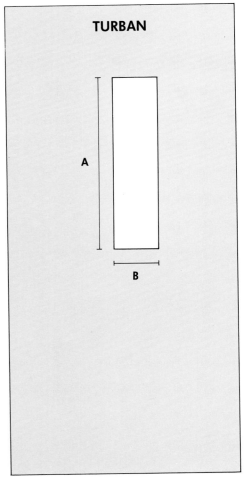

TURBAN

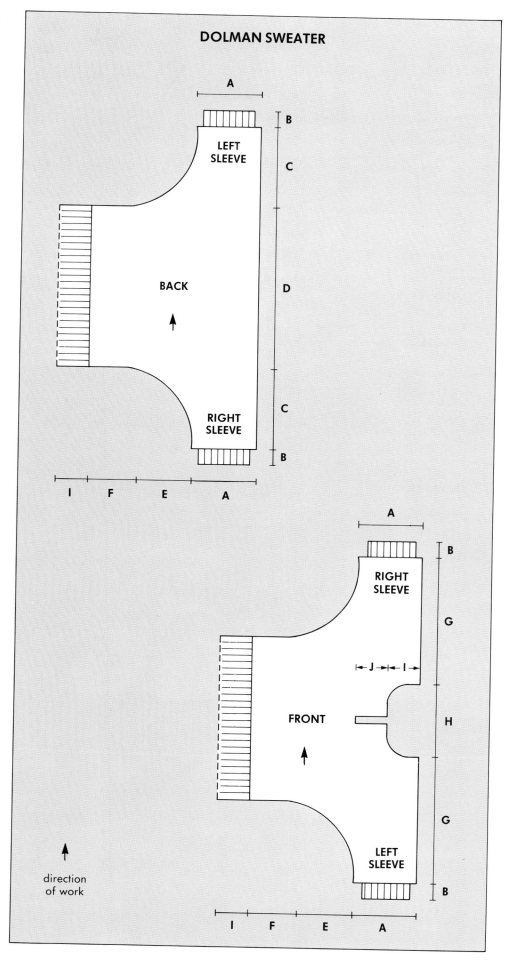

DOLMAN SWEATER
(p 63)

A 20(23)cm/8(9)in
B 5cm/2in
C 25(24)cm/10(9½)in
D 46(48)cm/18(19)in
E 16.5(15.5)cm/6½(6)in
F 15.5(16.5)cm/6(6½)in
G 39cm/15¼in
H 18cm/7in
I 10cm/4in
J 12cm/4¾in

DOLMAN SWEATER

A

B

LEFT
SLEEVE

C

BACK

D

C

RIGHT
SLEEVE

B

I   F   E   A

A

B

RIGHT
SLEEVE

G

J ← → ← I

FRONT

H

G

LEFT
SLEEVE

B

direction
of work

I   F   E   A

JAPAN

A 20cm/8in
B 17.5(19.5:21)cm/7 (7¾:8¼)in
C 2.5cm/1in
D 53(55:57)cm/21 (21¾:22½)in
E 43cm/17in
F 41(45:48)cm/ 16¼(17¾:19)in
G 55(59:62)cm/21¾ (23¼:24½)in
H 8.5cm/3½in
I 47(49:51)cm/ 18½(19¼:20)in
J 26(28:30)cm/ 10¼(11:11¾)in
K 33(35:37)cm/ 13(13¾:14½)in
L 106(110:114)cm/41¾ (43¼:45)in
M 37(38:40)cm/ 14½(15:15¾)in
N 8cm/3in
O 1.5cm/½in
P 24cm/9½in
Q 39(42:46)cm/ 15½(16½:18)in
R 4cm/1½in
S 5cm/2in

HEADBAND (p 72)

A 5cm/2in
B approx 50cm/19¾in

SHOULDER BAG (p 73)

A 17cm/6¾in
B 63cm/25in
C 5cm/2in
D 20cm/8in
E 6cm/2½in

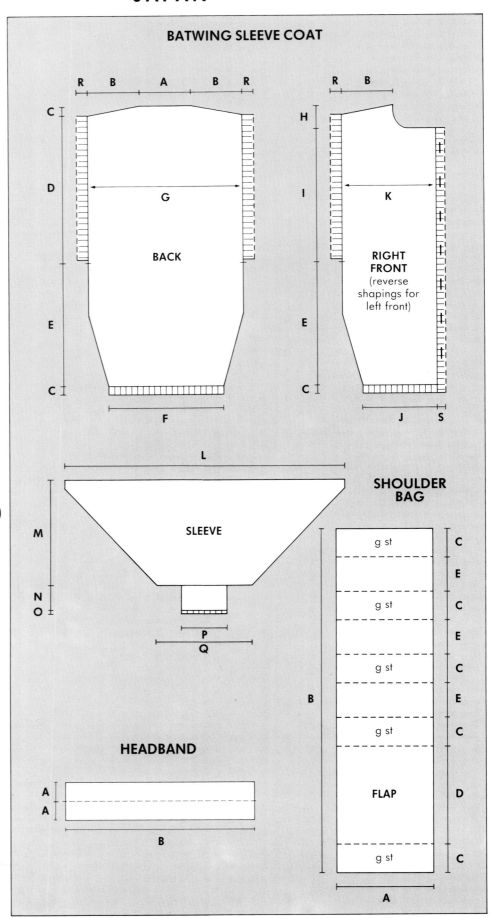

BATWING SLEEVE COAT

BACK

RIGHT FRONT (reverse shapings for left front)

SLEEVE

HEADBAND

SHOULDER BAG

FLAP

g st

PATCHWORK SWEATER (p 76)

- **A** 16cm/6¼in
- **B** 10(11.25:12.5)cm/ 4(4½:5)in
- **C** 2cm/¾in
- **D** 36cm/14¼in
- **E** 15(16.5:18)cm/6(6½:7)in
- **F** 10cm/4in
- **G** 49(51.5:54)cm/ 19¼(20¼:21¼)in
- **H** 6.5cm/2½in
- **I** 20.5cm/8in
- **J** 17.5cm/7in
- **K** 30cm/11¾in
- **L** 35(35:37)cm/13¾ (13¾:14½)in
- **M** 70cm/27½in
- **N** approx 73cm/28¾in

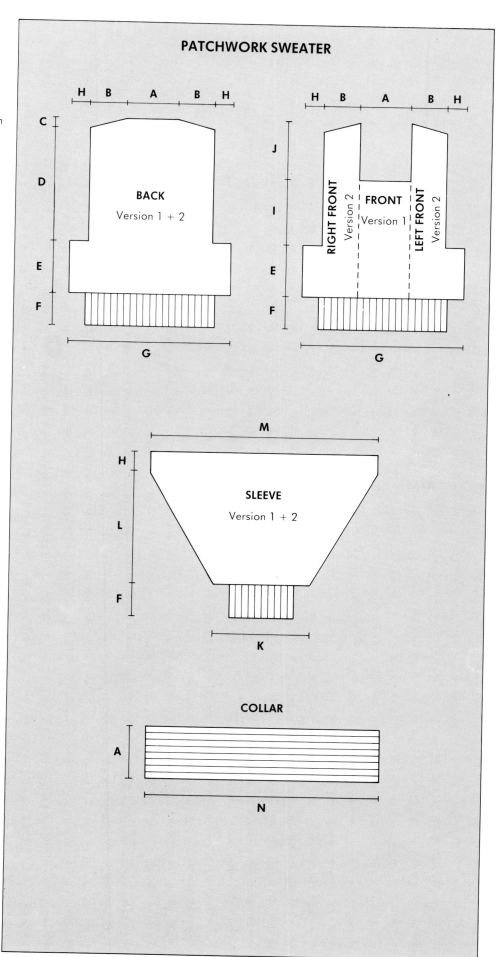

BUTTERFLY AND BAMBOO SWEATER (p 79)

- A 14(15)cm/5½(6)in
- B 34(36)cm/13½(14¼)in
- C 36cm/14¼in
- D 4cm/1½in
- E 55(58)cm/21½(23)in
- F 7cm/2¾in
- G 26(28)cm/10¼(11)in
- H 25cm/10in
- I 2.5/3cm/1(1¼)in
- J 21cm/8¼in
- K 8cm/3in
- L 30(33)cm/12(13)in
- M 51(54)cm/20(21¼)in
- N 11cm/4¼in
- O 45cm/17¾in

STRIPED SYMBOL SWEATER (p 82)

- A 21cm/8¼in
- B 14(16:18.5)cm/ 5½(6¼:7¼)in
- C 3cm/1¼in
- D 51(53:55)cm/ 20(21:21¾)in
- E 8cm/3in
- F 49(53:58)cm/ 19¼(21:23)in
- G 43(45:47)cm/ 17(17¾:18½)in
- H 11cm/4¼in
- I 58cm/22¾in
- J 32(34:36)cm/12½ (13½:14¼)in
- K 10cm/4in
- L 35cm/13¾in

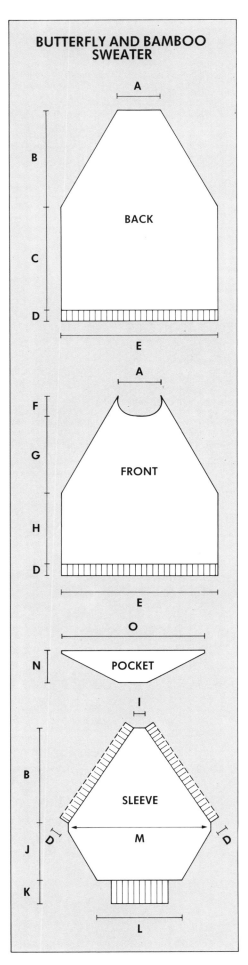

BUTTERFLY AND BAMBOO SWEATER

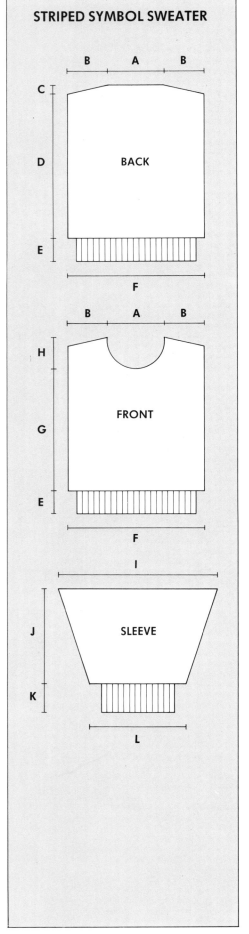

STRIPED SYMBOL SWEATER

AUSTRALASIA

ABORIGINAL BARK PAINTING JACKET (p 90)

A 57(61)cm/22½(24)in
B 6cm/2¼in
C 13cm/5in
D 16cm/6¼in
E 55(57)cm/21½(22½)in
F 3cm/1¼in
G 21cm/8¼in
H 18(20)cm/7(8)in
I 27(28.5)cm/10½(11¼)in
J 49(51)cm/19¼(20)in
K 9cm/3½in
L 36cm/14¼in
M 35(37)cm/13¾(14½)in
N 54.5cm/21½in

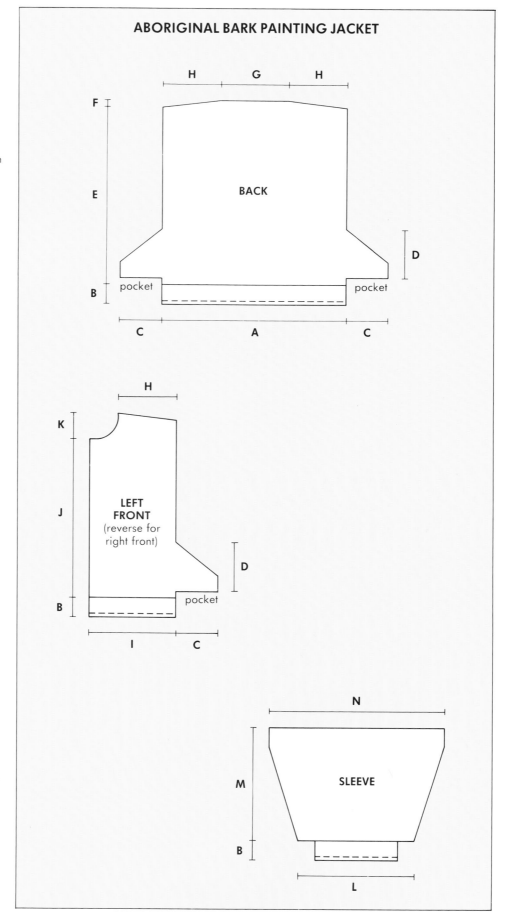

ABORIGINAL BARK PAINTING JACKET

TRAILING LEAF
SWEATER (p 93)

A 50(54)cm/19¾(21¼)in
B 8cm/3in
C 37cm/14½
D 16cm/6¼in
E 3cm/1¼in
F 21.5(22)cm/8½(8¾)in
G 53cm/21in
H 46cm/18in
I 5cm/2in
J 23cm/9in
K 50cm/19¾in
L 32cm/12½in

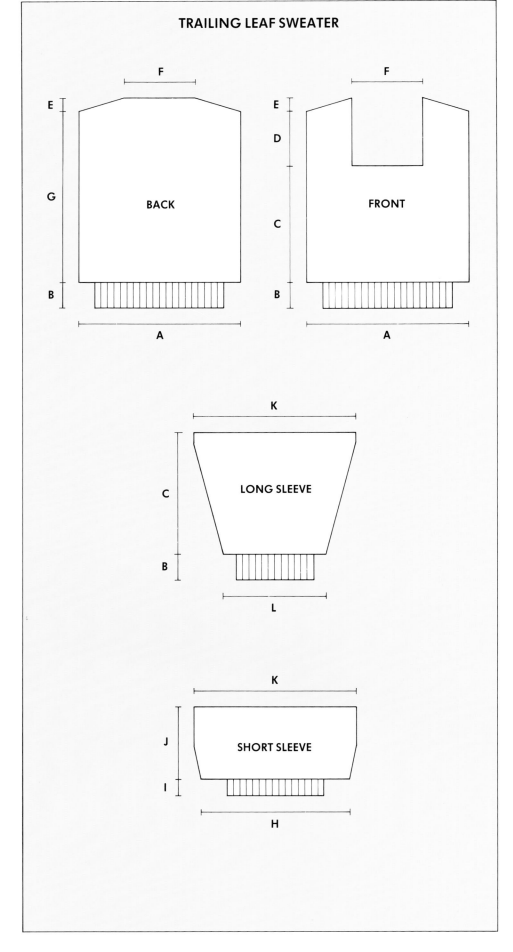

TRAILING LEAF SWEATER

BACK

FRONT

LONG SLEEVE

SHORT SLEEVE

WOOD CARVING
SWEATER (p 94)

A 48(53:57)cm/
   19(21:22½)in
B 10cm/4in
C 46cm/18in
D 6(8:10)cm/2½(3:4)in
E 39.5cm/15½in
F 5cm/2in
G 31cm/12¼in
H 52cm/20½in

STRIPED SKIRT (p 35)

A 8cm/3in
B 43cm/17in
C 4cm/1½in
D 82(86:91)cm/
   32¼(33¾:36)in

BANGLES (p 96)
VERSION 1

A 5.5cm/2¼in
B approx 24cm/9½in
   or length required

VERSIONS 2 and 3

A 9cm/3½in .
B approx 24cm/9½in
   or length required

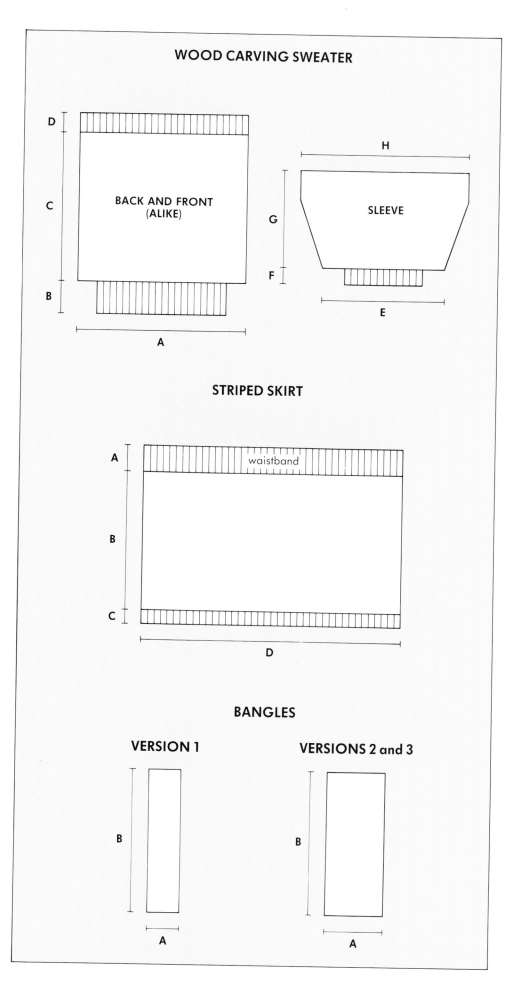

WOOD CARVING SWEATER

D
C
B
BACK AND FRONT
(ALIKE)
A

H
G
F
SLEEVE
E

STRIPED SKIRT

A
B
C
waistband
D

BANGLES

VERSION 1
B
A

VERSIONS 2 and 3
B
A

TEEPEE SWEATER (p 102)

A 53(55.5:58)cm/
   21(22:23)in
B 9cm/3½in
C 24.5cm/9¾in
D 24(25.5:27)cm/
   9½(10:10½)in
E 2cm/¾in
F 19cm/7½in
G 17(18.25:19.5)cm/6¾
   (7¼:7¾)in
H 17(18.5:20)cm/
   6¾(7½:8)in
I 38(41.5:45)cm/15
   (16¼:17¾)in
J 36(38.5:41)cm/
   14¼(15:16)in
K 48(51:54)cm/
   19(20:21¼)in

INDIAN SWEATER DRESS (p 104)

A 54(56:58)cm/
   21¼(22:22¾)in
B 7cm/2¾in
C 77(79.5:82)cm/30¼
   (31¼:32¼)in
D 2.5cm/1in
E 20cm/8in
F 17(18:19)cm/6¾(7:7½)in
G 69(71.5:74)cm/
   27(28:29)in
H 10.5cm/4in
I 34cm/13½in
J 40cm/15¾in
K 48(49.5:51)cm/
   19(19½:20)in

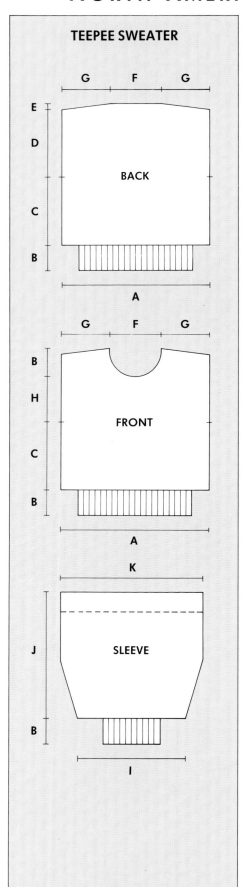

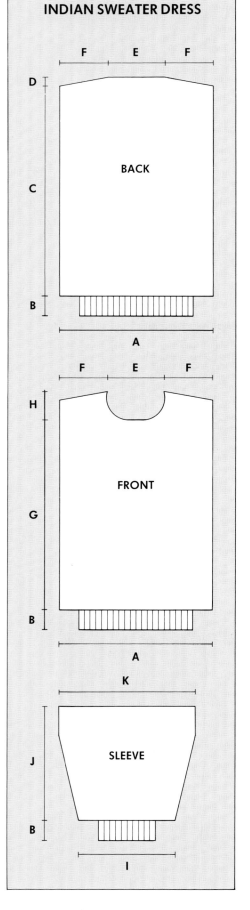

HEADBANDS (p 106)

VERSION 1
A 5.5cm/2¼in
B approx 50cm/19¾in
or length required

VERSION 2
A 8.5cm/3¼in
B approx 50cm/19¾in
or length required

EARRINGS (p 106)
A 4cm/1½in
B 4.5cm/1¾in

FRINGED COWBOY JACKET (p 109)

A 51(54:57)cm/
20(21¼:22½)in
B 4cm/1½in
C 74(76:78)cm/
29(30:30¾)in
D 2cm/¾in
E 14cm/5½in
F 18cm/7in
G 16.5(18:19.5)cm/
6½(7:7¾)in
H 24(25.5:27)cm/
9½(10:10½)in
I 66(68:70)cm/
26(26¾:27½)in
J 10cm/4in
K 26.5(30:33)cm/10½
(11¾:13)in
L 8cm/3in
M 36(38:40)cm/
14¼(15:15¾)in
N 44(47.5:51)cm/17¼
(18¾:20)in
O 3.5cm/1½in

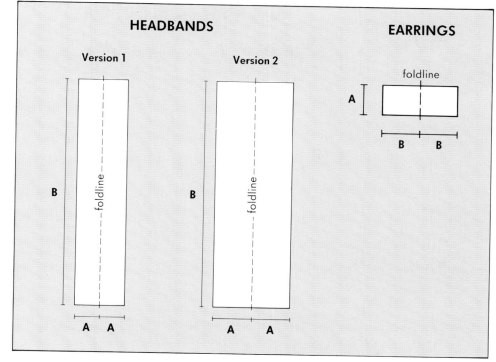

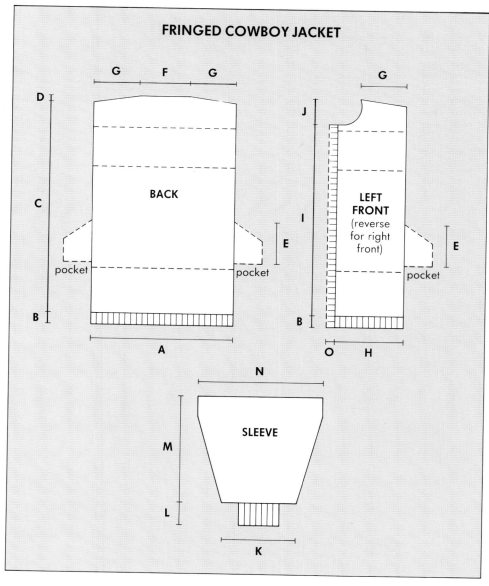

163

SOUTH AMERICA

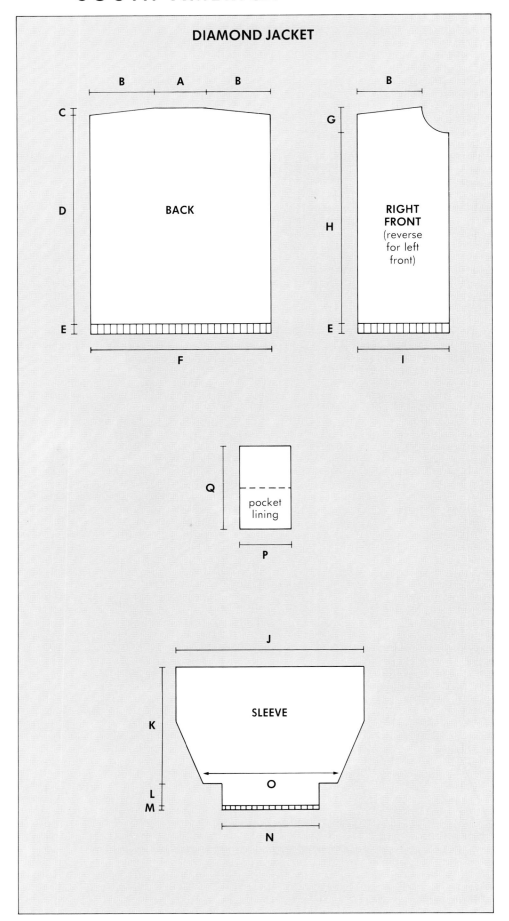

DIAMOND JACKET

BACK

RIGHT
FRONT
(reverse
for left
front)

pocket
lining

SLEEVE

MOTIF SWEATER
(p120)

A 12cm/4¾in
B 32(34)cm/12½(13½)in
C 22cm/8¾in
D 7cm/2¾in
E 55(58)cm/21¾(22¾)in
F 7(8)cm/2¾(3¼)in
G 25(26)cm/9¾(10¼)in
H 5(4)cm/2(1½)in
I 28(29)cm/11(11½)in
J 32(35)cm/12½(13¾)in
K 52(55)cm/20½(21¾)in
L 4cm/1½in

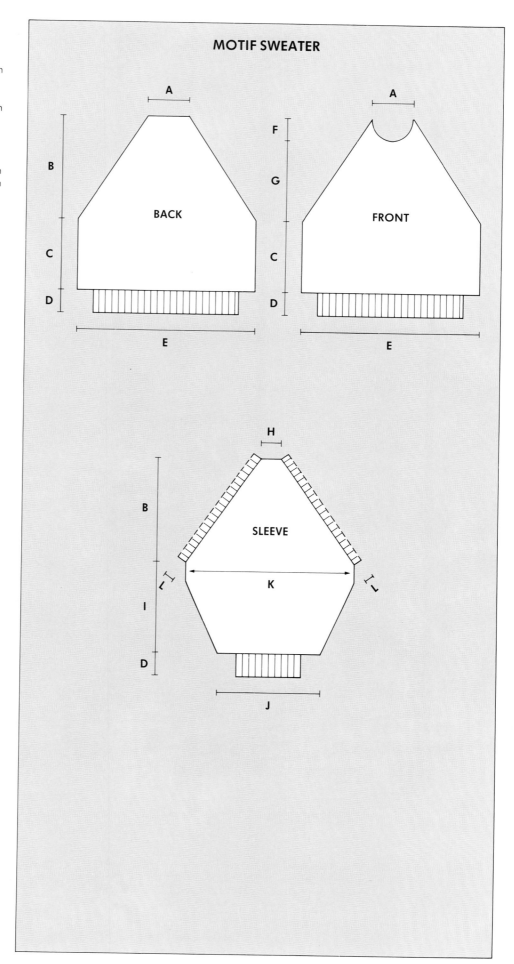

MOTIF SWEATER

BACK

FRONT

SLEEVE

PERUVIAN
DOLMAN JACKET
(p 123)

A 39cm/15½in
B 60cm/23¾in
C 26cm/10¼in
D 21cm/8¼in
E 16(19)cm/6¼(7½)in
F 138cm/54¼in
G 7cm/2¾in
H 19cm/7½in
I 144(150)cm/56¾(59)in
J 1cm/½in

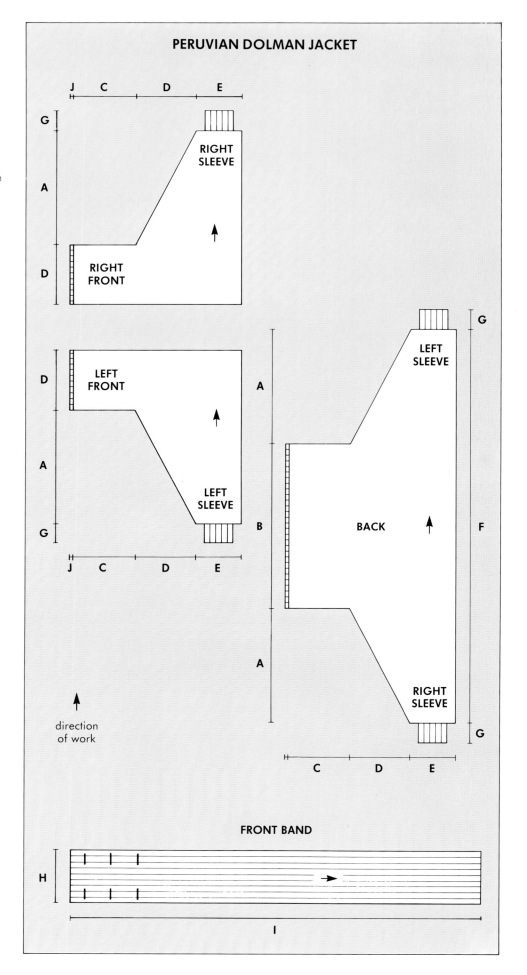

PERUVIAN DOLMAN JACKET

RIGHT SLEEVE

RIGHT FRONT

LEFT FRONT

LEFT SLEEVE

BACK

LEFT SLEEVE

RIGHT SLEEVE

direction of work

FRONT BAND

PERUVIAN SKIRT
(p 126)

A 69cm/27¼in
B 1cm/½in
C 15cm/6in
D 70cm/27½in
E 31(33)cm/12¼(13)in

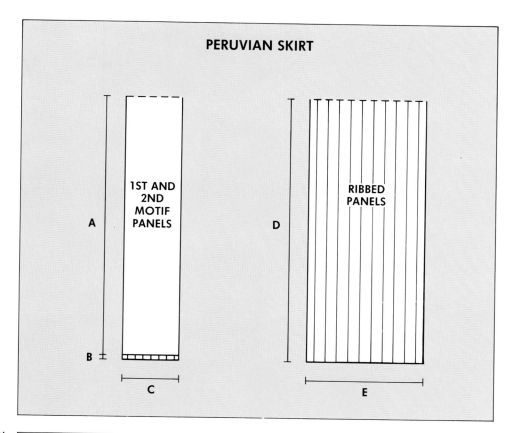

PERUVIAN HAT (p 126)

A 18cm/7in
B 1cm/½in
C 54cm/21¼in
D 16cm/6¼in
E 10cm/4in

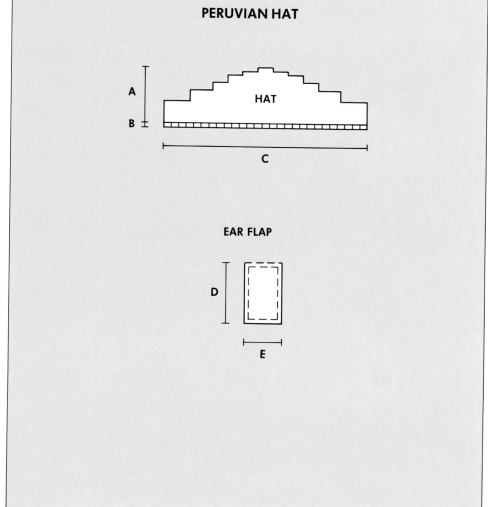

AFRICA

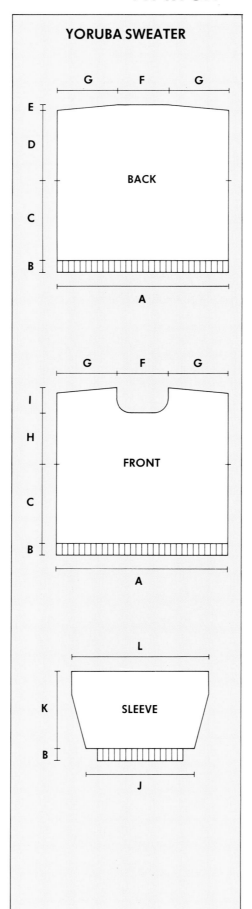

YORUBA SWEATER

BACK

FRONT

SLEEVE

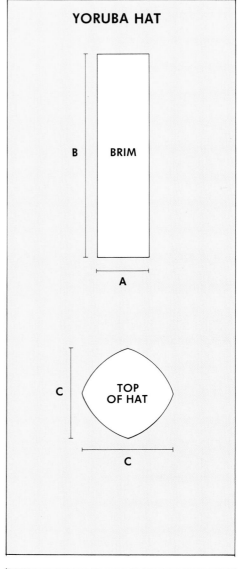

YORUBA HAT

BRIM

TOP OF HAT

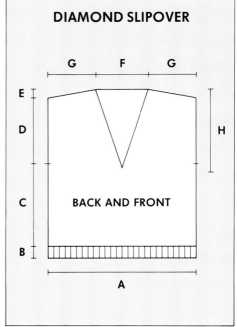

DIAMOND SLIPOVER

BACK AND FRONT

HAT (p 138)

A 7cm/2¾in
B approx 56cm/22in
C 19cm/7½in
D 17cm/6¾in

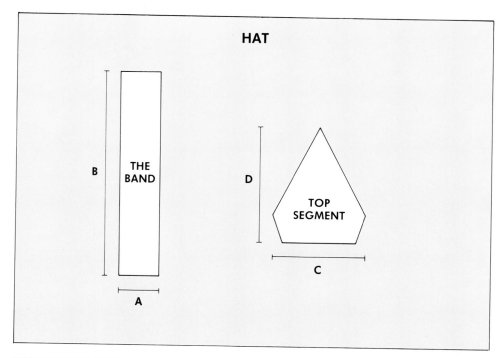

MASK JACKET (p 140)

A 61(65)cm/24(25½)in
B 5cm/2in
C 30(31)cm/11¾(12¼)in
D 26(27.5)cm/10¼(11)in
E 3cm/1¼in
F 17cm/6¾in
G 22(24)cm/8¾(9½)in
H 30(34)cm/11¾(13¼)in
I 10cm/4in
J 32(34)cm/12½(13¼)in
K 52(55)cm/20½(21¾)in
L 14cm/5½in

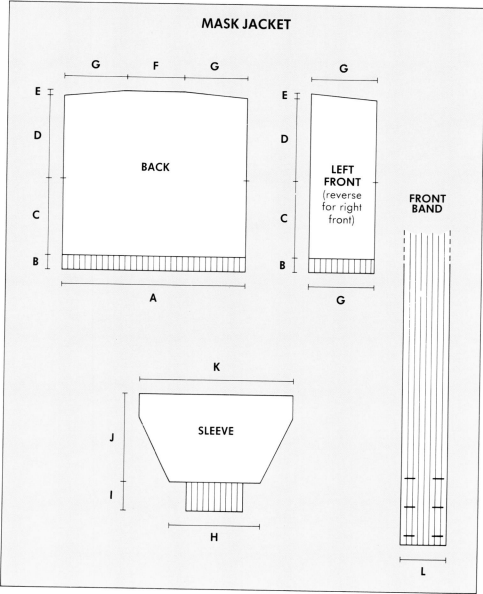

NOTES AND ABBREVIATIONS

YARN AMOUNTS

Because we do not specify a particular make of yarn for each garment and because different yarns are sometimes used together in this book, it is not possible to give exact quantities. The amounts of yarn given are based on average requirements and so are approximate. They are rounded up to the nearest gramme/ounce.

It is advisable to buy more yarn than you may need rather than run out and be unable to buy more of the same dye lot. You may have small amounts of yarn left over but these can always be used in the future.

TENSION

You should check your tension carefully before starting the garment. All measurements in these designs are based on the stated tension, therefore it is essential to maintain the correct tension throughout to achieve success.

The needle size specified is the one we have used to obtain the given tension, but as each knitter knits differently it may be necessary to change your needle size accordingly. If there are too many stitches to the cm/in then your tension is too tight and you should change to a larger needle size. If there are too few stitches to the cm/in, your tension is too loose and you should change to a smaller size.

Please note that these are designer patterns and as such the needle size and tension may be different from those recommended on the ball band.

CLEANING

Read the ball bands for general instructions on washing, etc. Do not wash any knitted fabric in hot water as this may cause shrinkage and matting. If the ball band advises hand-washing use lukewarm water and a mild liquid detergent. Rinse well and squeeze out excess moisture gently – do not wring. The drying process may be speeded up by spin-drying, but this is not advisable for garments with sequins or other trimmings. To prevent the garment stretching while spinning it can be put in a pillow-case (loosely closed with a few tacking stitches or safety-pins). After spinning the garment should be carefully pulled back into shape and laid flat to dry. Press under a damp cloth, referring to the instructions on the ball band.

If there are several different types of yarn in a garment or if it has sewn-on trimmings, it is safer to have it dry-cleaned.

CARE OF GARMENT

If the sweater has trimmings such as sequins it is worth buying a few extra to replace any that may be lost. Some yarns are prone to pilling (forming bobbles); these may be removed by hand or with Sellotape (Scotch tape). Mohair sweaters can be brushed with a teasel or a hair brush to keep them soft and fluffy. Never hang your sweater up on a clothes hanger as it will stretch – fold it carefully and store flat.

NOTES FOR ALL DESIGNS

When reading charts, work K rows (odd-numbered rows) from right to left and P rows (even-numbered rows) from left to right, unless instructed otherwise in a particular design.

When working the motifs, wind off small amounts of the required colours so that each motif can be worked separately, twisting yarns around each other on wrong side at joins to avoid a hole. Where possible, yarn can be carried over wrong side of work over not more than 3 stitches at a time to keep fabric elastic.

PATTERN NOTES

Every pattern is graded with one to four stars denoting the standard of knitting experience required:

★   easy

★★   average

★★★   for knitters with some experience

★★★★   for very experienced knitters

Figures in brackets refer to the larger size(s). Where only one figure is given, this refers to both (all) sizes.

NOTES FOR AMERICAN KNITTERS

● Both metric and imperial measurements are used throughout the book; American needle sizes are also given, so the patterns should be easily followed by American knitters. However, there are a few differences in knitting terminology and yarn names which are given below.

Knitting terminology

UK	US
Aran	fisherman/medium weight
chunky	bulky
double knitting	knitting worsted
4-ply	lightweight

ABBREVIATIONS USED THROUGHOUT THE DESIGNS IN THIS BOOK

alt	alternate
approx	approximately
beg	beginning
cm	centimetres
cont	continue
dec	decrease
foll	following
g	grammes
g st	garter stitch
in	inches
inc	increase
K	knit
LH	left-hand
mm	millimetres
oz	ounces
P	purl
patt	pattern
psso	pass slipped st over
rem	remaining
rep	repeat
RH	right-hand
RS	right-side
sl	slip
st(s)	stitch(es)
st st	stocking stitch
tbl	through back of loop
tog	together
WS	wrong side
yf	yarn forward
yrn	yarn round needle
ABCDEFGHIJK	contrasting colours

NEEDLE CONVERSION CHART

UK and Australian metric	UK and Australian original, Canada, S. Africa	USA
2mm	14	00
2¼mm	13	0
2¾mm	12	1
3mm	11	2
3¼mm	10	3
3¾mm	9	4
4mm	8	5
4½mm	7	6
5mm	6	7
5½mm	5	8
6mm	4	9
6½mm	3	10
7mm	2	10½
7½mm	1	11
8mm	0	12
9mm	00	13
10mm	000	15

LIST OF SUPPLIERS

UK YARN SUPPLIERS

Colourtwist Ltd
10 Mayfield Avenue Ind. Park
Weyhill
Andover
Hants SP11 8HU
tel: (026 477) 3369

Brinion Heaton Ltd
30 High Street
Saltford
Bristol BS18 3EJ
tel: (0225) 873142

Naturally Beautiful Ltd
Main Street
Dent
Cumbria LA10 5QL
tel: (05875) 421

Rowan Yarns
Green Lane Mill
Holmfirth
West Yorkshire HD7 1RW
tel: (0484) 681881

Smallwares Ltd
17 Galena Road
King Street
Hammersmith
London W6 0LU
tel: (01) 748 8511

Texere Yarns
College Mill
Barkerend Road
Bradford BD3 9AQ
tel: (0274) 22191

Pamela Wise
101-105 Goswell Road
London EC1V 7ER
tel: (01) 490 0037

UK RETAIL OUTLETS

Colourway
112a Westbourne Grove
London W2 5RU
tel: (01) 229 1432

Creativity
45 New Oxford Street
London WC1
tel: (01) 240 2945

Ries Wools
242 High Holborn
London WC1V 7DZ
tel: (01) 242 7721

Shepherds Purse
2 John Street
Bath BA1 2JL
tel: (0225) 310790

BUTTONS
The Button Box
44 Bedford Street
Covent Garden
London WC2E 9HA
tel: (01) 240 2716/2841
(send SAE for catologue)

USA AND CANADA YARN SUPPLIERS

Noro Yarns
Agent: Mr Sion Elaluf
Knitting Fever
180 Babylon Turnpike
Roosevelt
New York, NY 11575
tel: (516) 546 3600
    (800) 645 3457

Rowan Yarns (USA & Canada)
Agents:
Westminster Trading
5 Northern Boulevard
Amherst
New Hampshire 03031
tel: (603) 886 5041

William Unger & Co Inc
P.O. Box 1621
2478 Main Street
Bridgeport
Connecticut 06601
tel: (203) 335 5000

Estelle Designs and Sales Ltd
38 Continental Place
Scarborough
Ontario
Canada MIR 2TA
tel: (416) 2989922

USA RETAIL OUTLETS

Fiber Works
313 East 45th Street
New York NY 10017
tel: (212) 286 9116

School Products Co Inc
1201 Broadway
New York NY 10001
tel: (212)679 3516

BUTTONS
Tender Buttons
143 East 62nd Street
New York NY 10021

ACKNOWLEDGEMENTS

Editors: Louisa McDonnell and Gabrielle Townsend
Original design concept: Clare Finlaison
Designer: Anne Fisher
Charts: Danny Robins and Barry Walsh
Artwork: Barry Walsh
Pattern checker: Janet Bentley
Proofreaders: Fred and Kathie Gill
Location photography: Chris Craymer
Studio photography: Steve Tanner
Location finders: LocationWorks
Make-up: Mary-Ellen Lamb and Maureen Barrymore
Hair: Simon Robinson/Michaeljohn
Models: Valérie Heyfen and Gina/Synchro; Natasha
Maddox/Laraine Ashton; Lara/Profile; Barbara/
Premiere; Kate Bracher, Lisa Jay and Nina Grøvlen/
Models 1

With special thanks to the following knitters for making
the garments in this book:
Pat Bradley, Mary Colbeck, Barbara Davis, John Heath,
Rosemary Heath, Valerie Ruddle, Lila Selman.